THE UNEASY STATE

THE
Uneasy State

THE

UNITED STATES

FROM

1915 TO 1945

Barry D. Karl

THE UNIVERSITY OF CHICAGO PRESS

Chicago & London

BARRY D. KARL
is the Norman and Edna Freehling Professor in the
Department of History and a member of the
Committee on Public Policy at the University of Chicago.
He is the author of *Executive Reorganization and Reform
in the New Deal* and *Charles Merriam
and the Study of Politics*.

The University of Chicago Press, Chicago 60637
The University of Chicago Press, Ltd., London

973.91
K 18u

221018

Library of Congress Cataloging in Publication Data

Karl, Barry Dean.
  The uneasy state.

  Includes index.
  1. United States—History—20th century.
I. Title.
E741.K33   1983   973.91   83-9134
ISBN 0-226-42519-3

For ELISABETH and SARAH

Contents

Acknowledgments

THIS BOOK has undergone more revision than anything else I have ever written, and R. Jackson Wilson has read all but the very last version. While one is expected ordinarily to absolve such advisers from responsibility for the final result—or at least to credit them with the virtues but not the defects—he will understand my reluctance to do so in his case. David Brody, Eliot Brownlee, James Henretta, and James Gilbert read with collegial patience at a crucial stage and helped me formulate my ideas. Both they and David Follmer are responsible for the possibility that a few more readers will understand what I am trying to say than might once have been the case. Neil Harris, Stanley Katz, and Frank Freidel were particularly helpful as I neared the end, which is, of course, where I most needed support.

Since much of what is in this book has grown out of some twenty years of teaching, I have special debts to colleagues like John L. Thomas, whose skeptical questioning is matched only by his support once he is convinced, and to years of students like Mark Leff, Steven Wheatley, Beth Bailey, and Renée Borden, who are willing to support even when they are not convinced. David Farber's reading of the final manuscript was particularly important. And I have benefitted much from the responses of friends like Audrey and Ron Gryzwinski and George Ranney, Jr. Dena Epstein of the Regenstein Library of the University of Chicago was especially helpful in tracking down references to music of the period.

Marnie Veghte and Margaret Browning have slaved over the task of typing revision after revision, and all of the cutting and pasting that has entailed, with a grace and humor I have not always deserved.

My wife, Alice Woodard Karl, has borne the burden of my indebtedness to her so well for so long now that I suppose I could take it for granted. But since both the burden and the debt seem to increase, I won't. She and the daughters to whom I have dedicated this book have been able to accept most of what I am, and indefatigable in their willingness to improve the rest.

Prologue

THIS BOOK IS INTENDED as an effort to strike a balance rather than to
reverse directions or attack other points of view. It is not intended as a
revisionist statement, although readers familiar with the historiography of the
period it discusses may be inclined to see it that way. Simply put, its argument
is this: Americans have had a peculiar problem when it comes to identifying
themselves as a nation. The diversity of their geography, the origin of their
government in an alliance of states, and the waves of immigration that settled
many different racial and ethnic groups within the wide reaches of the country
established divisions and differences that have made "the American" a citizen
unlike any other citizen on earth.

On the other hand, the effort to achieve a sense of national unity has not
been blocked in this young country by the kind of historically fixed hatreds
between ethnic or racial groups, sustained by memories stretching back into a
mythologized past, like those that set Protestants against Catholics in Northern Ireland or Uzbeks against Russians in the Soviet Union. This is not to
ignore the outbreaks of anti-Catholicism that fueled the Know-Nothing movement in mid-nineteenth-century America or the anti-black sentiments that
have run through our entire history. It is rather to call attention to the
flexibility with which each generation has transformed such issues by reshaping institutions and popular attitudes.

Americans have thus not been tied so tightly to particular localities and
have not felt themselves so fixed in their loyalties as to be immobilized by
hostilities that remain unchanged over time. Internal migration, not only to
the open land of the frontier but from countryside to city, from city to suburb,
and now to the so-called Sun Belt, has continued to insure Americans one of

the oldest, perhaps, of their freedoms: the freedom to moderate the conflicts that enraged their parents.

Still, the need for national unity has come into conflict with local traditions in American society; and while the Civil War is the most obvious indication of that fact, it is in some respects too obvious. The sense that that conflict had to be gotten out of the way in order to make national unity possible, that it did indeed make national unity possible, is one of the cornerstones of our view of our own history, despite the questions that historians have asked about the real effects of the war, the real unity it achieved, the real beginning of racial equality. Americans have continued to assert a national unity, even a national identity, and historians have supported them by describing what some have gone so far as to call the growth of an American civilization.

This book is an effort to provide a sustained questioning of the historical reality of that nationalism. Other historians have done this over the past decade or so by writing what one might call "exceptionalist" history; that is, they have looked into local history for examples that enable them to take exception to one or another of the "nationalist" generalizations that historians have proposed. But the exceptions have been drawn from nineteenth-century history for the most part. The view that in the twentieth century the American nation has been successfully unified is still—despite the acknowledged cracks in the melting pot—the accepted interpretation. Our success in the two world wars is said to have proved this, as does the fact that we have survived intervals of internal crisis. We have a national history because we have to have a national history, one that will support our status as a world power and our claims to the utopian promises of equality, opportunity, and individual freedom.

Historians have come to understand the New Deal as the central event in the creation of America as a national society. For example, historians of the Progressive Era have defined it as essentially the forerunner of New Deal nationalism, just as historians of the emergence of the United States as an international power have looked on the two world wars as central to that development.

The effort to define America as a nation is not new. One of the first major acts of the American Historical Association, founded in 1884, was to call for a new, definitive, and *national* history; the result was the American Nation Series, edited by Albert Bushnell Hart. The authors of this collection of professional texts sought a firmer foundation for nationalism than the expansionist patriotism of Bancroft, Prescott, Parkman, and Motley, and they did so by finding very early evidences of progressivism in the American past. The resurgence of a scholarly emphasis on nationalism in the years after World War II produced a similar series, the New American Nation volumes edited by Henry Steele Commager and Richard B. Morris. As in the earlier series, United States history was viewed as a whole, not as a collection of state or even regional histories, although the South and the West were allowed to play their traditional roles as distinctive elements in the emergence of the nation. Yet it is precisely that—the emergence of the nation—that is the essential history being projected.

American historians have thus been peculiarly preoccupied with American nationalism, as though its existence needed, somehow, to be proved—that to assert it was somehow essential to its preservation. What most traditional nation-states had long since assumed to be their history, which they supported through symbols and myths, Americans had to establish through research. The symbols and myths were there, but they were not enough; indeed, they were often unacceptable to those who sought to sustain through scholarship a national unity that must have been more elusive than they were willing to admit.

Working from another perspective, American social scientists in fields like political science and public administration provided historians with major intellectual tools for tracing the development of an American nationalism; of prime importance here is analysis of the movement toward bureaucratic and economic centralization that is associated with what some mean by the term "modernization." The growth of national political parties and nation-wide industries laid the groundwork for defining the economic and political outlines of a national state that transcends state lines and regional commitments. Again, the Progressive Era and the New Deal served as the major periods of centralization, and the development of national "elites"—an "establishment" that manages the national system—was linked to the development of the United States as a world power.

Several major historical reinterpretations have resulted from this approach. Samuel Hays's *The Response to Industrialism* (1957), covering the period between 1885 and 1914, shows the impact of the process of industrialization on the building of the nation. Robert Wiebe's *The Search for Order* (1966) takes 1920 as its stopping point because, Wiebe argues, by that date bureaucratic centralization had transformed the country from a collection of island communities into a nation poised for the onset of the Depression and salvation by the New Deal. Rowland Berthoff's *An Unsettled People* (1971) traces the creation of a national social order set on its course, finally, by the New Deal.

Different though they are, such analyses define the historiographical outlines of the major post–World War II interpretations of the past. Richard Hofstadter's view of progressivism in his *The Age of Reform* (1955), Arthur Schlesinger, Jr.'s, interpretations of the New Deal, and the major studies contributed to the New American Nation Series by George Mowry, Arthur Link, and William Leuchtenburg are all consistent with a view of the American past that tends to equate nationalism with centralization and centralization with progress. Most of these authors avoid the simple dichotomies between "the interests" and "the people" set up by the Progressive historians, but, in the consensual base on which they rest their assertion of American nationalism, localism, states rights, congressional hegemony, regional autonomy, and the various "blocs" that reflect local interests are all regarded as potholes on the road to progress, and "leadership," variously defined, is seen as the key to the future.

Contemporary historians of the left have tended to see these nationalist historians as apologists for American capitalism, but they themselves have equally nationalist conceptions. Thus Gabriel Kolko sees progressivism as *The Triumph of Conservatism* (1963) rather than a failure of nationalism. Barton Bernstein's essays have emphasized the conservatism of Franklin Roosevelt but acknowledge his success in concealing it. Paul Conkin, in *The New Deal* (1967), criticizes the failure of the New Deal to establish a popularly controlled welfare state and assumes that the power to do so was actually there. Soviet historians like Nikolai Sivachev, who have the greatest stake in explaining the New Deal because of the revolution it did or did not produce, still accept the nationalist theses used to describe what they now see as an adventure in "state capitalism."

Ellis Hawley, in his analyses of the various forms of "associationalism" in the 1920s, came closer to the heart of the matter by speaking of America's effort to come to grips with the problem of how the functions of management and control, which are necessary in modern industrial society, can be performed without violating commitments to individualism and self-government. His *The New Deal and the Problem of Monopoly* (1966) suggests the problems such an analysis might pose when extended into the New Deal period.

Other New Deal historians have chipped away at this problem by questioning the degree of centralization and control that was actually achieved by the New Deal. James Patterson, in *Congressional Conservatism and the New Deal* (1967), thinks that opposition to control began earlier than the first New Deal historians had thought. In a suggestive little book entitled *The New Deal and the States: Federalism in Transition* (1969), he also warned historians that they might want to be more cautious in making broad generalizations about the effects of New Deal programs on state policies. Subsequent state studies have proved him right, although neither he nor the authors of these studies have tried to find an alternative generalization capable of acknowledging the New Deal's centralization of government without overemphasizing its role in influencing the lives Americans have continued to lead. Otis Graham's *Encore for Reform: The Old Progressives and the New Deal* (1967) covers much the same ground, but in his later work, *Toward a Planned Society* (1975), he seems to accept the idea that a more organized conception of executive management was possible in the New Deal and that New Deal efforts were at best primitive, at worst abortive.

More recent studies of the period 1915–45, some of them from the left, are beginning to question both the degree of centralization that was achieved and the effectiveness of the national elites who managed it. Martin Schiesl and John D. Buenker, in their studies of municipal reform in the Progressive Era, do not support the notion that the efficiency experts had any great influence on the governmental reforms that were actually achieved, while Stephen Skowronek, in his *Building a New American State* (1982), asserts the same of the managers who sought to impose bureaucratic systems at the national level. Theda Skocpol's recent studies of the New Deal suggest that American government does not easily respond to Marxist analysis because the American political system is an independent variable rather than a dependent one; by this she means that efforts to see political structure in the United States as a response either to an underlying economic order or to an overbearing managerial control simply do not fit the facts of American political life. To the extent that she still thinks along classic Progressive lines, however, she tends to see the possibility of structural reform in American political organization as the answer to social and economic problems.

Meanwhile, leftist writers like those who publish in *Democracy: A Journal of Political Renewal and Radical Change* have expressed the strongest reaction against nationalism; their hope for radical reform rests on a new decentralization of government in the United States. Ronald Reagan's New Federalism seems to embody the same hope. Thus, for one of those rare moments in history, the right and the left are in agreement. Centralization is now the problem. Decentralization is now the answer.

Americans, typically, have come to view these two things as alternatives, and political debate encourages this sense of choice. Centralization is associated with the managerial state, with international adventure, and with the threat of bureaucratic dictatorship. Decentralization is associated now with freedom of choice, with the survival of democracy, and with the preservation of individualism. Yet, throughout the period covered by this book, something of the reverse has been true, at least to the extent that centralization has been associated with liberal reform, decentralization with local inequality and suppression of rights. One can scarcely avoid wondering how such a remarkable reversal of ideas can be explained.

It may be that the habit not only of viewing centralization and decentralization as alternatives but of thinking that a choice between them must be made results from our experience with a federal system that seems to provide us with the freedom to make that choice. There may be less freedom than we think, now that industrialization and technology face us with problems our faith in individual choice will not allow us to resolve. It is for this reason that an awareness of the problematic nature of our nationalism might help us to understand both the seriousness and the importance of our dilemma.

What may distinguish my argument from others I have cited is the fact that I do not believe that this dilemma is going to be resolved, either by a new national crusade or by a revolutionary transformation of the federal structure that produced the dilemma in the first place. Federalism and localism are not simply convenient governmental instruments for the management of a large society, though that surely is where they began. And the international responsibilities of the United States no longer permit withdrawal into local enclaves of self-interest, no matter how we define them. My belief in our inability to resolve our greatest national problem, then, may be what distinguishes me as a historian from those who see in the lessons of history the blueprints for reform. I do not, and I feel committed to explaining why.

There is at the heart of American utopianism a flaw that the ancient Greeks would have understood as tragic—that is, beyond repentance, beyond prayer, too essential to the human condition to encourage the search for redemption. That flaw is our commitment to the autonomous individual as the fundamental element in American democracy. Generations of American philosophers have struggled with the problems that that commitment raises, the limits it places on the ability of our society to act collectively, the idealistic demands it places on human rationality. It is the siren song that has brought others to our shores to seek freedom in our land and gold in our streets. It is the energy that fuels mobility and gives hope to those who seek to transcend the confinements of class and region. It is our dream, and it is our curse. It is what makes our debate over gun control such a seeming anomaly to members of other civilized cultures and turns the regulatory power of government into a shambles. It is the lifeblood of corruption in government, the single most effective threat to efficiency; yet it is the one most fundamental tenet in the American belief in self-government, in the state that serves its citizens and meets their demands, legitimate or not.

It is not going to change, and for one very good reason. It works. And it works in ways that are not at all mysterious, however much they may upset the carefully worked out plans of planners and the scientific hypotheses developed during the past century by the world's most sophisticated and influential social scientists. For generations American technicians in industry and academia have had more success in persuading other nations to adopt their theories of industrial management and their conceptions of the political process than they have had with their own countrymen, who continue to pursue self-interest in ways that would probably not have surprised James Madison. The American ethos today is not very different from the one Tocqueville observed with his very special mixture of worry and admiration: it is still the world's most political. Rationality, scientific or otherwise, is still subjected to the only test Americans recognize: a count of the ballots, a count they accept even when they suspect it may have been rigged. It was politics that helped a squabbling collection of colonies form themselves into a union of states, and it preserved them. It made possible a pioneer expansion that throbbed with violence and an industrial revolution as raw and disorderly as any in the world. A central state would not have helped; but a central ethos was needed to justify, explain, and paper over the most glaring defects. We had it. We still do.

Most important of all, this belief helped create what may be the world's most successful—perhaps the only successful—multiethnic, multiracial democracy. The shock with which we discover our violent past, from time to time, and the horror with which we look upon injustices to blacks, women, and others are part of our past and also part of our triumph. For we discover that we have changed. We have used the banner of individualism both to spearhead change and to step back from it.

This interpretation is as close to an understanding of our past as I am able to come. Some may find this a timid nationalism, a pallid defense of a glorious past. But then, that is my point. There is no glorious past. There may be a glorious future. But that is not yet history.

1

Introduction

In September 1932, as Americans awaited an election they prayed would save them from the seemingly endless Depression, the president of Dartmouth said, in a letter to a recent graduate, "I don't believe we can go on much longer without a very major change in our form of government." He hoped that the alternative might be a parliamentary form, but he was willing to accept even more revolutionary changes—changes that would involve picking strong leaders and giving them the authority to lead "rather than having them street-runners to whom we signal our will and from whom we expect immediate obedience."

The thirty-two-year-old president of the University of Chicago, Robert Maynard Hutchins, was speaking both to and for his own generation when he reminded an audience made up of Young Democratic Club members in June 1932 of the "mess our predecessors have made of things. After attacking us as the younger generation for ten years after the war they caused they are now compelling us to earn our living in, and are preparing to pass on to us, a world wrecked by that colossal blunder and their inability to cope with its consequences. Their stupidity, selfishness, and rapacity in the postwar period have matched the criminal lightheartedness with which they sent us into battle."

Others, equally alarmed by the nation's seeming paralysis, were resigned to accepting a variety of alternatives to certain chaos. They were prepared to deal with the crisis as an unparalleled emergency, requiring remedies that would, if only for the moment, end government as Americans had known it; then, when calmer times and confidence returned, the nation could once again enjoy the luxury of democracy.

The belief that democracy was a luxury that industrialized nations could no longer afford or an error the world's masses had been forced by eighteenth-century idealists and nineteenth-century capitalists to endure was not central to the beliefs of concerned Americans, but the possibility that their government might cease to work most certainly was. Those who wanted to blame that possibility on outmoded theories of government or an inhumane economic system were free to do so. Mussolini's fascism governed Italy. Stalin's more tyrannical version of communism had replaced that of Lenin, the "Little Father." Hitler stood at the edge of power in Germany, and the young and popular Prince of Wales, the future Edward VIII, toured the working-class neighborhoods of depression-bound England and spoke the words that summed up the feelings of millions in nations throughout the world: "Something must be done."

If the dramatic sense of urgency that flooded the world of the thirties was new in its intensity, the international market crashes, the unemployment, and the "hard times" were not. Such episodes had occurred throughout the nineteenth century and had then seemingly corrected themselves. "Booms" had followed "busts" with sufficient regularity to lead experienced observers to speak of "business cycles" and to believe that such seminatural processes were good for the health of modern society. They were measurable, predictable, even partly controllable. Some believed that, like the raging rivers produced by the cycles of the weather, they could be harnessed and made productive. If the Great Depression of the thirties was indeed great and therefore different, that was in part the product of a new attitude toward the conditions that had produced it and the methods that would bring it to an end.

The relation between confidence in new mechanisms of economics for controlling the international economy and confidence in new forms of government for controlling the way people lived is not as easy to explain as it might seem. New intellectual conceptions of government had been emerging as significant revolutionary forces in many parts of the world for over half a century. Political organizations defining themselves as socialist, communist, anarchist, and syndicalist, to mention only the leading ones, had been working to organize opposition to established governments of all kinds. Immediate economic conditions affected the size and energy of their followings; but such movements were continuous throughout the nineteenth century, regardless of the state of the world economy. Their leaders predicted revolutions in good times as well as bad, and the political changes they called for reflected a belief that changes in the economic order required them. Urban industrial societies could not be governed by constitutions created in preindustrial eras, they believed. The legislative bodies and political party organizations established by such constitutions had long since been taken over by groups serving their own special interests, not the needs of the nation and its masses. Legislatures and parties were either manipulated by their leaders or, paralyzed by internal oppositions, fell into stalemates that served no one or compromises that served everyone badly.

Since the 1890s reformers and political analysts in all parts of the world had been calling for changes in government, either to create democracy where it had not previously existed or to preserve existing democracies from their enemies. While the different national cultures in which such arguments were raised defined both the enemy and the methods required for conquering him in very different ways, there were similarities that transcended national boundaries and historical differences as great as those, say, between China, Russia, and the United States. Industrialization had produced new conditions everywhere. Science and technology required new knowledge, new elites to lead, new forms of social and economic management, and new attitudes on the part of the nation's citizenry, including a new commitment to the state.

The universality of this point of view is surprising when one considers both the range of cultures in which it appeared and the range of ideologies that it produced. Communism and fascism were Manichean opposites that nonetheless called for similar destructions of the old order and its replacement by a centralized state served by the masses in return for the promise of order. Individualism had to be destroyed and some form of collectivism put in its place. The battles between labor and capital had to be ended. One had to be absorbed by the other, either by giving industrial ownership to the laboring masses or by making capital the monopoly of the state. At their extremes, it became difficult to distinguish between the two, though on the long continuum that connected them there were, to be sure, certain differences.

Americans observed the European scene with a sense of protection that obscured their own changing attitudes. From 1885 on, for example, writers like Woodrow Wilson and Theodore Roosevelt looked to changes in presidential power and congressional organization as the answer to threatened chaos or to the conspiratorial usurpation they called "corruption" or "political patronage" or "invisible government" in their reform literature. The political parties, which in the early nineteenth century had been Americans' chief route to political power, had become the enemy of the popular will. "Robber barons" and "trusts" were terms that focused hostility on the nation's system of economic management without necessarily calling for its overthrow.

Americans interested in such problems protected themselves from the need for revolutionary action by believing that the Constitution of 1787 had already provided them with the means for retaking the power they had supposedly lost. Some argued that a few changes here and there—some by constitutional amendment, some simply by reinterpreting "inherent" constitutional powers—would do. Thus the amendment calling for the direct election of senators was intended to take power away from the corrupt state legislatures and give it to the people. In the years following his presidency, Theodore Roosevelt insisted that he had greatly expanded presidential authority simply by taking actions the Constitution did not explicitly forbid him to take. In local and state governments reformers succeeded in strengthening the control governors could have over state finances; they were also calling for city government by hired business managers rather than by elected councils and mayors. Increasingly, politics came to be looked on as a bad profession, the refuge of the unsuccessful, the lazy, and the dishonest; yet Americans still looked to politics for the satisfaction of their individual needs. Even those who found socialism attractive were convinced that one could have socialist city governments and selective government ownership—chiefly of public utilities, like power plants or public transportation—without disturbing the status quo. One political scientist argued that if Americans could elect a socialist Congress and a socialist president, who would in turn appoint socialists to the Supreme Court, American government would begin to behave differently without having undergone a revolutionary change.

Despite their protections from the revolutionary implications of their ideas, Americans were coping with the same problems that were leading to revolutionary upheavals in other parts of the world. Labor unrest, a growing consciousness of poverty as a form of injustice rather than a condition of life, and, above all, a sense that the complexities of modern life required a kind of observation and control of the lives of others that threatened older ideas of freedom led Americans to examine many of the same questions Europeans were asking.

Other factors, too, brought American society up against the same problems that were unsettling the rest of the world. Technological change was making it apparent that more education was needed, and at increasingly higher levels. The influence of scientific knowledge on medicine, engineering, transportation, and even household management transformed attitudes toward health care, longevity, child-rearing, and family mobility. The relative isolation and stability of community life, reflected in the small town and the cultural and historical cohesion traditionally represented by regions like New England and the South, were giving way to a new national self-awareness. By 1900 America's growing international power had encouraged some of the nation's leaders to use that power in imperial adventures, to increase expenditure on naval and military developments, and to become directly involved in the diplomatic disputes of European and Asian powers. These ambitions seemed to them to require a consciousness of national citizenship and a willingness to make sacrifices, if necessary—in short, a devotion to the state that Americans had traditionally hedged with qualifications. The Civil War was still a living memory for many, and states rights continued to be invoked against the encroachments of federal power. Communities still protected their authority to educate their children, care for their sick and aged, and exercise their rights to determine social customs even if those customs discriminated against some and limited opportunities for others. The historical nationalism that leaders elsewhere in the world could use to unite their people as Englishmen, Germans, or French was compounded of many myths, to be sure. But Americans had taken all of their lands from someone else and had populated them with diverse ethnic groups. The vibrant nationalism with which other countries justified their international adventures and imperial ambitions was difficult for American leaders to create, however necessary they felt it to be.

Nonetheless, by the turn of the century the rapid development of national news media and book publishing, fueled by improvements in printing and photography and manned by the growing number of newswriters whose national reputations gave them status among readers in small towns as well as big cities, meant that a national opinion was emerging on a variety of issues. In politics the power of parties to organize voter attitudes on important issues was being eroded by the skill with which individual leaders could shape popular opinion. This was the result of new inventions that came into use in the first decades of the new century—inventions whose political significance no one at the time could have foreseen. Radio and movies brought leaders into homes and local moviehouses in a kind of direct communication never before possible. The potentiality of individual leaders to do battle with opponents and to lead rebellions became a reality that transformed traditional political debate.

Although it is difficult to speak of changes in psychological perceptions on a national scale, it is necessary to try to do so if one is to attempt to understand the character of the collapse that struck all of Western society in the 1930s. Reformers of the 1890s had moved forward with a seemingly relentless optimism that steadfastly rejected the growing body of literature that questioned the capacity of mass humanity to improve itself or to be improved by the rational persuasion of others. These reformers knew, or were learning, the ideas of Nietzsche, Freud, and Sorel, but they thought them wrongheaded; still, their ideas might be turned to therapeutic use. Then the terrible brutality of World War I shook the reformers' optimism; nonetheless, they approached the 1920s in the hope that further scientific exploration into the causes of human behavior would bring new support to their religious convictions about the perfectability of man, though perhaps in a more limited way. The onset of the Depression was a challenge that at first disturbed these optimists as they watched the world become progressively more paralyzed by economic catastrophe. Franklin Roosevelt and the New Deal promised a new salvation, but by 1939 that too began to look doubtful. Spectacularly unprepared, by comparison to other nations, for yet a second world war, they struggled to build a war machine they could not help fearing. At the war's end they saw their fellow countrymen turn their backs once again on schemes for major social reform, while their government continued to muddle through.

By now the New Deal had become the symbol of American reform idealism, taking over from the old progressivism the responsibility of representing the hopes of reformers. But in the postwar period, the reformers felt themselves temporarily rejected, if not by their countrymen, then by conservative forces in business and government. The possibility that Americans in general were basically unsympathetic to reform, or at best had only short-term commitments to it, did not seem to occur to them. Leadership, they continued to believe, was the key to American reform; so they searched for another Roosevelt and bided their time.

The tendency to look on the years between 1915 and 1945 as a sequence of episodes of energetic reform energy interspersed by periods of exhaustion is understandable. The two world wars give the era an especially episodic character if one considers it from the perspective of a generation that thought of wars as events that had distinct beginnings and endings, starting with resounding declarations and ending in legally and morally binding treaties. That same generation of Americans also thought of international involvement as a genuine choice, open to a people who still could think of "the world" as being a great distance away, "over there." Yet both of the postwar periods may also show the degree to which such conceptions were tragically outdated if not altogether inaccurate descriptions of the world the United States was actually engaged in influencing and being influenced by. The emergence of the United States into world politics and world economic and social conditions was a fact that foreclosed the option of withdrawal that Americans believed was still open to them. The difference between the United States and other nations, even the optimism with which its people approached the twentieth century as their moment of triumph on the stage of world history, may not be as great as most Americans believed.

It is perhaps one of our history's major ironies that Americans have been forced to adapt themselves to a world history that they and their ancestors migrated to the New World to escape. As the impossibility of that escape has been pressed upon us by advances in transportation and communication we ourselves have been eager to promote, the frustrations of the adjustment have grown greater. They have led us to attempt to define ourselves and our purposes as different from those of other nations and to grieve when our definitions have not been accepted.

The years between 1915 and 1945 were the years when the major transformations of our modern history took place. This book is an effort to recount that history from a perspective that will take into account the international background against which American attitudes toward themselves and the world were transformed. They are also the years that witnessed major changes in the attitude of the rest of the world toward the United States. For it may be another one of history's ironies that the war "to make the world safe for democracy" came at a time when America's own conception of democracy was under more serious question than it had been for almost a century.

For European intellectuals in the first half of the nineteenth century, the United States was the harbinger of democratic liberation, the model of the future that worked. By the end of the century that sense of the future had begun to change. A younger generation of social critics looked to the relation between capitalism and mass democracy and found disturbing signs that the old ideals were no longer viable. The presence of seemingly intractable poverty, inequality, and social injustice, perpetuated by the very legal structures once heralded as the new salvation, gave birth to a new skepticism. The United States was also moving onto the international stage as a world power, a competitor in the old colonial contests, however idealistically it may have sought to state its case. With international power came criticism and, with criticism, a new and disturbing reexamination of the meaning of American ambitions in the world. At home the new American imperialism was seen by many as a genuine reversal of American values, a new course inconsistent with democratic traditions. Abroad, the new American internationalism was looked on in confusion as the United States appeared to claim an authority in World War I it then rejected in the intervening years, only to seek it again after 1941.

These are crucial years, then, especially when they are viewed as a whole rather than in the bits and pieces that are more familiar to us. The bits and pieces may indeed more accurately reflect the indecision in our attitudes toward reform, domestic as well as international; but it is the indecision itself that has operated most effectively to define the United States in the modern world. It has made us flexible and responsive but erratic and unpredictable. It has made us difficult to understand, even to ourselves. And, for better or for worse, it has made our struggle to write our history important.

2

Militant Progressivism

Progressivism was the nineteenth century's last reform movement and the twentieth century's first. The striving for equality of opportunity, an essential element of political reform movements from the nation's earliest years, had taken forms ranging from popular demands for land, tariffs, and an expanded currency to fervent calls for the abolition of slavery and for educational opportunities for the young of all classes. Although such demands would take new forms in the new century, they were part of a tradition Americans associated with the dreams they believed were embodied in their revolution and in their nineteenth-century struggle to preserve the union of the states.

By the end of the century, however, developments in science and technology were raising new problems, and many wondered whether the old methods of democratic reform could cope with the problems of a rapidly expanding nation. The kind of life that was lived in small towns and on the family farms that clustered around them was ceasing to be the dominant American mode of life. Linked by railroads to the major coastal markets and the international economy to which these markets, in turn, were tied, farm communities found themselves caught up in the transformations later writers would call "modernization." They felt compelled to profit by selling goods on the new national and international markets, but they wanted to sustain values that depended on generations of attachment to local communities. Such communities were a rich amalgam of family history and sectarian religious organizations, and the landscapes in which they flourished were as different from each other as the hills of New England and the fertile plains of the trans-Mississippi West.

Persons who moved from such communities to the cities, to seek new opportunities in the labor-hungry industrial empires, found themselves competing with European immigrants struggling for the same advantages. The barriers to communication between these groups, created by cultural and language differences, were often painful. The traditional practices of local American democracy—the town meetings and local political party organizations that assumed common agreement on the methods and purposes of governing—functioned differently in the backrooms of urban politics. Small-town Americans in the nineteenth century believed that they governed themselves, educated their children, and cared for one another, just as they came together on Sunday to pray for their common salvation. The circumstances that crowded them in cities seemed to isolate them in spirit; for them there was no urban organization to supply the authority of the old communities. They remembered an agrarian past more idyllic than it had really been, and they grew increasingly fearful of the decline in participatory democracy. Some sought to restore it with such devices as initiative, referendum, and recall. Others were more willing to acknowledge revolutionary changes in the very nature of democracy and to seek more effective managerial and technological methods for coping with the disturbing disorganization of modern life. The contrast between old and new was sharp and confusing; but it could also be harsh and threatening. The old reformers had sought to expand democracy; the new sought to preserve it within limits now imposed by science and technology. The two groups had a common history, even if they did not always remember it the same way.

A faith in state and local government as the centers of participatory democracy was being eroded by corrupt leaders and self-serving local interests, increasingly controlled by political parties and those who managed them. A growing consciousness of the unequal distribution of the resources on which economic opportunity depended was symbolized by the closing of the frontier, the once free land of the West. Increasingly, opportunity was coming to depend on technical skills—specifically, engineering and business management—which combined learning and experience in ways that agriculture, seemingly, had not. While celebration of the self-made man and the triumphant progress from rags to riches would remain part of the popular conception of America as the land of opportunity, its status as myth grew apace as the realities of modern life set limits on success.

Even those reformers who engaged in relentless attack on local political leaders were tempted to look to federal regulation and legislation as one way of assuring progress. Federal management promised uniformity of rules from state to state, as well as a certain amount of protection against the corruption of local politics, even though it threatened local autonomy. If civil-service reform always promised more than it achieved in its efforts to professionalize public service, the national media who took up the cause succeeded in keeping it before a national public that often despaired of local improvement. The high status accorded national political leaders, whether or not it was always deserved, contrasted sharply with the perception of local politicians as enmired in patronage and spoils. Yet the vast reaches of the still incompletely settled nation, the diversity of its population, and the cultural differences that gave regional identity to distinct areas like the South and the West continued to make it difficult for Americans to accept a central government with any-thing more than the limited powers permitted it by strict interpretation of the Constitution. What nineteenth-century Americans expected the distant federal government to do was to provide basic protection for the democracy they preferred to act out in the statehouses and city halls, close to home.

The conditions that weakened that preference are part of the history of nineteenth-century America and the key to the debates of the twentieth century. The rise of the cities and the large and powerful national industries that pressed uneasily against traditional political boundaries is a history of expansion and modernization in transportation and communication. Progres-sive reform began as a continuation of reform movements that had sought to improve the quality of state and local government, but it spread with the speed of a tidal wave to Washington itself. Riding that wave were leaders whose rhetorical skills combined religious fervor, embodied in the traditional American belief that God favored their political enterprise above all others, with a pragmatic commitment to politics as the one method that could solve all problems.

The religious tone of progressivism had been set as early as August 1910, when Theodore Roosevelt opened his Bull Moose campaign before a crowd of angry Kansans assembled to dedicate a monument to John Brown on the battlefield at Osawatomie. Brown's crusade had begun there and had ended on the gallows, a martyrdom that established him as one of the saints of the Civil War. If Roosevelt intended any parallels, he limited them to the mood his opening words evoked: "We come here today to commemorate one of the epoch-making events of the long struggle for the rights of man—the long struggle for the uplift of humanity." The insurgency that had been seething within the Republican party was now an open rebellion that for over a year threatened to destroy the majority strength the organized Republicans had built. Roosevelt, one of the architects of that strength, became the leader of the revolution and of the new party. He would ultimately become, in his own ebullient way, its martyred saint.

Roosevelt's opening sally was a call for a moral reordering in the wake of political disputes marked by attacks on "bosses," political machines, and the various forms of economic organization that could be brought together under the term "invisible government." The term underscored the sense of con-spiracy that had led one writer to speak of the "treason" of the Senate. Protesters, who designated themselves "Progressive Republicans," began to organize a revolution of purification within the party. When the Republican convention of 1912 renominated President William Howard Taft, Roosevelt's own carefully chosen successor, and rejected Progressive Republican pressures for an alternative to the leader they had come to associate with all the villainies of the regulars, dissidents formed the Progressive party and nominated a candidate of their own, Theodore Roosevelt. Roosevelt was not only an ex-president but an ex-regular, a professional politician deeply committed to the Republican party he now sought to purge. This was Armageddon, he shouted. "We battle for the Lord."

The creation of the Progressive party in the political campaign of 1912 gave the reform movement a sense of program and specificity it had not had before and was not destined to sustain. The multiplicity of reform programs put forward in the years after 1890 could not be systematically organized for a political campaign except by the extraordinary energies and manipulative talents of a man like Theodore Roosevelt. Even he could not maintain control of his erstwhile disciples in the aftermath of his defeat. As his followers picked among the rubble in the battlefields of state and urban politics, where progressivism had seemed so promising, they found the conflicts and inconsistencies the campaign had papered over. Those who favored industrial reorganization were not necessarily agreed on what role labor should play in that reorganization. Those who sought control over banks and currency did not have to see women's suffrage or prohibition as important to their argument. One could be willing to fight for public management of utilities and be concerned about the growing use of natural gas and electricity without wanting to preserve the natural forests or the purity of the nation's lakes and rivers. Lumber companies and coal mines were ravaging the nation's hillsides and depleting its resources; but they were employing working people to do it, feeding giant industries, fueling transportation for endlessly itinerant Americans, and providing housing and heating for all classes of citizens. The web of causes and effects was tangled and confusing. The momentary sense of simplicity generated by and for the 1912 political campaign gave way to complexities and quarrels. Once in power, the Democrats and their minority leader, Woodrow Wilson, could pick up the pieces and pass legislation that created banking boards, stiffer regulation of the trusts, and a commission to exercise some regulatory control over business practices. By excluding labor unions from antitrust prosecution, the Clayton Anti-Trust Act created a degree of government support for union organization, though it proved ineffective in the decades that followed. The newly created Federal Reserve System was not the central bank the banking community had sought; but banking power still gravitated toward New York, and the Federal Reserve itself remained just out of reach of political control.

The struggle to adapt traditional historical attitudes to the conditions of industrialization and urbanization was by no means uniquely American.

American progressivism was part of an awareness in all of the industrializing societies of the Western world that rapid technological change had social consequences. Science and industry were transforming nations from traditional organizations of classes and interest groups to large-scale industrial systems controlling masses of urban workers and managed by increasingly professionalized specialists. The owner who put his own money into his business and worked side by side with his craftsmen had been replaced by investors who scarcely knew the managers they hired, let alone the people who did the work.

The agony of such transformations had been apparent throughout the second half of the nineteenth century as religious groups throughout the world joined middle-class reformers of all ideological persuasions in rejecting the traditional justifications for poverty and suffering. The notion that the poor were responsible for their own poverty became as unacceptable as the belief that the ill were responsible for illness or the aged for age. Reformers began to put forward the concept of social justice, the idea that justice should not be limited to the traditional legal and economic relationships involved in the ownership of property but should extend to conditions under which people were required to live, the hopes they could entertain for themselves and their children, and their right to what Americans called "the pursuit of happiness."

Pope Leo XIII was one of the late nineteenth-century Roman pontiffs who called for a moral reordering of industrial relationships. Such religious pronouncements suggested that churches could become forces for alleviating poverty itself instead of simply providing charity to the poor. Bismarck's social policies in Germany established new forms of welfare in response not only to socialist pressures but to the realization that the conditions that produced labor unrest and social disorder were the results of decisions made by men— decisions that other men could change for greater social benefit.

Charles Dickens's novels depicted the injustices to women and children in industrial England, as Ibsen's plays did for Norwegians and other European audiences. Audiences who first saw A Doll's House knew that it was a tragedy, not a story of liberation. Nora's final exit was not into a world that freed her from bondage to her husband but into a world governed by a legal system that supported that bondage and left her nothing. George Bernard Shaw's play Mrs. Warren's Profession dealt with similar problems, more humorously but just as bitingly. The American novelist Kate Chopin shocked her readers with The Awakening, a novel about a woman whose effort to liberate herself from marriage and family servitude led to her suicide.

The problems of industrialism, and the personal tragedies it sometimes produced, were not confined to stories about women and children, although for reformers these remained the most moving themes for generations who believed that men were ultimately responsible for what happened in society.

Frank Norris's trilogy, of which only *The Pit* and *The Octopus* were completed, described a system of grain-trading that ultimately destroyed all who engaged in it, from the manipulators of grain prices on the Chicago Board of Trade to the railroaders who transported the grain and the farmers who produced it. His earlier novel, *McTeague,* had focused on a less ambitious but just as poignant problem. The story here is of a self-taught dentist forced out of the only profession he knows by new laws defining and regulating his profession; the end result for him is poverty and death.

Of all the American writers, it is perhaps Theodore Dreiser who best reveals the ambiguity in American attitudes toward industrial progress. In his novels *The Financier* and *The Genius* the author's affection and admiration for the supposedly "natural" qualities of business leadership in the battles of the market are tempered, if not contradicted, by his criticism of the system that twists and distorts that leadership. That ambiguity suggests, perhaps, that many Americans were still close enough to their agrarian origins to retain a strong sense of the values those origins provided. Agriculture contributed significantly then, as now, to our foreign trade. Thus, if it was a reality that could be romanticized, it was a reality nonetheless.

The transition from an agrarian to an industrial society threatened traditional values everywhere it occurred, whether the agrarians were established farmers, who resented the decline of their power, new agricultural entrepreneurs caught in shifting economic conditions they could not control, hired hands, working on lands owned by others, or, at the bottom of the heap, the sharecroppers and migrant workers.

American progressivism, nonetheless, like all American reform movements, differed in significant ways from its European counterparts. American reform had always taken place in the context of American expansion, as waves of people spread across a landscape they persisted in treating as unoccupied frontier even as they pushed its native occupants, the American Indian tribes, off their traditional lands. "God's country," they called it, or "virgin land," as though the generations of native habitation had been an error of nature they had been appointed to correct. Part of the problem lay in the definition of "occupancy" and "habitation" created by industrialization and expansion. For centuries the colonization of lands inhabited by peoples believed to be "primitive" had been justified by conceptions of race and hierarchies of social order, which were in turn justified by the achievements of European culture, science, and technology. But these justifications seemed more obvious to the Europeans who colonized Africa or the British who colonized Australia and New Zealand. They were leaving their traditional homes to seek new worlds, as they had done for centuries. The American view of the West had come to be somewhat different. Even before the Mississippi had been crossed, Americans had accepted their ownership of the West as part of their national destiny.

Yet American westward expansion was a process of conquest and coloniza-tion, and when it was completed, in 1890, historians lamented its ending. Frederick Jackson Turner's response to the closing of the frontier was to romanticize the effect the frontier experience had had on the establishment of democracy. He argued that frontier life had produced a unique form of democracy, and he suggested, somewhat more obliquely, that Americans might miss so essential an influence in their efforts to sustain that democracy.

Turner was by no means alone in his sense not only of transformation but of the ending of something essential to American life. Theodore Roosevelt's *The Winning of the West* had prefigured some of Turner's conclusions in its description of the first stages of westward expansion. Roosevelt's sense of the West was personal. He had gone there as a young man in not very good health, and the experience had transformed his life; he regarded it as his rite of passage to a sturdy, ebullient adulthood. This notion, that the rugged natural landscape was something important, something to be preserved—that it was the stage on which the proper education of the young should take place—played an important role in the conservation movement, which sought, among other things, to preserve natural park lands. Roosevelt was one of the leaders of that movement.

Conservation had its less romantic side, too. Railroadman James J. Hill worried about the depletion of the nation's resources, about the lumber, iron, and coal that were being destroyed the way the buffalo had been destroyed. As part of his effort to conserve resources that were being plundered without regard for the nation's future needs, he urged reforestation programs on the lumber companies. Although the term "planning" was not yet in use, many in the conservation movement were beginning to think of it, if only to lament the absence of managerial foresight.

As presidents, both Theodore Roosevelt and William Howard Taft worked to organize meetings of the nation's leaders to discuss not only conservation but the decline of agrarian life as the base of American culture. The Country Life movement was, like conservation, an effort to sustain important aspects of the past that were now being threatened; what is more, it sought to preserve not only values but practical realities. Like the progressive side of the conservation movement, it looked to science and technology not only to maintain agrarian life but to modernize it. Americans had to continue to eat, and farms were still the producers of food. Both the White House Conference on Conservation in 1908 and the Country Life Commission were examples of the way a president could influence events by appointing commissions to examine problems, to recommend solutions, and, above all, to publicize issues nationally. Federal intervention would remain limited to what presi-dents could persuade people to do, but presidential concern for planning had begun.

The American progressive movement was thus born at a point in American history when writers in a variety of ways were raising questions about the future of democratic government in the United States. The book known as the "bible" of the Progressive Era, Herbert Croly's *Promise of American Life*, appeared in 1909. Croly called for a more conscious ordering of American life and warned that failure to take his advice would lead to catastrophe. Walter Lippmann's title of 1914, *Drift and Mastery*, spoke of a similar crisis of choice and need for direction. While use of the term "planning" was still confined largely to the urban geographers, the concept itself was clearly in the wind.

The economist Thorstein Veblen was also writing at this time. In books like *The Theory of the Leisure Class* and in the series of critical essays he produced over the next two decades, Veblen combined a commentary on the tendency of businessmen to accumulate capital at the expense of efficient and stable production with a call for moral responsibility on the part of the nation's new technological elite, its "engineers," who could, from his perspective, play a much more important role in the rational ordering of society than the out-dated tactics of the "captains of industry" were willing to allow them.

For many European reformers the choice was clearer than it was for Americans. With constitutional monarchies still governing England and most of the Continent, reformers could adopt various forms of socialism as clear alternatives to traditional governments. Socialism would create a managerial control different from the upper-class controls still evident even in democratically modified monarchies. For Americans the fact that class oligarchies had to consist of figures like John D. Rockefeller and Andrew Carnegie, who sought little actual control over the operation of the federal government, made the problem more complex. One could point to the millionaires in the United States Senate, as David Graham Phillips did in his *Treason of the Senate*, but that amounted to a vast oversimplification of the problem. National wealth in America had changed hands for generations, and efforts to establish clear links between wealth and national political power, however tempting, could not produce evidence of continuous and long associations between the nation's rich families and its political leadership. American politicians may have been corrupt from time to time, but their ties to party organizations were closer than their ties to traditional wealth, to the extent that such wealth even existed.

Many writers at this time talked about the need to improve the quality of American management. Woodrow Wilson defined "leadership" as one of the essentials, and "statesmanship" was the key word in a series of American political biographies edited by J. T. Morse; the latter were exemplary accounts of individual development, written by amateur historians like Theodore Roosevelt, Henry Cabot Lodge, and Henry Adams, whose object was to provide readers with a pantheon of American saints. Such books were part of a movement to educate and inspire the young to be leaders, and they provided part of the basis for conceptions of leadership whose emphasis on mystical personal qualities and intuitive skills marked a new generation of "warriors." Such mysticism did not threaten the democratic tradition, it appeared, for the leadership it marked was widely dispersed; as the books themselves demonstrated, it was capable of being acquired on training grounds as far apart as the plantations of Virginia and the forests of the frontier.

The government created by the Constitution of 1787 was thus perceived as a democratic government already in place. Any connections between that government and upper-class wealth were understood as insidious corruptions of popular control, not as inherent defects in governmental form. Revolutions, therefore, were not necessary. One had only to "turn the rascals out" and retake the power. Although such aspects of socialism as government ownership of railroads and utilities were attractive to some progressives and populists, they were attractive more as methods than as parts of a revolutionary ideology. Textbook writers like David Saville Muzzey could predict in 1911 that some form of socialist-like government ownership was on the way in the United States, but revolutionary socialism was not. "Violence," the term that described the antithesis of the American conception of political action, was unacceptable as a method of reform. Americans had had their democratic revolution. All that was necessary was to make it work; and progressives set about accomplishing that task.

For progressives, then, the threat to democracy was not the existing government but the failure to use it properly. That failure could be remedied by attacking the hidden centers of antidemocratic power through legislation. Banking reform and business regulation were the chief methods, and progressives argued for greater control over banking and for revision of the Sherman Anti-Trust Act. The creation of the Federal Reserve System in 1913 and the passage of the Clayton Anti-Trust Act were the results. The Seventeenth Amendment to the Constitution, calling for direct election of senators, was intended to give voters rather than state legislators authority to elect senators and thus limit the number of wealthy individuals who could supposedly buy Senate seats. The Sixteenth Amendment, providing for a federal tax on incomes, though quite modest in its effects, was viewed as a triumph by the progressives, who thought they saw in its very limited attachment of wealth a foot in the door for redistribution.

Nonetheless, it is probably at the level of state and local government that one sees not only the greatest impact of progressivism but the sharpest contrast with European experience. Westward expansion had made the formation and reformation of new governments a habit for Americans. While changes in state constitutions caused political ferment whenever they occurred, they were familiar matters and they occurred with relative frequency. Urban governments, too, responded to reform moods, not only by changing leaders but by changing methods of governing. By the end of the century greater managerial control over expenditures, the establishment of budgets, and the creation of local agencies to look after citizens in need had joined local schools and state institutions of higher education as subjects of political debate. Local business and philanthropic elites managed such agencies, entered reform politics, and began to fight for such governmental innovations as the council-manager system of city government, which took the management of the city away from politicians elected by partisan political processes and turned it over to a nonpolitical professional and a board of business leaders. State governments, too, were being reformed, with closer attention paid to the managerial functions of executives, to more efficient systems of budgeting and accounting and a clearer division of responsibility.

The battle against partisan politics, which was so central to progressive ideology, thus took place at the level of local and state, not national, politics. If the victories were often short-lived—as in many instances they were—they were still victories, and they did more to fuel the energies of progressive reformers than any of their limited national triumphs. By contrast with Great Britain and Europe, where the aim of reformers was to centralize national authority over antiquated local bodies, American reformers, for the most part, were ambivalent about using the federal government as an agency of social reform; they concentrated on increasing the effectiveness of state and local systems by modernizing them. In that sense, the tradition of American federalism did as much as any single factor to shape the direction of progressive reform in the United States. The close connection between local wealth and local government was more often looked on as a virtue than as a sign of insidious control. The fact that so many of the reforms increased the power of executives at the expense of legislatures and sought to replace partisan politics and political opportunism with systematic controls and technological efficiency was not necessarily looked on as undemocratic by citizens, who thought that the protection of democracy and individual rights was up to the federal government. Executives were now perceived as superdemocrats, leaders with special democratic insights. The president of the United States was president of all the people; he alone was selected by the votes of the whole nation. This left Congress its role to play in preserving the prerogatives of localism. Communities retained control over those areas of life understood to be of local concern alone. Community custom often determined rights, and various forms of repression were often part of local religious and racial custom.

In many ways, Woodrow Wilson's career illustrates the complex elements that characterized the progressive leadership. As a professor of history and political science, he argued for the need to reshape attitudes toward government to make it more effective. He found British cabinet government attractive, as did many of his academic contemporaries, and he believed that the structures of government in the United States could, with little constitutional change, be made to provide responsible leadership and management. As president of Princeton University he joined a generation of university presidents who counseled the nation's reform leaders and accepted the task of training new leaders in the elite institutions of higher education they managed. Wilson in this period became a familiar speaker on the circuit of eastern dining clubs and reform political organizations. His addresses to the graduating classes of a number of law schools called for greater social responsibility on the part of the nation's most political profession. When he left Princeton in 1910 to become governor of New Jersey, it was as a reformer but also as an expert on politics and government; and in the eyes of many of his followers, he was headed for the presidency. A southerner by birth, the son of a Presbyterian minister, he held the appropriate WASP credentials among Democrats. His eloquence on the platform and the anecdotal humor that made him popular in informal political gatherings gave him an authority and a charm that captivated a wide range of audiences. As a Democrat he was obviously not identified as a progressive when the Republican party split over the issue of progressivism, but he was clearly an alternative to the conservative Taft; on the other hand, he was sufficiently progressive to draw votes from Roosevelt, whose tone became increasingly radical.

As a minority president, Wilson was faced with the task of rebuilding the fortunes of a minority political party—the Democrats—that was still dominated by the South, at the same time that he acknowledged the nation's rapid urbanization by building Democratic parties in the nation's northern and midwestern cities. The young Democrats he attracted to his administration—Franklin D. Roosevelt of New York is a prime example—were useful for that purpose. The awareness of the potential impact of urbanization on party politics and the willingness to use it in effective, practical terms was crucial to the development of the majority party that Franklin Roosevelt himself was going to lead.

At the same time, however, the South's domination of Congress increased the burden on Negroes, who lost their patronage jobs with the change in administration and found themselves faced with newly segregated facilities in the Washington offices they still occupied. Such evidences of racial prejudice were perfectly consistent with Wilson's interpretation of the Reconstruction era. As a historian he had already placed himself in opposition to Negro suffrage. Like progressivism itself, Wilson stood between old traditions and new realities, attempting to adjust the one to the other.

Thus Wilson, like Theodore Roosevelt and William Howard Taft, reflected the limits of progressive leadership as well as its strengths. Each had experienced in one way or another the profound sense of division and amalgamation that had so marked nineteenth-century America. Roosevelt, the son of a New York banker and a Mississippi lady who had steadfastly maintained her secessionist principles throughout the Civil War, had become an ardent advocate of American nationalism. Taft, a product of the Ohio River aristocracy that built mercantile centers like Cincinnati, had gone on to a successful legal career and had distinguished himself as the mediator of the complex racial and military problems involved in the American takeover of the Philippines. Wilson's earliest recollections were of the victorious Union troops marching through his hometown of Staunton, Virginia, and of his visits to Ohio relatives who called him "the little rebel."

Their sense of American nationalism thus rested on strong commitments to a nation of fundamentally diverse cultures that had to be unified, regardless of differences. Each reflected the complex of upper-middle-class elites that had guided American reform from its beginnings. If early American leaders like Washington and Jefferson looked to the development of some kind of national elite to which lesser citizens would defer, the rise of the politics of the common man in the Jacksonian era seemed to have blocked it. But not completely. For what had emerged by the end of the century was an American-Victorian class of national leaders whose common sense of social responsibility and whose attachment to middle-class values were underscored by their commitment to English and Protestant approaches to education and charity that enabled them to practice their Americanism without feeling that they were oppressing anyone. They knew what Americanism meant, and they believed it was their mission in life not only to maintain standards but to educate the nation's newcomers to an understanding and support of the image of American society as they saw it. They were not the extravagant millionaires to whom the term "elite" would more often be applied, but they did much to shape the direction of progressive reform.

The fact that American society had changed a great deal in the years of their upbringing and the formation of their political careers only reaffirmed their certainty about the rightness of their endeavors, and this helped to establish the range of criticism that later observers would employ in attempting to explain them. Wilson, in particular, was destined to be viewed as a man of rigid moralistic commitments and prejudices that limited his insights and his effectiveness, but such criticisms lift him out of his generation and underestimate the seriousness of the problems that committed progressives were now trying to cope with.

At the center of the new problems was a sense that American values were being threatened, and not only in the burgeoning cities. The new generation of immigrants were no longer European farmers seeking new land to farm but immigrants who were themselves either urban workers or peasants too poor to look for, let alone to buy, now, what land might be left. Older patterns of European migration had often tended to distribute newcomers across the nation in communities of friends or former compatriots. Ethnic and religious homogeneity, even the preservation of native languages from generation to generation, supported continuities and customs. Urban migration had followed similar patterns, for countrymen sought each other out for companionship.

In the cities dramatic conflicts often occurred at the borders between one enclave and another, but the rural communities, too, were experiencing intrusion as trainloads of newcomers willing to work in the fields or mines for lower wages confronted traditional communities unaccustomed to accepting differences in race—Indians and blacks were an old object of hostility in many western communities—let alone differences in language and culture. The sense of being invaded by a different culture was thus not new; but the magnitude of the problem seemed greater, and so did its seeming inescapability.

The movement of young people from rural communities to the cities to seek new opportunities, particularly in times of agricultural depression, was spurred by a literature that described industrial growth in Alger-like terms. The movement from rags to riches depended on the classical American faith in Yankee ingenuity and opportunism. If Mark Twain, in his *A Connecticut Yankee in King Arthur's Court*, cast doubt on the success such indigenous wit might produce, it did so with cynical humor.

Mark Twain's Yankee, attempting to introduce technology to medieval England, is almost a parody of the progressives' problem. How much change in basic character did modern advance require? If an American nation was going to be created out of the new immigrants moving in, the process would have to satisfy the older Americans who were pursuing their own ambitions in the nation's cities. Industrial growth and technological developments were the source of jobs for both groups, but the assumption that city jobs would solve all problems—as free land had once seemed to—did not turn out to be true. Clashes were inevitable. The new immigrants became competitors at the bottom of the labor force, resented not only by those who utilized their services but by those whose jobs they had taken. Although the ethnic enclaves formed in large cities were sometimes looked back on by later sociologists as cohesive communities of like-minded and supportive newcomers, helping one another, that view romanticizes a life that was often hard and brutal. The growing numbers of professional social workers who climbed the stairs of tenement buildings knew the reality of the grim and unhealthy environments created by the poverty of immigration and the sense of utter displacement of those whose lives in Europe, while poor, had at least been supported by familiar settings and traditions.

Americans borrowed the English idea of settlement houses, gathering places devised and managed by charitable members of the upper middle class for improving the condition of the urban poor through education and "friendly" advice; but the American effort was complicated by the essential foreignness of the new immigrants and the Americans' corresponding unfamiliarity with and lack of sympathy for the European lives led by those they were committed to helping. Turning immigrants into Americans as quickly as possible seemed to be the answer, no matter what problems that might cause for those whose ethnic identities were being transformed. Moreover, the public schoolteachers, who bore the brunt of the Americanization effort, were not interested in understanding the different cultural traditions assembled in their classrooms. Their aim was to replace them with their own version of American cultural norms.

Later critics of the Americanizing process would be inclined to see it as the imposition of white, Anglo-Saxon, Protestant cultural values on the nation's immigrants, but the teachers and social workers of the progressive era saw themselves as doing no more than their counterparts in other world cultures had always done in their efforts to nurture the young and improve the condition of the poor in their societies. Yet there was a difference. In the more or less homogeneous national cultures of England and the Continent, educators and welfare workers dealt primarily with internal migrants, whose cultural attitudes and values, language, and, in many instances, religion were the same as their own. The aim of these reformers was improvement, not total transformation. On the other hand, they were often less hospitable to genuine foreigners than Americans were. Expulsion and repression of foreigners had been common in Europe for centuries. By contrast, what the American reformers were after was not simply the transmission of cultural values but a total transformation in language and social behavior. It was not a process that placed great value on ethnic identity or the survival of alien cultures; but it was not perceived as repressive by those who championed what was coming to be called "assimilation," and many immigrants accepted the ideal of immersion in the "melting pot."

It is difficult to recapture in their own terms the reformers' understanding of what they were doing. What appears today as condescension at best, bigotry at worst, was in fact based on the idea that social behavior is traceable to national origins. As we will see in later chapters, this idea did not give way easily. Given their belief that behavior was ethnically, even genetically, determined, the reformers' essential humanitarianism lies in their conviction that Americanizing could even be done. Many in their generation did not share that conviction, as is evident from the recurring proposals that immigration be halted. The reformers were responsible, too, for founding the religiously based charitable associations that pioneered in the study of ethnicity and assimilation at the same time that they provided help in ways that were acceptable, if not kind. What is important about the urban crisis at the turn of the century is not the fact that it existed but that so many responsible people were committed to doing something about it.

That commitment is perhaps one of the most distinctive elements of the reform movements here and abroad. In a sense, it could be argued that the breakdown of the traditional class structures, and the class values on which those structures rested, had led to a growing consciousness of the injustices on which class differences were based. This sense of injustice was clearest where it was most obvious. A new perception of industrial violence was part of it. Efforts to improve the conditions under which factory workers worked had been part of reform movements for years, but the hazards of some occupations had been enshrined in folklore in ways that made them seem part of the natural world and hence irremediable. Whaling was such an occupation—indeed, all maritime service was; and the families and communities that depended on the sea accepted not only the hazards of the work but the peculiar harshness of life aboard ship. Herman Melville described the injustices in *White-Jacket*, and in *Moby-Dick* he raised the whole subject to the level of myth.

In the late nineteenth century mining was perhaps the most hazardous occupation; there were few safety regulations, and enforcement of those that did exist was lax. Moreover, life in the "company towns" was poor and mean. These isolated rural communities existed solely to support the mine, and everything in them, including the homes and the stores, was owned by the mining companies. Railroading was also hazardous, and here, too, the owners and managers were unwilling to adopt safety devices or provide adequate living conditions for the nomadic workers who manned the system. As the ballad of Casey Jones testifies, railroad wrecks were part of a mythology that could create heroes; but the wrecks were often due to inadequate maintenance of roadbeds and equipment and lack of realistic and controlled schedules.

At the turn of the century there was a great deal of labor unrest, and work hazards were one of the issues. Strikes called attention to the need for safety regulations, but this kind of protest was not welcomed by middle- and upper-class reformers, who tended to look on labor organizations as something foreign, un-American. The use of immigrant labor in railroading and mining contributed to that attitude. Nor were rural Americans who read about the Haymarket Massacre in 1886, the Homestead Massacre of 1892, or the Pullman Strike of 1894 likely to learn the workingman's side of the story. Haymarket, which occurred in Chicago, was the result of a police attempt to break up an anarchist meeting. It ended in the killing of seven policemen and the execution of four of the leaders. The Homestead incident occurred during a strike at the Carnegie Steel Company plant. Pinkerton detectives hired by the company killed seven of the strikers. The Pullman strike was ended when President Grover Cleveland sent in federal troops. Lurid newspaper accounts of all these events, obviously reflecting newspaper hostility to unions, helped fuel public concern over the growing incidence of violence.

In New York City the Triangle Shirtwaist Factory fire in March 1911 was an event whose horror inspired a generation of progressive reformers. One hundred forty-six persons died, most of them young women who were trapped in the workrooms, barred from access to the fire escapes. The management had locked the doors to keep them at their sewing machines every minute of the workday. Those who saw and heard those screaming girls, leaping to their deaths to escape the flames, never forgot it. The New York codes covering building safety were drastically revised in the aftermath of the fire, but one can still wonder if men leaping to their deaths would have aroused the same sympathy. It had happened before, and it was going to happen again.

The wounding of women and children in the Ludlow incident in 1913 may also have helped, finally, to inspire a national response. The Ludlow strike at a Rockefeller mine holding in Colorado was the last of a series of events that finally led President Wilson to appoint an Industrial Relations Commission. The hearings before this commission, which brought together the major critics and supporters of the labor movement in the United States, provided the publicity that was needed to transform public opinion.

By 1915 two major changes in American attitudes toward labor were taking place. One was the view that work, as the progressive social reformers understood it, influenced the stability of the whole social order. Labor could no longer be conceived of as a commodity to be controlled by industry, acting in its own interest alone. Labor unrest was not confined to one factory or one industry; it affected society as a whole. Mrs. Russell Sage, widow and sole heir of one of that generation's most unsympathetic industrialists (his only contribution to business literature was an essay condemning vacations) used his fortune to establish the Russell Sage Foundation, which sponsored research in the new field of social work and in labor economics and related subjects. Like other millionaire philanthropists of her era, she was acknowledging the need for a more comprehensive view of the social order and its discontents, as well as the need for more systematic knowledge in dealing with the problems of the industrial order. Although neither she nor her contemporary philanthropists, John D. Rockefeller, Sr., and Andrew Carnegie, would have called themselves "progressives," they were laying the groundwork for the development of the methods and instruments in the social sciences that would make progressivism work and would, indeed, be one of its chief legacies.

The other change in American attitudes was the idea that there had to be national policy on the problems of industrialization. Hammering out that policy was something Americans would cope with for the next two decades, as the federal government debated its relation to labor unions in particular and to social welfare in general; but the need for a policy had now been recognized. There would be steps backward and forward but never as far back as the conditions that had produced the crisis in the first place, and the coming of World War I produced notable steps forward when the nation, hard pressed to build a national war machine, looked to labor to help produce it.

The building of the industrial war machine also provided national awareness of the need for more efficient management of the nation's industries. For almost two decades the name of an industrial engineer, Frederick Winslow

Taylor, had been associated with concepts embodied in the term he had popularized, "scientific management." Taylor had become the champion of more effective managerial control over the actions of workers in the industrial process itself; he created what were known as "time and motion studies"— scientific studies of the necessary motions that a given task required and of the precise amount of time needed to complete each one. These provided standards for measuring workers' efficiency. Thus, efficiency depended on judgments made by technical experts observing the workers' actions, not on what workers believed to be their own best methods of working. Called before the Industrial Relations Commission and forced to defend himself against charges that he was antilabor, Taylor insisted that what he was looking for was a cooperative relation between management and labor, one based on objective "science," available for study by both sides, and subject to rational judgment—and acceptance. Enforcement, he insisted, was not necessary if rationality prevailed; but his writings made it clear that shop management should deal decisively with "irrationality" on the part of the workforce. Taylorism would ultimately be broadened into a social conception of industrial cooperation, intended as an ideological substitute for class conflict and union-management hostility. Taylor himself remained more interested in promoting efficient planning by management and greater industrial productivity. European observers over the next decade would be inclined to see a striking resemblance between Taylorism and some of the arguments proposed by theorists of industrial fascism, the ideological counter to socialism and communism, but Americans were not inclined to mark the resemblance. Nor were they inclined to take Taylor seriously as an ideologue of anything more revolutionary than more efficient systems of industrial production. Experiments with Taylor's methods in war industry were sporadic and incomplete, but they played an important part in making the nation aware, during the war years, of what critics would see as the wastefulness and inefficiency of the American industrial system. Such criticisms emphasized duplication of effort, poor management methods, and reluctance to adopt cost- and labor-saving improvements designed by the growing number of industrial engineers. There had been critics in the prewar years, but the war provided the first opportunity to think of the nation's industries as part of a whole system.

Although many progressives at first resisted American involvement in the war—the editors of the recently founded *New Republic* were among the most articulate—they ultimately allied themselves with the management engineers as they began to see an opportunity to use the war to bring about the national transformation that progressivism by itself had been unable to achieve. The war effort required some kind of national industrial system. That system, they reasoned, could be used to effect social and economic charges the political system had been reluctant to adopt. Yet the progressives had never really been forced to ask themselves whether or not the national culture they seemed committed to imposing on American society violated any of the traditions of democracy and individualism they were also determined to preserve. "One nation, indivisible, with liberty and justice for all" had scarcely been perceived as a contradiction, but the wartime imposition of nationalism was going to raise some disturbing questions.

Progressive reforms did, in fact, impose regulatory limits on economic, social, and political behavior—behavior that Americans were accustomed to regarding as matters of individual choice. That industrialization, science, and technology required such limits was obvious only if one had to see the nation's industries as a system, an integrated whole, bent on achieving a single national purpose. Progressive ideologues like Herbert Croly and Walter Lippmann had been implying that a single national purpose was essential to the industrial well-being of American society, but they had not been required to spell out that purpose, let alone to face the consequences of achieving their aims. Now the war effort spelled it out for them. The need to enforce a national unity, however imperfect it may in fact have been, was sufficient to reveal the consequences of imposing controls not only on the behavior of industry and labor but on the rights of individuals to say what they thought and to act on their beliefs.

In a sense, the fact that the war was perceived as foreign, hence alien to the American experience, made it possible to separate the war experience from the experience of American life itself and, at the war's end, to reject it. But the relation between the war and progressivism was dangerously close. The refusal to see a threat to traditional liberal democracy in the logic of science or in the complex demands of technological advance was part of an American commitment to the universal application of democracy and individual rights to all human endeavors, including science and technological advance. That commitment produced one of the essential differences between American progressives and their counterparts in European reform movements. European proponents of a new industrial order did not accept a fixed relation between liberal democracy and the technological transformations fueled by science and industry; they were inclined to think rather of redefining democracy in terms of revolutionary new conceptions of mass society or else of discarding it altogether in the search for a new industrial state.

If Americans were on their way to understanding the implications of progressivism, the war stopped them. Wartime nationalism and progressive nationalism had to be different from each other. In any case, the end of wartime nationalism meant the end of progressivism. It was dangerous to speculate on the relation between them, even to admit that it existed. For the next four decades—even up to the present, one might argue—the relationships between war and reform, nationalism and internationalism, traditional individualist democracy and the centralized industrial state would continue to provide Americans with a puzzle to contemplate, at least for those brave enough to try.

3

Managing War

THE OUTBREAK OF WAR in Europe in August 1914 was not looked on by most Americans as an event that urgently affected the interests of the United States. Businessmen involved in international trade of course wondered what the consequences of so widespread a conflict might be, and when they saw foreign trade come to a virtual halt in the first few months of the war, they became intensely concerned. The general public followed the war in the newspapers, but it was probably more troubled by disturbances immediately to our southwest, where Mexican revolutions seemed threatening. Few serious observers would have predicted that in less than two and a half years American soldiers, drafted by an aroused and angry citizenry, would be crossing the Atlantic to fight on European soil. The transformation of popular attitudes in so brief a period of time was as remarkable as the experience of the war itself. American interest in international affairs entered a new phase as public opinion shifted from its familiar focus on protection of "our" hemisphere to salvation of the world.

Foreign trade and world salvation seem distinctly different issues, but their persistent entanglement as reflections of reality and idealism had been part of American history from its beginnings. As a major producer of such world-market crops as cotton, tobacco, and wheat, the United States had long played a significant role in international trade. And as a country committed to its own industrialization, it had had the experience of debating tariffs and their effects on American consumers of foreign goods. By 1914, certainly, the arguments were familiar, however heated they may have tended to become from time to time. Duties on sugar, for example, had helped provoke the successive crises in Cuba and Puerto Rico that resulted in the Spanish-American War. A battle over duties on Canadian wheat and its effect on American wheat producers had split the Progressives and Republicans in 1911. Americans wanted the freedom to compete on international markets at the same time that they wanted government protection from competition of cheaper goods from abroad.

When the outbreak of war in Europe threatened to bring trade to a halt, it introduced a set of factors that American policymakers had not had to deal with on such a scale for years—indeed, not since the Napoleonic era. Ever since the early nineteenth century, international law had provided codes of procedure for enabling trade to continue during wartime and for protecting the status of nonbelligerent nations. Rules defining "contraband" and governing "search and seizure" had all been methods of controlling that trade in ways that would limit the shipment of armaments to countries at war without destroying international shipment of nonwar items.

The breakdown of that system under the peculiar demands of World War I and its new technologies was what actually drew the United States in, although that was not foreseen at the beginning. The "neutrality" Wilson proclaimed in August 1914 accurately reflected American attitudes. The term not only meant that Americans felt no consensus on the causes of the war, on the rights or wrongs being committed on either side; it also meant that they wanted to continue to deal as openly as possible with all of the participants. American philanthropists organized shipments of food and clothing to supply homes and families in need, wherever they might be. The Wilson government offered its services as mediator; and, gradually, American suppliers of materials of all kinds seized the opportunity to expand their markets abroad. Banks facilitated loans while the Wilson government stood nervously by, fearful of the outcome of such involvement but inexperienced at managing it. After the initial period of paralysis, international trade took off. Americans were benefiting from the war, no matter how much they deplored it.

Within a year it was clear that a shift was taking place. Americans were still following journalistic descriptions of the battle scenes of Europe, the horrors of trench warfare and poison gas, and the terror wrought by new weapons like "Big Bertha," a huge German cannon that hurled its missiles over previously unheard-of distances; but on the sea lanes of the North Atlantic a new war and a new weapon were now perceived by the European belligerents as the key influences on the outcome. The submarine had become a crucial weapon in determining what would ultimately happen in the land battles in Europe.

Thus, while Americans were reading accounts of village invasions like Gertrude Abernathy's *House on the Marne* and speculating on the damage being done to the great continental cathedrals, it was becoming clear to the belligerent governments that the outcome of the war depended as much on the power to blockade shipments of supplies as on any other single factor. Americans considered their shipments of food and clothing to the starving children of France and Belgium as acts of mercy, despite the fact that this relief, by weakening the blockade, had the effect of prolonging the war. Great Britain's island isolation made them in some respects vulnerable, but the British navy's control of the North Atlantic and the success of its blockade of Germany at first were serious irritants to American policymakers, who persisted in refusing to consider the consequences of their "charity."

Germany, unable to compete with the British navy, countered with the submarine, a weapon that effectively destroyed the nineteenth-century tradition of naval warfare. The submarine's power depended on secrecy and surprise. "Search and seizure" and other methods of humanizing military encounters were simply ignored by the new attack vessel. On the surface it had relatively little power and virtually no defenses. Underwater it was a monster, a hidden beast of prey against which there was seemingly no defense. Like the Continental troops of the colonial era, arrayed in colors, accompanied by fifes and drums, and organized in neat lines, the ships of the traditional navies faced an enemy not unlike the Indians, hidden behind trees and aware of the utility of silence and surprise. The equation of the submarine with barbarism was thus not difficult to make. Indeed, the notion of surprise attack as somehow immoral, a violation of the legal practices and moral commitments by which international-law theorists had been attempting to civilize modern warfare, would remain a problem for American public opinion for many years to come.

On 7 May 1915 a German submarine sank the British ship *Lusitania*. Among the 1,198 passengers and crew who died were 128 Americans. The fact that the vessel was British and hence, by German definition, an "enemy" did not mollify American feelings, which ran high. It was, morever, a passenger vessel, not a purely merchant ship, a fact that occasioned much argument, not only in the United States but within the German General Staff, where it was clear that the novelty of the submarine as a weapon had reduced many of the formal definitions to rubble. The ship had been sunk without warning, despite the fact that it was unarmed. No effort had been made to find out what, in fact, it might have been carrying.

For Americans the event could be distinguished even from the sinking of vessels known to be carrying goods and supplies. The *Lusitania*, whatever its cargo, was loaded with passengers; and the freedom of Americans to travel the seas, even on the ships of nations at war, became the issue that galvanized popular response and began the crucial shift in the official position, which was no longer to be based on the freedom of neutral states to engage in trade in wartime but on the freedom of American citizens to travel as they chose. The first was a legal issue, already badly disturbed by the novel method of attack but amenable, at least, to some redefinition of the older rules. The second became an emotional issue of such intensity that its legal status rapidly lost meaning. The American secretary of state, William Jennings Bryan, could still see the distinction, and he argued against Woodrow Wilson's taking a strong stand; but Wilson, pressed by public opinion and perhaps by his own sense of outrage, insisted on a harsh and threatening response. Bryan resigned.

The debate that raged from May 1915 to the American declaration of war on 6 April 1917 reveals the gradual escalation of emotions on all sides. Great Britain was growing increasingly dependent on American supplies. Germany could not continue to allow its enemies to be supported by a supposed neutral. German strategy, dependent as it was on speed and surprise, could not be maintained indefinitely. The stalemated war in the trenches of Europe had developed into a ghastly inferno, where soldiers crawled in mud and darkness, lit only by the rocket flares, to achieve little but mutual destruction. The German decision to engage in unrestricted submarine warfare was based on an acceptance of the fact that the United States would probably intervene; but the Germans also calculated that internal divisions in the United States and the disorganized state of American industry, already revealed by Wilson's efforts at "preparedness," would render America's entry irrelevant. The benefits of halting Atlantic shipping, they reasoned, would outweigh any direct American involvement.

The Germans should have been right. The fact that they were not—and the reasons why they were not—reveals important aspects both of America's experience in the war and of the ways that experience affected postwar American thought. The sinking of the *Lusitania* had shown the inherent weaknesses of "neutrality," but Wilson's attempts to persuade Americans to prepare themselves by adopting even a limited form of military conscription, like his attempts to get American industry to organize itself voluntarily for war production, had demonstrated the profound limits of presidential power over the nation's industrial system. What is more, it revealed that there was no national system capable of centralized management.

Readers of American newspapers and journals of various political persuasions and ethnic identifications would also have noted deep divisions in public opinion. It was, initially at least, not easy to hate the Germans. After all, they were Anglo-Saxons, like the English. Their contributions to American intellectual development were clear, not only to Americans of German origin but to the generation of American scientists and social scientists who had gone to Germany to work for higher degrees. Moreover, the American Irish sympathized with the Irish revolutionaries, who were seeking to win independence from Great Britain; they were contributing money as well as young fighters to what had become a bloody battle for the kind of freedom Americans of older English stock felt they had won from the mother country. Their concern for British interests on the continent of Europe were obviously very limited. Pro-British enthusiasts like Henry James and, ultimately, Theodore Roosevelt reflected a WASP America in decline, particularly to young intellectuals like Walter Lippmann and the editors of the *New Republic*, who opposed involvement on a variety of grounds. Popular political leaders associated with midwestern and western progressivism—men like Robert M. La Follette, William E. Borah, and Hiram Johnson—were part of an older antiinternationalism that would ultimately be defined as isolationist. Some, like Borah, favored an American imperial stance but resisted the notion that America should defend any interest but its own. All in all, observers of the American scene from abroad would have had difficulty in detecting a national consensus on the war.

The American war machine gradually took shape, but it did so like a lumbering leviathan, willing to respond to the demands the new age was making upon it but slow and clumsy in its efforts to do so. The assumption that so vast a national program could be built on a voluntary basis, that Americans, from the top industrial managers down to the lowliest factory laborers, would organize themselves to serve the national war purpose, required the creation of a national will far more purposeful and far more self-sacrificing than Americans had ever before been asked to sustain. The insistence, too, that a significant portion of the cost of the war should be borne by public subscription through the sale of bonds also required a national consciousness different from that demanded by any previous crisis. The belief that all such things could be done with the minimum of legal coercion rested on a willingness to use the maximum of rhetorical persuasion and popular pressure to bring them about. Yet, long before the American decision to intervene, the tone had been irrevocably set. The war that no one could justify in 1914 had become a national crusade for aims no one could define in 1917; but everyone knew they were right, that they reflected a justice to which all Americans would have to subscribe. The Great War had been transformed. A puzzle in international power relationships had become a new democratic revolution; for the world, as Wilson put it, was going to be made "safe for democracy."

The American declaration of war against Germany on 7 April 1917 could be viewed as the culmination of one process of development and its transformation into something else. "Freedom of the seas" and the assertion of neutral rights had been the key concepts in the early years of the war, when America's interests in international trade had been, for better or for worse, transformed by the unprecedented expansion of American trade with Great Britain and France. The crusade to "make the world safe for democracy," however, was another matter. By asserting its rights not only to protect its own interests but to change the basic international structures that had presumably placed those interests under threat in the first place, the United States was seeking a new role for itself in international affairs, a role much closer to that of the sympathetic revolutionary state it had so often tried to be in nineteenth-century international politics. Whether Wilson and the military-industrial state he assembled reflected a national consensus was, as we have seen, highly questionable, but it was absolutely necessary that such a state be created, consensus or not. In fact, it became necessary that the consensus itself be created. Wilson's speeches were all calculated to produce a fervent national agreement, to call upon all Americans to help him fight not only the war but internal opposition to it. The Allied victory was produced by the power of an American industrial system created specifically for that purpose and placed under the command of a national administration with powers the United States had never before granted to its federal government. While the process of getting the system in place was slow and awkward, at the peak of its power, from December 1917 to November 1918, it exercised extraordinary control over American industrial life.

Wilson's decision to staff the war administration with volunteers recruited from the nation's industries was crucial not only to the way the war effort was ultimately organized but to the American approach to the war itself. Selecting leaders from the nation's railroad industry and its clothing and manufacturing concerns, as well as key figures in banking and finance, meant that Wilson would have an experienced cadre of industrial managers to work with. Given the fact that there was no alternative group in the federal government itself, the decision was less a matter of choice than a quickness to take advantage of the options open to him. These leaders in turn brought a younger group of executives with them. The top echelon consisted of men who, wealthy in their own right, could work for the government for "a dollar a year," the phrase used to characterize their patriotism.

Equally important, the private managerial system was inspired by a nationalism just as intense in its control of the life of the nation as the patriotism that justified wartime service. The need to "win the war" produced a sense of urgency that veiled a fear, not simply that the war might be lost or that the consequences of losing it would be dire, but that the cause of failure would be the internal divisions that the years from 1914 to 1917 had revealed so clearly. The war abroad had to be won; but that victory seemed to many to depend on winning the other war—the war at home.

On 14 April 1917, a week after his address requesting a declaration of war, President Wilson issued an executive order creating the Committee on Public Information. Headed by a newspaperman and magazine writer, George Creel, the committee was intended to organize the distribution of information required to keep the public properly informed on the course of the war. While part of the initial intention, at least on the part of Wilson, was to provide Americans with alternatives to the propaganda with which they were being bombarded from all sides, the committee in fact became a propaganda agency itself; that is, it assumed responsibility not only for informing public opinion but for controlling it. Members of the new advertising industry joined with journalists and academicians to promote the war effort. The public schools were provided with pamphlets to distribute to schoolchildren, explaining America's role in the war and the need for loyalty to the American cause. Local committees tapped citizen volunteers to speak on behalf of the war effort to schoolchildren, clubs, and other organized citizen groups and in movie theaters between the end of the film and the beginning of the vaudeville acts. Such "four-minute men," as they were called (partly because they promised to speak for only four minutes and partly to recall the volunteer fighters of Revolutionary days), exhorted audiences to all forms of engagement in the war, from military service to volunteer activity, like rolling bandages for the Red Cross, knitting sweaters and scarves for servicemen, serving in the coffee and cookie canteens that sprang up in cities and towns near military camps and railroad transfer points, and, ultimately, purchasing the bonds with which the war was financed.

The promotion of Americanism and a spirit of wartime loyalty inevitably focused on the dissenters, the un-American and the disloyal, who opposed the war for whatever reason. The line between promotion and coercion dimmed as the effort to define loyalty intensified. A failure to volunteer for service, even an inability to do so for legally acceptable reasons, became tantamount to opposition in the eyes of a community aroused to furor against the enemy. Freedom of the seas, rights of neutrals, competition of national empires for world markets—all of the issues that had been central to the debates of the previous three years—were pushed aside in the turmoil of the war effort, replaced now by a rage against Germans and things German. The German language was removed from school curricula, German operas and symphonies were cut from repertoires, German street names were changed, often being replaced with some form of the term "Liberty," and "von" vanished from family names, where it had once signified some proudly remembered identification with nobility. The British royal family of Saxe-Coburg-Gothas became Windsors, the Battenbergs became Mountbattens, and Americans with German names followed suit.

The actual organization of the war effort itself brought many of the progressives' arguments to the fore. The financing of the war had played no role as an issue in any of the preparedness debates. A tacit understanding that American industry and American agriculture would benefit from expanded war trade rested on the assumption that the Allies were customers with funds of their own to pay for what they bought or with borrowing capacities attractive to American bankers willing to lend. The possibility that the war would become dependent on the American public for funding was not seriously considered in advance. The income tax was still a novelty, and the initial rates were still set by the compromises made by the progressives. Thus it did not weigh heavily on the wealthy, and it bypassed all Americans with incomes of less than $4,000—the vast majority. By 1916, increases in military expenditures had begun to produce a national deficit, but Congress was unwilling to increase taxes.

The War Revenue Act of 4 October 1917 was in some respects a progressive triumph. It authorized a graduated income tax beginning at 4 percent on personal incomes of more than $1,000, raised the corporation tax, and placed an excess-profits tax on corporate and personal income. Excise taxes on alcohol and tobacco were increased, and new excise taxes were levied on luxuries, amusements, and transportation. This triumph was short-lived, but the progressive principle was nonetheless established: almost three-quarters of the cost of the war was to be borne by corporations and those with large incomes, not by the consumption taxes conservatives had tried to promote. The costs skyrocketed far beyond what was envisaged at the beginning. Ultimately, a third of the money came from war-bond subscriptions; the rest was charged to future generations of Americans. War-financing was a mixed experience, and few on either the progressive or the conservative side of the debate were satisfied. The issue was destined to return in the aftermath of the war as critics reexamined the experience and tried to assess its meaning.

The effective management of the war was again a subject of dispute. It was clear by the winter of 1917 that volunteerism was not working. The collapse of the nation's railroad system was the most threatening sign. It was also the oldest and most familiar example of American industrial inefficiency. The railroads had led in the creation of virtually every aspect of national American industry, but they had done so like Hannibal's elephants lumbering over Alpine passes they would never have chosen to traverse, not like the innovational industries their supporters claimed them to be. Reluctant pioneers, they had been forced to face the development of a national labor force, the pressures of regional customer demand, the puzzles of technological innovation in materials and equipment, and, above all, the impact of federal regulation well ahead of their companions in the American technological revolution. They had also served as the most logical target of those who called for government ownership of public utilities. Even William Jennings Bryan had returned from Europe convinced that public ownership of the railroads was a national need, and, by the eve of the war, that conviction was shared by a sizable segment of informed public opinion.

By 1917, the American railroads had experienced almost thirty years of federal regulation, but this had been administered, by and large, with their advice and consent. As critics had been pointing out for more than two decades, railroad ownership had become centralized to a degree that had disturbed trust-busters without eliciting clear judicial decisions on what the government's response ought to be. The American railroad system was not a "system" in any serious sense. The lack of standardization in such obvious mechanisms as the couplings that attached one car to another made it impossible to ship a loaded car across the country without several reloadings into cars of different lines. Shippers complained about rates, while local railyards maintained platoons of workers whose job it was to reload cars. Gossip about wage differentials was carried along the same lines that carried cargo. Railroad managers rejected innovations and safety features as too costly and insisted that they could not raise wages or rationalize rates. Centralization in fact had produced few of the efficiencies the proponents of centralization claimed. The United States had a national railroad system in one sense only: the rail lines spanned the nation.

The war effort compelled the adoption of a national system. Shipments of troops and materials had to be organized for one basic purpose: support of the war effort. The demands of war exposed the inner workings of the rail system as they had never been seen before, and the strain on the system was already very great when the weather—December 1917 was an unusually snowy month—produced the straw that broke the old camel's back. The federal government took over the running of the railroads the day after Christmas. Secretary of the Treasury William Gibbs McAdoo became director-general of the Railroad Administration, which controlled almost 400,000 miles of track operated by 3,000 companies. The progressives cheered. Innovative managers moved in. They introduced technical improvements, modernized the system, rationalized rates, and raised wages, not only to keep the system going but to keep it going well. But again the progressives, who had seen all this as a needed revolution, turned out to be wrong; for the government did not choose to go on managing the reformed system after the war. The Transportation Act of 1920, against President Wilson's advice, returned the system to its private owners, much improved, more efficient, and more profitable. The war, and the public, had bailed out the railroads. They had also created the necessary transportation system for making the war effort work, and that, when all was said and done, was all they had intended to do.

The War Industries Board, established in July 1917, is another example of a centralized administrative control replacing a failed volunteer effort. In March 1918, President Wilson authorized a sweeping reorganization that placed financier Bernard M. Baruch in charge of the group that controlled war industry, set priorities, and fixed prices. Congress had already authorized strict presidential control over food production and fuel, and it moved now to take over patents and other property of enemy aliens and to control all trade with enemy nations. The creation of a War Finance Corporation to lend money to financial institutions, who would in turn lend money to industries engaged in war work, was another dramatic step in the process of government intervention, while the National War Labor Board and the War Labor Policies Board were presidential efforts to resolve labor disputes in war industries.

Progressives pressed all of the industrial boards and committees to follow progressive principles and to use their power to institute the reforms that progressives had long been advocating. Economists on the War Industries Board had their first opportunity to acquire systematic information on the economics of national industrial production and to push for standardized reporting. The Labor Board, under the joint chairmanship of Frank P. Walsh and former president William Howard Taft, committed itself to the ideal of a living wage, carrying a significant step further the argument against the treatment of labor as a commodity in the production system whose compensation was determined only by the law of supply and demand. The Labor Policies Board under Felix Frankfurter made important strides by requiring accurate and realistic reports on labor conditions and gave great impetus to the idea of justifiable grievance. Presidential threats to use war power to take over industries whose management refused to negotiate with labor were effective in forcing bargaining and in gaining support from the leaders of the labor movement. Yet, as the experience in the twenties was to demonstrate, the balance between wartime fervor and commitment to progressive ideals was considerably more uneven than even the most knowledgeable of the progressives were inclined to believe in the heat of what some preferred to see as a wartime revolution. At the same time, the experience was there. It was intense, and it was available for later use in the New Deal decades. Even so, it was the sense of emergency, one could argue, that could be appealed to, not any commitment to reform.

Federal support of farm prices, to encourage expanded production, posed a similar problem for those who would later look back on the war years. It answered an immediate wartime purpose in a nation responsible for supplying not only its own needs but those of its allies; and price was no object. But when price became an object, as world production returned to normal, the experience of price supports was there to be appealed to, not necessarily in recollection of the emergency but certainly in recollection of the prosperity it had produced. No one would have argued for a return to war emergency, but the mechanism, many thought, could be reshaped for peacetime use if only one could figure out how.

All in all, the war was a disruptive experience that swept across the American landscape like a firestorm feeding on every source of energy it touched. Prohibition had been an issue for more generations than anyone could remember. Wartime morality, plus the belief that most American manufacturers of alcohol were German, gave the Eighteenth Amendment movement the edge it needed. The intensity of the need to create and sustain a national sentiment in favor of the war was based on a fear that failure to do so would make victory impossible; but it led to repressive legislation that severely limited any criticism of the war or of the nation's conduct of it. The Espionage Act of June 1917 was intended to control treasonable or disloyal activities, and the coupling of treason and loyalty is the key to the difficulties that were encountered in interpreting and administering the law. Treason could be defined by forms of behavior determinable by law as treasonous. The same standard could not be applied to loyalty, a concept that depended on beliefs and on statements in speech or writing. The act empowered the postmaster general to exclude from the mails anything he deemed treasonable or seditious. Its constitutionality was upheld by the Supreme Court, even though Oliver Wendell Holmes's ringing dissent became the standard, ultimately, by which the Court would defend free speech. Before the war was over, the act was amended to make it even more severe, particularly in its penalties against socialists and pacifists.

Faced with congressional pressures to create a national war cabinet to build a more effective war machine, Wilson himself wrote the legislation that became the Overman Act of 1918, which granted the president greater administrative authority than any previous president had ever had. Passed in May 1918, the Overman Act gave Wilson enormous powers of reorganization and concentration of government where war activities were concerned. The American war machine had reached its peak. It could now win the war, but it would do so at a price that many were beginning to consider much more costly than anyone had anticipated. Americans had nationalized themselves to face threats that had gradually become more internal than external, although it grew increasingly difficult to see the distinction. Even the Zimmerman Note—Germany's effort in March 1917 to enlist Mexico against the United States in the event that America entered the war against Germany—paled as a threat when Americans faced the thought that they might lose the war through failure to achieve a national consensus on the effort required to win it. The enemy at home became the most visible enemy to attack.

Part of the problem lay in the initial inability of any of the combatants to explain the reasons for the war in the first place. Wilson had pointed to the problem in his earliest efforts to negotiate a settlement, long before America's entry. Neither side would define its war aims. Wilson's attempt to promote what he called "peace without victory" had failed to stimulate even a rudimentary list of the demands each side would make as the price of settlement. After America entered the war, Wilson sought to establish a list—the famous Fourteen Points—but by then it was clear that, at least as far as America was concerned, the list was no longer negotiable. The Fourteen Points were, he asserted, "the only possible program." Basic attitudes toward war in general and this war in particular had undergone changes, and these had begun to differentiate this war from previous wars. To the extent that previous wars had reflected a nineteenth-century view of war as an extension of diplomatic policy, designed to bring about specific aims with regard to borders and territorial authority, they had been managed by governments as policymaking activities. From such a perspective, the proponents of perpetual world peace were characterized as dreamers, out of touch with the realities of world politics.

The transformation of Wilson's attitude toward the war from "peace without victory" to "the war to end war" and then to a "war to make the world safe for democracy" was a transformation from the instrumental realism of much of the nineteenth century to a dramatic idealism that became much more of a religious crusade. Nor was this simply an American aberration, traceable to a unique American idealism or to Wilson's personal naïveté. Russia's withdrawal from the war, following the November 1917 revolution, led to the enunciation of similar criticisms of the aims of the war. Couched in Marxist terms, they held little appeal for Americans, even though they spoke to some of the same issues of international politics and to the ultimate uselessness of war as a policy instrument. Instead of arousing American sympathies, the Bolshevik position exacerbated American fears; for Russia's withdrawal liberated German troops for service on the Western front and underscored the growing fear that the antiwar movement, led by socialist and pacifist groups in other countries, would lead other allies to withdraw. The Committee on Public Information opened an office in Rome for the precise purpose of influencing Italian public opinion and countering the antiwar literature being circulated there. In the United States the hostility to socialism and to immigrant groups who were identified, rightly or wrongly, with leftist ideological positions came to be tied directly to the commitment to winning the war. It appeared to be a simple step in logic to argue that socialism and communism alike were pro-German.

The entry of the United States determined the outcome of the war; but the United States did not win the war. The victory went to the Allies, who dictated the terms of the peace. Germany had agreed to an armistice on the understanding that the United States would dictate the terms of the peace and that Wilson's Fourteen Points would serve as the basis of the terms. But Wilson joined the Versailles Conference as only one of the four heads of state who drafted the terms, and his influence was limited, especially given his inexperience and given the fact that the election in November 1918 had turned control of Congress over to the Republicans. Those who considered the election results a repudiation of Wilson seemed to forget that none of Wilson's political victories had been clear-cut. The Democrats had not been a majority party in 1912 and they were not one in 1918. The factors that had given them their slender margins had quite possibly been balanced by the experience of the war. The return to normal politics was on the way, and normal politics meant Republican majorities at the polls.

For so brief an experience, even if one dates it from 1914 rather than 1917, the American involvement in World War I was as intense and as significant as any since the Civil War. The regular army in 1917 consisted of about two hundred thousand men. By 1919 that number had reached more than four million, over two million of whom had gone to France.

For the first time since the Civil War Americans had been drafted to serve in the armed services. Fearing riots like those that had attended the Civil War draft, particularly in cities with large German populations, Wilson had dis-

tributed registration forms through the sheriffs' offices, but there was no need
for concern. The patriotic mood held. Public hostility to "slackers" and
"draft-dodgers" had its effects, while management and selection by local
boards helped smooth the transition from the old nineteenth-century system
of locally recruited units to the establishment of a national army.

That Americans were fighting on the battlefields of Europe was something
new and shocking, both for those who went and for those who joined the labor
force to serve the nation's industrial needs. American industry responded,
too, to its first major taste of government intervention; but even that was an
experience of gradual escalation of control. One could remember the voluntary beginnings or the coercive last months and be remembering something
quite different. The new industrial efficiency, developed along lines recommended by Frederick Winslow Taylor, gave some an opportunity to see what
might come of scientific management; but the tests were too sporadic and too
incomplete for anyone to draw clear conclusions.

The introduction of psychological testing brought professionals from a new
academic field into consulting positions where industrial managers could see
the possible effects of their methods. An experimental field hospital funded by
the Rockefeller Foundation advanced medical knowledge of burn and wound
treatment. Modernization in the teaching of foreign languages was hastily
adopted to meet the needs of those who had to learn quickly to communicate
by word of mouth rather than to read the literature or comprehend the
subtleties of the grammar. Historical and cultural knowledge of Europe was
necessary to guide policymakers faced with the responsibility of advising the
first president to engage in face-to-face negotiation with the leaders of the
victorious powers of the wartime alliance. Yet, in virtually every field, the
lesson was always the same. From the economists who worked for the War
Industries Board to the historians and political scientists who advised the
president at Versailles, the issue boiled down to one basic problem: American
specialization in such fields was essentially in its infancy. American energy
was great. The creation of the industrial machine that won the war had
supplied an undeniable demonstration of that energy. But efficient management of the machine had depended entirely on the emergency of the war, on
the fear of losing it, and on the support of a popular fervor the government
worked desperately to sustain. The speed with which Congress dismantled
the machine at the war's end, to the point of leaving Washington office
workers to find money for their passage home when federal funds were
abruptly cut off, suggests that national management was basically viewed as
something temporary, even dangerous.

Yet progressives had argued, long before the war emergency gave them
what they took to be their opportunity, that American society was seriously
threatened by its inability to organize its resources and rationalize its industrial system. From the conservationists to the scientific industrial managers,
the depth of concern was profound. The war had revealed the precarious

condition of the American industrial system. Concerned Americans who lamented the closing of the frontier, the disorganization of the industrial labor force, the weaknesses of the transportation system, the pointless duplications and inefficiencies in agricultural and industrial production methods, the pockets of illiteracy and substandard health among the young, and the lack of technical information on national finance and industry found that they had indeed been correct in their assessment of conditions. They looked to the war to make their point for them, to prove to public opinion and even the most backward congressmen that their prescriptions would have to be followed. Nothing could have been further off the mark. All down the line, from their conviction that the new wave of American internationalism could not now be turned back to their belief that the war had put industrial management on a new course, with government firmly in command, the progressives simply turned out to be wrong.

The war had become a reform movement of its own, sweeping up all of the reform interests in one way or another but turning them to the one central purpose, winning the war. Still, what really destroyed the reform movement was not just the excesses generated by that purpose but the exhaustion produced by the war effort itself. Trench warfare had been a nightmare. As if to be certain that civilian populations would share the nightmare, an influenza pandemic, which originated on the Western front, spread to the United States with extraordinarily devastating effect in the winter of 1918–19. The high mortality rate from the disease accounted for more than half of the 112,432 American war fatalities and for thousands more at home.

The failure to consolidate, let alone to extend, wartime gains was nowhere more apparent than in the American labor movement. Spurred by an immediate postwar inflation, which by 1919 had driven the cost of living 77 percent above its prewar level, labor unions began to organize strikes. The most dramatic were the strike in the steel industry, where workers had for years suffered conditions among the worst in American industry, and the strike of the Boston police. Public reaction to both was colored by the antiradical hysteria of the period. Violence in the steel strike and the threat of violence in the police strike touched old nerves in the American public's general suspicion of unionization and its association with radical ideas. Yet these two were among 2,665 strikes involving more than four million workers, while the cost of living rose to 105 percent above prewar levels by 1920. Faced with the opposition first of state officials and ultimately of the United States attorney general, labor backed down. That it was forced to do so during the immediate period of postwar prosperity suggests something markedly antilabor in the public response. The Boston police strike became the symbol. Public protectors had no right to strike; they must have been led to do so by insidious forces.

The war effort demanded and enforced a national unity unlike anything Americans had ever known. The Civil War had been fought to define the Union. No one who looked honestly at the aftermath of that divisive explosion wanted to reexamine the nation's queasy unity. Foreign observers like James Bryce were forever trying to explain to their countrymen the sensitivity Americans felt about the rights of their state governments—"*these* United States" they persisted in reminding anyone who wanted to describe the American nation. The creation of a unity sufficient for the successful prosecution of World War I revealed the costly divisions that still existed in the form of regional differences, ethnic and racial hostilities, and urban and agrarian competitions.

Former wartime managers, when writing of their part in the war effort, continued to extol the voluntarism with which Americans had joined together to forget their differences and win the war; but even many of those who praised that victory still insisted that the national industrial system should not be required to undertake such a burden again. Businessmen and labor leaders had not found government intervention in their interest, and neither side thought that the government had been even-handed. Even the language used to urge cooperation, like the repeated exhortations to make "sacrifices," suggested that wars were temporary emergencies that required the violation of some basic principles, chiefly the primacy of self-interest. The progressives' use of the war as an occasion for achieving the reforms they had failed to achieve in peacetime was more than a failure; for by linking the war with a fearful centralization, they proved the point about reformers that their critics had so often made: they were seen as oppressive zealots seeking to impress a national unity on an inherently free people. In the years to come, Prohibition would be taken as another proof of this point. And when the crisis of the thirties began, the reluctance to go back to wartime measures of national control was based in part on recollection of what had happened before. The fear that leaders used emergencies to justify the imposition of state controls was part of a historical experience with war that had nothing to do with voluntarism. Like children whistling past a cemetery, postwar memoirists praised voluntarism, but there was always a gnawing fear that it had not really worked. The truth of the matter was that it hadn't.

Americans were willing to assert their national commitments when they celebrated the Fourth of July; but there were many who still mourned the dead of the Confederacy. Now there would be Armistice Day to celebrate on November 11th and a monument to an Unknown Soldier to visit in the nation's national cemetery at Arlington. But behind occasions and monuments there was a multitude of commitments to local needs, regional prejudices, and ethnic practices and attitudes, and there were widely differing points of view that were not capable of resolution in the melting pot. In the rural and urban landscape alike there were sheltered enclaves of citizens who looked to one another for identity first, and who gathered together to sustain one another in their daily lives.

The war to end all wars had ended. The brief sense of triumph gave way to bickering as Wilson and the supporters of the League of Nations attempted to revive the wartime fervor, now for an international agency to preserve peace. But they failed. Like a rubber band stretched beyond its breaking point, the idea snapped back to injure both those who fought the League and those who defended it, while the majority of Americans looked on in puzzlement and waited for the future to begin. Throughout the 1920s and '30s the response to the war resonated like a distant sound in a literature that talked about something other than the war. *The Enormous Room* (1922), a novel by e. e. cummings, described the war as an experience in a French prison among the outcasts of Europe, a kind of pilgrim's progress for an American who went to France to drive an ambulance and wound up in jail as the result of a bureaucratic and legal goof. Ernest Hemingway's stories published as *In Our Time* (1924) and William Faulkner's *Soldier's Pay* (1926) deal with the war as an experience suffered by those who return home, are unable to manage the world to which they have returned, and are wounded far more deeply than anyone understands. Katherine Anne Porter's novella *Pale Horse, Pale Rider* (1936) is perhaps the most recollective work of the war as a domestic experience, in which enforced patriotism, the ravages of war, and the flu epidemic are all tangled together in one feverish nightmare.

Many of those who backed Warren Harding for the presidency in 1920 did so in the belief that he would support the League; but his assertion in his inaugural address that Americans wanted "not nostrums but normalcy" suggested a stepping-back not only from the war experience itself but from the whole reform mood that had been part of it. And when the stimulus to general economic conditions, supplied by Europe's reconstruction needs, ended in 1921, the depression that followed, while brief, seemed to prove that the costs of international adventure might be higher than Americans could afford. The fact that Americans had afforded it, that they had invested heavily in the economic future of Europe through loans and investments, was brought home to them now by the remaining war debts. The war-debts issue would remain beyond resolution. The responsibilities the United States had assumed by involving itself in the war were beyond popular understanding. Americans still preferred to consider themselves independent of the fortunes of Europe, but they were not. Wartime America had not been a familiar America, in a sense, but it was undeniably American. Efforts to blame Europe and Europeans would continue to override the possibility that something in American society itself had generated the hostilities and threats revealed by the war.

4

Middle America

UNCERTAINTY AT THE CROSSROADS

F EW DECADES in American history are as sharply separated from the events that preceded and followed them as the decade of the 1920s. Even for historians, the twenties seem to erupt. The war ends and the decade begins. The decade ends with a similar abruptness: the Crash occurs in October 1929 and the Depression begins.

Certainly part of the illusion of sharp separation is underscored by the distinction between Woodrow Wilson and Warren Harding, the one a heroic, even tragic, leader, the other a party politician ultimately associated with one of the more corrupt periods of American history. But part comes from the distinctive character of the American involvement in the war. Americans did not *see* the war itself, however much they may have felt its presence in their lives. Unaccustomed to maintaining a significant military system to support a colonial empire, they looked on their soldiers as citizens called to the service of their country in time of war, not as members of a familiar national profession. American shores were never threatened, and most Americans never saw an enemy face to face.

The war nonetheless exerted its influence on the decade that followed, at times like some invisible planet whose presence can be detected only by its effect on the motion of other bodies. The war debts, for example, were renegotiated in a series of conferences that took on all the public trappings of business meetings rather than discussions of international aims. Farmers, accustomed to the price supports generated by the war, sought ways of using government sales of produce abroad as a way of maintaining protected prices at home, but without government control of production. The old issue of immigration restriction, newly awakened by the intense fear of foreign radical influences sparked by the Russian Revolution, took on a nativist hostility that echoed the wartime calls for 100 percent Americanism.

Business leaders, attracted by what they recalled as the voluntarism of wartime business associations and labor-management relations, began to search for comparable methods of organizing more systematic controls of production and merchandising. The War Industries Board had helped to rationalize production in many industries, standardizing sizes of threads for nuts and bolts, pipe-fittings and the like, even colors and shapes of typewriter ribbons. Peacetime trade associations sought to extend that process into the twenties, without government regulation, of course, and without triggering concern that they were violating the antitrust laws. By calling attention to the national scope of many industries, wartime management had created a nation-wide communications network in industry that made greater efficiency seem possible.

Yet government, it seemed, had to be there, just as it had really had to be there during the war. In new industries like radio and air transport the need for a governmental presence was more obvious than the actual form that presence ought to take. Key people in both the administration and Congress quickly recognized that state-by-state regulation could not cope with the rapidly developing radio corporations. The radio networks were national in scope, and Washington was forced to determine that the national airwaves were public, not private, and therefore subject to some kind of public control. The same thing was true of air transport. Commercial aviation was not going to go through the clumsy evolution from state to federal regulation that had made the railroads a chaotic industry.

Although the sense of a need for federal management of the new technologies pervaded the twenties, there was no consensus on what that management would appropriately be. Radio could enter every home. Did that require federal standards of quality to assure morality, even to assure that radio would be an educational medium? The federal government said yes. Then what about movies? The rapid development of national chains of movie theaters and the centralizing of movie production in Hollywood seemed to suggest a similar response, but the answer was no. The movie industry finally established its own censorship board with its own guidelines, but it did so in part to forestall federal controls.

The growing use of electricity raised similar issues. To some it seemed even more appropriate that the federal government should intervene in the development of electric power, since a number the companies involved used federally controlled waterways, including dams constructed by the Army Corps of Engineers. But the production of electricity remained private, despite its importance for the development of all industry and despite the tendency of all utilities to be monopolies. Like the telephone and telegraph before it, electricity became a regulated monopoly, but the question of who would do the regulating—the federal government or the states—was left in abeyance.

Thus it would be difficult to find another era in American history quite as revolutionary as the twenties in the pace of its technological development and in its uncertainty about how to manage that development. The war had, almost by inadvertence, introduced a brief period of federal management of technological change. Everything from railroad management and labor relations to electrical production and news management had come under federal regulation. The fact that regulation had been part of the building of a war machine had made it appear to be a temporary expedient, but in the postwar years it became an issue again and again.

In a sense, Americans in the twenties faced the consequences of progressivism, for the vivid recollections of wartime government intervention served as both a warning and a temptation. The prewar progressives, for example, had wanted to use the public schools as their agency for Americanization. The wartime Committee on Public Information had expanded that idea beyond their wildest dreams—dreams that turned to nightmares after the war, when vigilante committees investigated textbooks for everything from their treatment of George Washington (they did not want him called "a revolutionary") to their teaching of Darwinian theories of evolution. Prohibition, long the buzzword in the battle between nativists and immigrants, had become a legal fact. Yet it remained the most important urban political issue in the twenties, not because anyone was yet willing to believe that the constitutional amendment could be revoked but because it was so convenient a weapon for politicians out for the ethnic vote to use against the progressive reformers.

Individualism became the battlecry in an effort to create a new reform concept, one that freed the individual from group control, whether of dress, hairstyle, or sexual behavior. John Dewey's impact on education rested in part on his concept of treating the child as an individual. The popularization of Freudian psychiatry was part of a similar drive for individual liberation. Sinclair Lewis's *Main Street* (1920) and *Babbitt* (1922) attacked the standards imposed by small-minded communities on those who dared to try to liberate themselves.

The search for forms of business association that could be free of government coercion and the search for ways of liberating the individual from community coercion both suggest the fear that progressivism inspired. Industrialization and technology promised unlimited opportunities for all, but they threatened chaos and destruction if left unregulated. Evangelist Aimee Semple McPherson provided an amusing example of the problem when she refused to abide by the new standards that confined her to a single radio frequency in broadcasting her sermons. They were God's airways, she insisted, as she spread her message across the dial. One could resent the laws that governed technological advance even as one sought to benefit from those advances.

Throughout the twenties, various groups continued to form national associations to provide meetings for the exchange of information and to establish professional standards. Such practices, already used by doctors, lawyers and academics in earlier periods, were now enjoyed by city managers, police and fire chiefs, and a host of state and urban professionals, from mayors and governors to tax-rate surveyors. Such groups were committed to the belief that there were uniform methods of problem-solving that could be applied by all communities to all kinds of problems. Such uniform standards could be evoked without having to be enforced. Rational persuasion was always preferable to any kind of national control. Yet the issue was always there: how much national control would in fact be necessary? Prohibition became the chief example of a uniform national control. Could there also be uniform criminal codes, uniform licensing practices, and the like? Federal power, many still insisted, was not a police power; but if the federal government continued to enter areas where practical enforcement was required, then some kind of federal police would be necessary. In 1921 the establishment of a Bureau of Investigation in the Justice Department began the movement toward some kind of national police force; it was supposed to devote itself to investigation, not enforcement, but the line was difficult to draw. Under the leadership of J. Edgar Hoover and under the extraordinary pressures generated by the need to enforce prohibition, the G-men became popular heroes of law enforcement, like the federal marshals in the old western territories.

If prewar progressives accepted the necessity of building a *national* America, of bringing the federal government into the solving of problems that crossed state lines, postwar Americans were considerably more cautious. Certain issues could be dramatized, to be sure. Public reaction against prostitution had made so-called white slavery a federal crime in 1910, and the kidnapping and murder of Charles A. Lindbergh's infant son in 1932 led to the inclusion of that crime in the federal canon; but again it was crimes against women and children that built sentiment for federal action.

The search for substitutes for federal control reawakened an interest in state compacts—agreements between neighboring states—that could lead to common solutions to shared problems. The Constitution allowed for such treaty-like arrangements; but the attempts in this direction by the states that shared the Connecticut River were not successful, nor were those of the southwestern states, where common water resources raised similar problems. The expansion of electrical power and its dependence on river dams meant that one community's dam changed the way another community lived. The growth of regional planning associations in the twenties was prompted by an awareness of larger common interests and of the inherent inability of the older political units to cope with regional problems. The same awareness grew when cities and satellite suburbs squabbled over their relationships; annexation fights often erupted. Suburban communities recognized their dependence on the city; they viewed traditional city politics and politicians as corrupt, and they suspected that compromise would lead to a loss of control over the life of their own community. Americans had always tended to look on taxation as a purchase of specific services, not as a support of government in general, let alone for services for someone else. They were increasingly willing in the twenties to respond to pleas from the growing number of Community Chests for social services for others, but that was charity, not taxation. The war had expanded the country's most visible national charity, the American Red Cross, but that, too, was looked on as an emergency agency, designed to help in time of natural disasters. The Salvation Army and other religious organizations were expected to provide services for those temporarily down on their luck. The services they provided to the poor, the unemployed, and the elderly were essential public services; but the philanthropic tradition that created them kept alive the illusion of voluntarism, the conviction that tax-supported agencies were not required. Yet even philanthropic good works required public support when philanthropists bestowed playgrounds, public parks, libraries, and hospitals but left it up to the communities to operate and maintain them.

Americans looked at European events in the twenties but did not compare their own experiences with what they saw happening abroad. The Versailles settlement had attempted to resolve a century of conflict between the needs of industrialized nations to consolidate and centralize the peoples and the borders they governed and the desire of historically identifiable ethnic groups to govern themselves independently. A Europe of little nations, defined by nationality, seemed the answer to a number of questions, not only of nationality but of the need to limit the growth of large, aggressively competitive states. The divisions did not sit well with leaders hungering for a new try at world power, but they did, for the moment, seem to settle the problem of cultural difference. The new Soviet Union faced similar problems of diversity of culture within its own borders but saw answers in various moves to assert a new revolutionary state by introducing vast plans to industrialize a backward nation rapidly and at whatever cost. Some Americans admired that effort, particularly in education, where the Soviet movement to wipe out illiteracy assumed an almost religious intensity.

New national media—*Time* magazine first appeared in 1923—spread news to a mass audience of readers across the country, and newsreels began to be offered to audiences of regular moviegoers, for whom a night at the movies was now a weekly social event. The addition of sound in 1927 carried the revolution one step further. A mass audience of Americans had come into being, an audience to be entertained, instructed, and, above all, influenced on a national scale by those who had access to the new world of film. While American political leaders of the twenties seemed reluctant to use the new media for anything more than the traditional purposes of communication, leaders elsewhere in the world were growing increasingly conscious of the possibilities of dramatizing politics for popular consumption.

These new national audiences also meant national markets: for goods, advertised in livingrooms across the nation on radio, and for personalities, whose screen portrayals and personal lives were almost equal in their power to draw ticket-buyers into the movie theaters. The same film that played in an exotically appointed movie palace in Chicago or New York drew audiences into lesser architectural imitations in the smaller towns. The movie became a universal experience for Americans, an experience designed for profit by a national system masterminded in Hollywood and New York.

The centralization of American culture in the 1920s was thus a process whose main purpose was profit, not social influence or government management. Even some purveyors of traditional high culture found themselves tempted by the possibility of national markets. Leaving it to new entrepreneurs to satisfy the needs of local literary circles in New York and Chicago, they began a search for a broader national taste at an intellectual level they could, they believed, help create. The *New Yorker* first appeared in 1925; not simply a national literary magazine, it was designed to show a particular circle of eastern intelligentsia to the nation through stories, gossip, cartoons, and criticism focused on events in Manhattan. The Book-of-the-Month Club offered readers across the nation too busy to select the best new books a board of experts to do it for them. Ambitious musicians fought their way onto the rosters of New York–based concert series that played in the nation's smaller cities and towns. The programs were designed to appeal to audiences supposedly not yet sophisticated enough to appreciate the kind of music enjoyed by critical audiences in Carnegie Hall.

The wave of wartime nationalism had subsided, but it had left in its wake a nation puzzled by its experience with unification and therefore equipped as never before to face a whole set of questions about the meaning of national identity. One song had asked "How you gonna keep 'em down on the farm, after they've seen Paree?" But you could push that question much further. Had the changes of the previous decades, and the changes now taking place, made adjustments to traditional American small-town life even more difficult than those who were returning to it understood?

Sociologists Robert and Helen Lynd spent the mid-1920s examining a place they called "Middletown," which was actually Muncie, Indiana. When their study appeared in 1929 it documented the uneasiness of the new era, the testiness of the response to mobility, technology, and the underlying crises produced by what William F. Ogburn was calling "cultural lag." The pace of technological change, Ogburn argued, outstripped the capacity of society to adjust its economic, political, and social mechanisms for maintaining stability and order. Ogburn believed that the adjustments could be made and without basic revolutionary change. Others were not that optimistic, and their arguments represented perhaps the first real questioning of the doctrine of progress from a liberal perspective. The conservative opposition to progressivism was familiar enough, but these new liberal doubts seemed, at least for the moment, to express something more profound. Adaptation to change, it seemed, could generate as much disruption as change itself, and it became difficult sometimes to separate the two. One could herald the automobile as a marvelous new harbinger of individual freedom, but its use had to be controlled by laws and traffic regulations, with officials to enforce them. Bureaucracies seemed inevitably to develop in the wake of social change. Americans in Middletown were beginning to feel insecure with their neighbors and with themselves. A willingness to accept more legislation, indeed, an eagerness to invent new legal methods of governing life, had been one of the fundamental tenets of progressivism. The movement for the protection of civil liberties that grew out of the war was evidence of an awareness that law might not be protection in itself, that it might provide new opportunities for oppression. Postwar liberals sometimes found themselves looking askance on their prewar progressivism.

The war experience had badly split the Republican party. The eastern internationalists backed General Leonard Wood as the successor to the late Theodore Roosevelt; the midwestern progressives backed former Illinois governor Frank O. Lowden. The deadlock to which these two groups fought each other in the Republican convention of 1920 produced Harding as the compromise, but it was a compromise that meant a rejection, at least in part, of the new liberal internationalism, supported by new magazines like *Time*, and the old progressivism, represented now by isolationist Hiram Johnson. The role that internationalism was destined to play in the split between east and west, the emergence of a midwestern conservatism, and the focus of the news media on promoting arguments on all sides were products of the war's effect on the party. Not only Henry Luce's *Time* but Colonel Robert McCormick's *Chicago Tribune* and William Randolph Hearst's growing newspaper chain continued to be public voices in the battle over the meaning of internationalism and its coming role in public policy. All three represented an urban America that, though rapidly expanding, was still only edging into dominance of the American scene.

Warren Harding's assertion of the need to return to "normalcy" was not the bland and simplistic political statement critics sometimes make of it. Harding was one of the nation's political professionals, a small-town Ohio newspaper publisher whose twenty years in political office had earned him a solid reputation among the party regulars. The nation to which he spoke in the campaign of 1920 found his soothing rhetoric gratifyingly empty of the demands and pressures they had been hearing from reformers for almost two decades. Listeners could relax, confident that Washington could be made to recede from view.

Small-town, local America may have been declining in statistical reality, but its spirit still commanded uncountable majorities. Harding looked like a leader. The cabinet he chose included petty manipulators like Harry Daugherty, his attorney general, and Albert Fall, his secretary of the interior, who was destined to end up in jail for his mismanagement of oil leases and acceptance of bribes, and their notoriety has obscured the fact that Harding's cabinet was one of the better teams of the period. It included Charles Evans Hughes as secretary of state, Andrew Mellon as secretary of the treasury, Henry C. Wallace as secretary of agriculture, and Herbert Hoover as secretary of commerce. Each in his own way represented aspects of the new technocratic mentality.

The Democrats had nominated the progressive governor of Ohio, James Cox, for the presidency, along with the attractive young Franklin D. Roosevelt as his running mate; but even the possibility of a Democratic victory was dimmed by the long hiatus of leadership produced by Woodrow Wilson's stroke in 1919 and by his slow recovery, plus the quarreling over the League in the Senate.

Harding's efforts to organize and simplify his administration's approach to the complex problems of the postwar reconversion were not superficial or unintelligent. Mellon, Hughes, and Hoover were empowered to build a new administrative apparatus for dealing with the new economic internationalism that had grown out of the war. Mellon's tax policies and his management of the serious economic downturn of 1921 seemed masterful by 1923, when the return of prosperity set the country on what appeared to all observers to be a healthy course of expansion. The problems that were going to eventuate in the Crash did not develop for another five years, and they were neither as predictable nor as interpretable as critics of Republican economic policy later fancied them, in the wake of the Crash.

The scandals revealed in the months just before and after Harding's death in 1923 cast a shadow over his entire administration, perhaps a bit unfairly; and his vice-president and successor, Calvin Coolidge, utilized the contrast between his own austere efficiency and Harding's jovial conviviality to good effect. Like Harding, Coolidge had come to the presidency from a life-long career in politics. A shrewd, laconic Yankee, his eligibility for the vice-presidential nomination in 1920 had been enhanced by his successful handling of the Boston police strike of 1919. That as governor of the state he had rejected not only the strikers' demands but their right to strike had made him a popular figure for a public not altogether sure what it thought of labor unions but very sure of its position on police protection. The same appeal to traditional values carried him into the presidency in his own right in 1924; he was a perfect foil for the Harding administration. The scandals had just begun to emerge—enough to provide a contrast, not enough to taint him.

Coolidge's much-commented-on silence was also agreeable to the public in the twenties. Economist Wesley Clair Mitchell had called for men of "facts," not men of "hunches," when he announced, in 1920, the establishment of the New School for Social Research in New York. He acknowledged that men of hunches were more dramatic, more likely to attract attention, but said that men of facts, while less attractive, were more useful. In 1928 political scientist Leonard White extolled the new city-manager profession as a "profession of doers, not talkers." Airplane hero Charles A. Lindbergh's modesty underscored his courage and his mastery of the new machinery. Magazine articles throughout the period approvingly described Herbert Hoover's demeanor, his unwillingness to bark commands, his dependence on a community of loyal associates to fulfill his mission. He had depth, not drama, according to his admirers. Coolidge reflected one image of leadership: simple virtue in rebellion against the growing complexities of industrial life. If, afterward, that image seemed unreal, it was the change in the public's sense of leadership that made it so, not its failure to meet the requirements of its own times.

American politics and politicians had faced periodic rebellions against what reformers called "partisan politics." What the term meant seemed clear enough at the time. Patronage, spoils, smoke-filled rooms, and the cigar-smoking party regulars who filled them with smoke were all familiar figures. It was sometimes forgotten that they provided the political system with continuity, stability, and even orderly management in the years between the sporadic reform sallies. Reformers sought to clean them up as though they were dirty defects in some otherwise pure process rather than essential parts of the process itself.

Part of the progressives' drive to transfer government reform from state and local government to Washington had been based on the belief that the federal government was relatively freer of partisan corruption and that civil-service reform could in any case succeed in protecting the federal government from the encroachments of partisan politics. The fact that their reform drives were far from victory in 1920 was brought painfully home by the scandals of the Harding administration. Petty though they were, the fact that they seemed to have involved the White House itself was a disheartening revelation.

Throughout the 1920s suspicions that the political process was ineffective were being documented by the new political scientists in studies that used sophisticated statistical sampling techniques to measure voter apathy and disillusionment. The quadrennial political conventions began to seem like unseemly circuses, particularly the Democratic conventions. H. L. Mencken enjoyed reporting the raucousness of these events, and if the anger and antipopulist sentiments that infused his writings were expressed in comic terms that entertained his readers, they still reflected the Nietzschean origins of his own doubts about democracy and public opinion as effective governmental forces.

When the Democrats decided to meet in New York City in 1924, they unwittingly unleashed a series of disputes so vicious that the raw divisions in America were revealed. WASP political dignitary Franklin D. Roosevelt, slowly recovering from the crippling attack of polio that most people thought had effectively ended his once promising political career, ventured forth on crutches to seek the presidential nomination for New York Governor Alfred E. Smith. The "Happy Warrior," as Roosevelt called him in his speech, was Catholic, Irish, an opponent of Prohibition, and an urban politician, from the accents in which he spoke to the derby hat he wore. An excellent reform administrator, he nonetheless bore the ethnic and religious stigmata many southern Democrats considered dangerously foreign.

His opponents had arrived in New York with yet another weapon for splitting the party: a commitment to the revived Ku Klux Klan. A product of the resurgent racial bigotry that had emerged on the eve of the war, the Klan was a far cry from the protective organizations that had been part of the Reconstruction. The movie *The Birth of a Nation*, with its racist images, helped make the connection with the past, while the burnings and mutilations the new Klan now added to its roster of coercive methods aroused even greater fears. Membership grew nationally, and a series of exposés and trials in the mid-twenties revealed the seriousness of the problem. The Democratic convention of 1924 finally included a plank condemning the Klan, but not until William Jennings Bryan, who attempted to mediate, was hooted down by his former followers. The fact that the convention deadlocked when it came to nominating its presidential candidate only confirmed the public's view of a party in disarray. The nomination of a conservative West Virginia lawyer, John W. Davis, seemed to make it clear that the liberals in the party had been driven back irrevocably from their triumphs of 1912 and 1916 and that they would be forever stymied by the Democrats' rule requiring a two-thirds majority for nomination. The Southern Democrats, it was thought, would never vote for an urban liberal.

The progressives' efforts to revive their party in the campaign of 1924 revealed their problems. They had no candidates with national constituencies. Hiram Johnson's hostility to Wilson and internationalism had weakened him. The party finally settled on Robert M. La Follette, who ran a fervent campaign, which his two opponents easily labeled as radical. Although he drew five million votes in the election, the limit of genuinely Progressive third-party strength had been reached. Only by tying themselves to one of the major parties could the progressives hope to attain their political aims. They were a critical minority, nothing more.

The progressives now devoted themselves to finding more sophisticated tools for measuring public attitudes and interests and more efficient ways of providing public services. Education, health care, and sanitation were sub-jects of careful analysis by private and public groups. A group of young lawyers, who identified themselves either as progressives or as followers of Brandeis and Wilson, turned to the courts and litigation as their answer to the problem of combatting their old enemies, the "interests." Politics was not perceived as the route to take. The voters' questioning of the utility of political participation in the twenties was for progressives—indeed, for partisans of all political persuasions—an unexpected phenomenon.

The two major parties were being reshaped by the growing political in-fluence of the big cities and by a consciousness of the need for greater managerial skills. Wilson's political tactics had helped urbanize the Demo-cratic party, broadening its base beyond the agrarian and southern constit-uencies on which it had rested and making it more attractive to local reform leaders who had left the Republicans to join the Progressive party. Smith, for example, represented not only the new importance of ethnic, urban voters, but a remarkable skill in combining new and efficient techniques of adminis-trative reform with the old practices of urban politics. Progressives had reformed state government in New York by increasing the power of the governor and his control over budgeting and management; but it was Al Smith who made it work.

Americans obviously still considered themselves a democratic people and refused to accept the idea that strong leadership and efficient government would lead to changes in their conception of self-government; but long before the crisis of the Depression began, many political observers were beginning to see that the new technologies required skills and controls that partisan politics could not provide. The increasing use of gas and electricity by house-holds as well as industry and the growing dependence on public transporta-tion raised the issue of who was going to control what were rapidly becoming essential services. The relation between education and a successful career, between access to medical knowledge and the quality of life—even survival itself—made individual achievement less the product of individual ambition and the accidents of life than the result of opportunities available to those who could afford them. Communities of all kinds were coming to expect the services of technically trained, efficient managers. If politics had ever been the way of producing such elites, it had done so in an earlier time; Americans who fondly remembered the aristocratic demeanor of a Washington or Jeffer-son would no longer have considered them suitable candidates for political office.

In some respects what the war had done was to help transform the progres-sives' moral fervor for reform into a reverence for scientific knowledge and technological innovation. The old and recurring fear of science that had long been associated with technological advance was, for the moment, replaced by a kind of mystical utopianism. Everything could now be solved by scientific research. All diseases could be cured. Poverty could be ended. Everyone could become rich. The new faith suffused the thinking of a wide range of Americans, from the new social scientists to the new and inexperienced speculators making a try at the stock market. The phenomenon of the chain letter suggests the quality of this faith. The recipient of a chain letter was ordered to send dollars (or handkerchiefs or neckties) to the top name on the enclosed list and to send copies of the letter to a new list of recipients, composed of his or her own acquaintances. In theory, one would be deluged with dollar bills (or handkerchiefs or neckties) as one's own name reached the top of numerous other lists. "Do not break the chain!" the letters warned, or one would not only forfeit one's own reward but destroy the system for everyone else. Progress, it seemed, had become just such a chain; and if there were many who rushed to take advantage of it, there were others who feared the ultimate collapse.

New scientific methodologies of child-rearing and educational development also made their appearance in the first half of the twenties. John Watson's impact on popular attitudes cannot be overstated (two decades later, of course, the pendulum swung to the opposite extreme of "permissiveness"). Watsonian behaviorism called for strict scheduling of infant life; feeding, sleep, play, and toilet-training were all to be regimented. In some respects Watson's rejection of heredity as the chief factor in determining human character and his emphasis on producing character by manipulating and conditioning behavior do provide a sharp, even liberal, contrast to the genetic, more or less racist, conceptions of behavior that were more characteristic of the period. At the same time, encouraging parents to let their children cry, to feed them measured amounts of food at carefully timed intervals, is distinctly Spartan. The Victorian idea of the utility of hardship in the training of the young was not part of the Watsonian argument, but the resemblance is there, and the relation to Taylor's theories of scientific management is obvious.

Watson was not the only one to try to define behavior precisely and to use that definition to measure training. E. L. Thorndike's research in psychological testing and the subsequent emergence of "intelligence quotients" seemed to show that mental power could be quantified. Later critics would question the objectivity of Thorndike's methods, but, at the time, his tests seemed capable of reducing the effects of social distinctions and cultural exclusiveness in the public schools. Reformers were also optimistic that, by defining the "normal," they could provide a precise scientific base from which to measure the social utility of education.

The commitment to measurement was at once simple and complex, popular and arcane. Its simplicity lay in the belief that everything measurable could be universally known, hence popular, available to all. Numbers were the key to true democracy, to advancement by merit and merit alone; opportunity would be available to all. At the same time, the mania for measuring things produced a new breed of experts to develop new measuring techniques and to interpret the results. Such experts had to be trained, certified, and controlled.

Increasingly, parents found themselves faced with the consequences of turning over the training of their children to experts whose motives they did not always understand. Periodic community outbursts over the schools' use of particular textbooks became one way of asserting traditional parental influence on the intellectual and social development of the young. Still, the growing profession of educators was taking over a broad range of socializing functions once controlled by the family.

Progressives, one could argue, had traditionally used accurate information, systematically collected, as their basic reform tool; but, as those in the twenties well knew, their achievements had usually fallen short of their ideals. Precisely for that reason, the new idealists of the twenties chose not to call themselves "progressives" and certainly not "reformers." They had moved out of the turbulent world of politics into the ordered world of science. Collections of data were to be used now not simply as ammunition in political debates; they were to be used in the real world, to help direct programs in educational psychology, criminology, and population studies. The latter led to what was perhaps the most dramatic policy transformation of the period, the closing of immigration. As a subject that had long been debated among progressives, immigration restriction brought the old and the new together.

In May 1921 Congress passed the first of the "Quota Laws," restricting immigration in any future year to 3 percent of each nationality represented in the census of 1910; in 1924 this became 2 percent of the census figures for 1890. The Quota Laws applied principles of statistical measurement to the shaping of American nationality. Later critics would see this as a "scientific" rationale for bigotry. Quota laws set up an implicit equation of nation and race that would supposedly provide the United States with a kind of "racial" culture of its own. Sharper restrictions on immigration from southern and eastern Europe and from Asia embodied the ethnic and racial hostilities of the framers of the legislation.

Immigration restriction had followed closely on the Red Scare of 1919–20. In that period of hysteria it was widely believed that a web of conspirators was at work, composed mainly of recent immigrants, thought to be anarchists or Bolsheviks. Great efforts were made to find and deport them. Yet the movement to restrict immigration—indeed, to bring it to an end—could be traced to subtler, more intellectually respectable theories about the state of American society, derived in part from progressivism and reinforced by the war experience. One did not have to be a racist or a bigot in the 1920s to believe that Europeans of all cultural backgrounds, even the formerly admired Anglo-Saxons, were no longer suitable candidates for American citizenship. The process of urbanization had aroused uncertainties about America's endless capacity to absorb new citizens. Census statistics showed that 1920 marked the first time that more Americans were living in cities than in the rural countryside. Even though census statisticians had used 2,500 as the population figure that defined "urban," the idea was as troubling as the announcement of the closing of the frontier. Immigrants in the immediate prewar period had increasingly located in cities to swell a labor force that could not be infinitely expanded. Urban schools, with decades of experience in the problems of "Americanizing" the foreign-born, had learned to live with one of progressivism's triumphs, compulsory education, but now did so with a growing consciousness of the costs. It cost money to keep children in schools. To be sure, schools kept children out of the labor force for a longer period of time. Yet they also required more plant, more teachers, and more advisers and administrators to guide and counsel children who would have been out earning their living had they been allowed to follow either their own desires or the dictates of family need. New laws defined lack of interest in education in effect as truancy and established officers to cope with the new offense.

Increased reporting of crime statistics, another product of the new wave of social-science reform, suggested what the growing popular literature on crime already encouraged readers to believe: that many of the leading figures in the crime world bore "ethnic" names. That many were also named Smith, Brown, and Jones was conveniently ignored.

Fears of urbanization and cultural mongrelization, and the closing of immigration that these produced, were related to the American version of the nineteenth century's perception of "race" and its association with nationality. Generations of Americans had come to believe that national character was genetically transmitted. Ideas that Hitler was soon to use so effectively and so catastrophically to rebuild German nationalism were difficult for Americans to employ as a device for describing an American character, but they had their own versions of what "American" meant. If it could not always be defined in positive terms, it could be defined negatively by characterizing various kinds of behavior, identified with national origins, as un-American.

The complex of attitudes toward political and social behavior that Americans associated with the races and nationalities of the nineteenth-century world is difficult to explain to Americans who no longer tend to think even of the Japanese and Chinese as constituting "races" and who think of "racism" as involving almost exclusively blacks. The characteristics attributed to the various nationalities often bordered on the absurd, but they were taken seriously enough to affect international policy as well as judgments about the behavior of would-be new Americans. Thus, the Germans were the "intellectuals" of Europe if one meant the Germany of Goethe, Kant, and Beethoven, but Germans were also a "militaristic" race, capable of drifting into the barbarities of their Niebelungun past. The French were the "democrats" of the race of Rousseau and the young Marquis de Lafayette, but they also tended toward decadence and libertine promiscuity. The Russians were emotionally intense musicians, ballet dancers, and writers of long tragic novels, but they were also radical peasants who could be identified with various anarchistic, possibly Jewish, movements. Jews were, paradoxically, both radical socialists and oppressive capitalists, as well as good family people, generous and intellectual, but greedy and crass. The Irish were fun-loving, brilliantly imaginative "naturals" who believed in fairies but drank too much and were unreliable workers. Even the English, of whom the most good could be said, were also, unfortunately, Puritans, whose rigid, Victorian morality could be insensitive and stifling.

The idea of a "natural," or historical, nationalism had been an important part of late nineteenth-century European thought, and the battles that various separatist national groups waged in middle and eastern Europe to keep from being absorbed in centralized empires was one of the factors that had led to World War I. The settlement at Versailles had at least paid lip service to these nationalist aspirations, and it had sanctioned the formation of a number of small states that would reflect the cultural homogeneity of the various Slavic groups fighting for ethnic and political identity. The effort to establish a Jewish state in the Middle East was perhaps the most extreme example of this whole movement, given the thousands of years of history that had to be bridged to justify returning the Jews to their point of origin. The American Jewish community had been divided on the issue of a Palestinian homeland. For some Jews, particularly those of German descent, a homeland threatened separation from the American nationality with which they preferred to identify. For others, a homeland provided the first sense of real nationality after all the centuries of wandering.

The awakening of ethnic identity in the various American communities that traced their origins to eastern Europe became part of an American political debate as the federal government now discussed economic supports for fledgling governments and entertained representatives of those governments, who did not hesitate to appeal for public support from their transplanted countrymen. The new Polish president, Ignace Paderewski, was also an accomplished pianist, and he skillfully combined his music and his political interests in his tours around the country. The American Irish, of course, had been supporting Irish nationalism against British suppression for years.

Separatism also affected the black community. Marcus Garvey presided over an international convention of his Universal Negro Improvement Association in 1920, and by 1925 he was advocating a back-to-Africa movement. His intense separatism was criticized by black intellectuals like W. E. B. DuBois and black union leader A. Philip Randolph; but it provided yet another example of the divisions among Americans seeking to define for themselves a nationalism inclusive enough to protect traditional senses of identity but exclusive enough to protect the United States from the world, which it seemed to have entered for the first time. Blacks in particular had coped for a long time with separatist ideas used as a means of getting rid of them, not as a device for supporting their identity; and the "go-back-where-you-belong" arguments had been used against virtually every ethnic group at some point in its Americanization experience.

Separatism, in all of its forms, was the barrier to the building of a national society; but it was also the source of a security on which Americans had for generations depended. The states with their independent political histories, the regions with their special geographies and cultural patterns, the towns that had resulted from the westward migrations of religious communities, all rested on a comfortable sense of homogeneity that made the idea of a melting pot a distant ideal. Such communities may have been perceived as islands, but they tended to be islands of likes, powerful enough to exclude unlikes, and to do so without guilt. The Nation was an abstraction, a distant idea.

But the distance was shrinking, and rapidly; the auto restructured ideas of personal space, while air travel provided a sense of the continent as a whole, but a whole whose traditional divisions no longer had the old meanings. In the years to come, even mountains would cease to be the divisions they once had been, let alone barriers to movement. If the sense of regional separation had remained, as indeed it did, the intellectual content signified by regionalism no longer fitted easily with geographical realities and the individual's access to opportunities available in different parts of the country.

Movies and radio brought images and sounds to all parts of the country, and they needed to define general heroes and heroines in order to appeal to the largest possible audience. Stereotypes remained. The first serialized radio entertainment was a program called "Amos and Andy," but the two white men portraying blacks emphasized human foibles that were universal, even amid echoes of minstrel blackface. Even Al Jolson's blackface song, "Sonny Boy," a highlight of the first "talking picture," was a kind of universal statement on the relation between parents and children. Movie star Rudolph Valentino played roles that curiously blended Latin and Middle Easterner.

Political leaders were also compelled to achieve a universal appeal that would attract national audiences at the same time that it met the needs of various communities and interests across the nation. Warren Harding "looked like a president" to his backers. ("No, he looks like a king," his wife insisted.) Theodore Roosevelt had exploited the political utility of fast photography, presenting himself to the camera in action rather than sitting only for formal portraits. Yet, as Harding and Coolidge clearly demonstrated, a regional identity and humble origins remained important. Hoover was a country boy from the West, whatever he had become in his years of involvement in the international business world. Al Smith's urban accent identified him all too well in his radio broadcasts; but so did Franklin Roosevelt's soon-to-be-familiar salutation to his radio listeners, "My friends." The patrician tones were more acceptable, it seemed.

The national audiences created by the new media exacerbated one of the country's oldest political problems, the creation of national leaders. Congress had always been an assembly of regional voices, even regional styles of dress and manners; habits that were not only acceptable to voters at home but even essential for election often looked parochial on the national scene. But candidates hungry for national office had to learn a variety of styles as they traveled. They were learning to eat strange foods and to be photographed pitching hay, wearing cowboy hats and Indian headdresses, and attempting to look comfortable in such settings. In one way or another, presidential candidates had always faced these problems—Martin Van Buren's attempts to identify himself with his supposed log-cabin roots were famous—but the scale had changed by the 1920s. American voters, many of them still resident in their traditional communities, wanted presidents who represented the interests of all the voters, but, given the kind of national scrutiny available to them now, they were threatened with a universal blandness in the candidates that might have suggested how diverse those interests really were—and how irreconcilable.

In the twenties leadership was, increasingly, the problem. Experts and the need for expertise helped to erode faith in the essentially simple kind of leadership represented by a Harding or a Coolidge. A growing awareness of the psychological implications of leadership had also begun to intrude itself, not always very subtly. Whether this took the form of a Freudian interpretation of the leader as father figure or a Weberian interpretation of the leader as worker of miracles, the "charismatic" figure, the idea that was being implied—that the people were insecure and needed a new kind of leader, endowed with special skills—was not comfortable for American democrats, but it was there. Americans had protected themselves from periodic lapses into hero worship, partly by the habit of creating temporary pantheons from which heroes could be evicted. William Jennings Bryan, Theodore Roosevelt, and Woodrow Wilson were subjected to critical attacks throughout the 1920s as popular analysts examined their personalities and found them defective. All had been models in their time and would ultimately suffer little historical damage. The process of promotion and demotion seemed necessary to maintaining faith in democracy, self-government, and endless opportunities for leaders to emerge from all classes and conditions of American life. It was an old process, fueled by revisionist biography, popular newspaper revelations of supposedly hidden scandals and misdeeds, and textbook accounts of great men and villains.

For years a growing literature of children's fiction based on contemporary experience had provided models of leadership for an audience of readers in small towns and cities alike. E. P. Roe and Horatio Alger described patterns of business success in terms of a morality of achievement that clearly associated wealth with virtue, the just due of the brave young man who did not succumb to temptation. Edward Stratemeyer, who published his first story in 1889, completed the last Alger novels when Alger died in 1899; he then devoted the next three decades of his life to transforming the genre. Alger's Gospel of Wealth became Stratemeyer's Gospel of Technology. By 1904, when he formed the Stratemeyer Syndicate, to bring mass production to the process, he had written more than a hundred fifty novels. By the time he died, in 1930, the syndicate had produced over seven hundred. As Arthur Winfield, he gave us the Rover Boys, a more or less traditional adventure series; but as Victor Appleton he invented Tom Swift, the boy genius, generating useful technological innovations at a decent profit. By contrast, the villain in the Swift saga is always the self-interested exploiter, the industrialist whose inefficiencies drain for personal gain the resources capable of providing a general, public benefit. Tom is successful but never rich, and the distinction is reflected in his modesty, his courage, and his emphasis on rationally conceived technological goals. Stratemeyer's heroes combine the virtues of the Alger tradition with the skills and expertise of the new technology. The new machines—the airplane, the automobile, the motorcycle, even the submarine—seemed to objectify the newest of popular social virtues, industrial efficiency. Stratemeyer kept up with the times. His daughters, who took over the operation, added Carolyn Keene to the roster of authors; her creation, Nancy Drew, gave young girls a model of detective ingenuity and effectiveness to follow. The Stratemeyer style emphasized simplicity in an age of technological change, the retention of small-town agrarian ideals in modern urban industrial settings. But the style of behavior, particularly Tom Swift's, supported the virtues of technological innovation and socially useful enterprise.

The war effort had dramatized a shift toward new conceptions of both industrial management and industrial managers. That the industrial recession that began in 1921 was ended by 1923 was taken as a triumph of fiscal management, as a crisis successfully weathered under policy forces commanded by government. As the master figure in presidential cabinets from Harding to Hoover, Treasury Secretary Mellon had followed the classic conservative model for managing the still new income tax: he lowered taxes to expand the supply of capital for investment. Popular news and magazine articles presented Mellon as a brilliant commander behind the scenes. A shy, somewhat introverted, and very private banker and art collector, virtually unknown outside Pittsburgh before his nomination to the cabinet, Mellon dominated economic policy in the twenties, not only at the Treasury but in agriculture, foreign affairs, and indeed any area where national interests were conceived of as economic. Even the scandals of the Harding era, which were minor in terms of their actual relation to the larger problem of liquidating the federal government's wartime involvement in the economy, underscored

Mellon's fundamental concern: to maintain, or to reestablish where necessary, the principle that the industrial system was a private system, operating with government support but without government interference. As a result of the war, that distinction was increasingly hard to make, especially in agriculture. During the war the government had accumulated resources useful to private enterprise; the western oil reserves and the unfinished dams and nitrate plant on the Tennessee River were among them. As in the Grant administration, and in every postwar administration since, the liquidation process became an invitation to corruption. Teapot Dome and the oil scandals were, certainly in Mellon's terms, a petty and pointlessly self-serving misuse of a relationship with the federal government that the industrial system would have to learn to use properly, according to some standard of public morality. At the same time, Mellon did not hesitate to use his position to purchase paintings for his private collection from the Soviet Union, even though he did not approve of the Bolshevik government's revolutionary confiscation of the paintings from their original owners. That he may even then have been planning ultimately to turn over his entire holdings to the government is beside the point.

The issue can be put more broadly. The great triumph of progressivism, dramatically underscored by the war, had been the increased interdependence of business and government, working together for purposes deemed beneficial to both. Yet that triumph had contributed to a fear, again underscored by the war, that the growing partnership threatened values on which American democracy rested: individualism, popular control of government, free enterprise, and privacy. The scandals of the Harding administration and the public outcry they ultimately provoked tended to obscure the more fundamental problems of the changing relationship between government policymaking and the private industrial system. The expansion of government involvement into a number of industrial areas, necessitated in part by the war, required reassessment in peacetime, particularly in light of the declining commitment to internationalism. The oil reserves set aside during the Taft and Wilson administrations to assure a continuing supply for naval and military use could now be returned to private use, many thought. The Veterans Administration was now providing expanded services to a larger constituency through its hospitals and other benefit programs. The Alien Property Custodian held control over patents and other useful assets of the wartime enemies. All together, government had expanded to support not only a war but an international responsibility that no longer existed. The redistribution of the resources it had commandeered for the war could obviously have been handled honestly and responsibly, but, just as it had in the aftermath of the Civil War and as it would again in the aftermath of World War II, temptation moved some individuals to take personal advantage of a situation that seemed to many to be without precedent. With one cabinet officer in jail and other officials under various indictments (the duped president was conveniently dead), the problem had somehow been resolved by being seen as a simple crime against the public, and a not very big one at that.

The general improvement of economic conditions in the years that followed were believed to be the result of shrewd management. Coolidge's election to a full term of his own in 1924 was not an accident or due to absence of choice. The slogan "Keep cool with Coolidge" reflected a popular approval of silent and effective political management. It was an era of expansion, of the development of new technologies, new sciences, and an optimism summed up in the phrase "New Era." The election of engineer-turned-philanthropist Herbert Clark Hoover to the presidency in 1928 was part of the same movement and reflected the modernization of progressivism from reform crusade to technological professionalism. As secretary of commerce through the previous eight years, Hoover had more than amply demonstrated his command of the particular range of competence Americans believed to be their key contribution to the new era: business acumen. Business leadership in the twenties reached a zenith in public repute that established it as the ultimate American profession; but these new business leaders must be differentiated from the old captains of industry, excoriated in the Progressive Era debates. The new leaders were part of a technological revolution that linked industrialization and science. Management of that linkage was a new, highly trained skill that promised success to those willing and able to learn it. That knowledge contributed a new utopian energy to the twenties; it signified the transformation of progressivism, not its death.

Business managers, breaking away from an entrepreneurial past that characterized them as manipulative exploiters, turned to science, as they understood it, to create new approaches to wealth. The manipulators of a single key extractive resource—one thinks of Andrew Carnegie and steel, of John D. Rockefeller and oil—were being replaced by systems managers of new technologies. Owen D. Young's organization of the Radio Corporation of America is a good illustration. Radio was a new technology produced by scientific invention rather than exploration and development. New skills were needed to maneuver for international patents and investment, to manage and promote technological research and laboratory study. Regulation by government was accepted in the beginning. Young, the New England small-town boy, became Ida Tarbell's new hero, an important contrast with her earlier muckraking portrait of Rockefeller and Standard Oil. Young's strength was in management, not in exploitation. Tarbell saw his interest as the public good, not as personal aggrandizement. He became the personification of the new service side of private enterprise.

Henry Ford pushed the image several steps further in his efforts not only to build cars for a mass public but to involve his workers in the economic benefits, as he saw them, of his enterprise. The Model T of 1909 (known affectionately as the "flivver") destroyed the luxury status of the automobile. Standardization of parts, production-line innovations, and an approach to pricing that depended on a mass market made the Ford a "people's car" through methods later emulated by the German developers of the Volkswagen. In 1914 he shocked industry and his stockholders by introducing an eight-hour day and a minimum wage of five dollars a day, which he supplemented with a profit-sharing scheme for his employees. Though he turned over the company presidency to his son Edsel in 1919, he was, by the twenties, a national figure, a symbol of rags-to-riches success. His efforts to take over a power plant on the Tennessee River, built by the wartime government to produce electricity and fertilizer (the system that became the core of the New Deal's TVA), increased his popularity among rural voters and seemed to be a viable base for a presidential bid; but his outspoken views on other subjects—most notably, perhaps, his anti-Semitism and various of his attitudes that many conservative businessmen considered radical—weakened his cause. Aldous Huxley's utopian novel of the thirties, *Brave New World*, sets up Ford as god in a futurist, technological society ("Our Ford who art in heaven," his characters pray). Ford the folk hero and public moralist could have stepped out of the boys' fiction of the twenties.

Like government leaders, the new business leadership did indeed look to greater service from the social sciences. Robert S. Brookings, a Saint Louis industrialist, had established Washington University in Saint Louis in the first decade of the century to place himself squarely in the camp of John D. Rockefeller, who had founded the University of Chicago a decade earlier. But Brookings' adoption of the Institution for Government Research in Washington, D.C., in 1920 marks a transition to a newer model: the private advisory system for public policy formulation. The research institutes founded in the 1920s were expected to provide information that would guide policymakers in making useful reforms—reforms that would maintain, not threaten, the political and economic system that had produced the philanthropists themselves. Like highly intellectualized Tom Swifts, they decried inefficient exploitation and called on business and government alike to respect the needs of the social system they shared.

No catalogue of the new leadership would be complete without the name of Samuel Insull, but not as he was known in the thirties, when he was often depicted as a revived Jay Gould or Jim Fisk, though they, at least, had robbed other robbers, while Insull, according to his critics, had robbed widows and orphans. As a leader, Insull has to be viewed as he was at the peak of his reputation in the twenties, when his innovations in the management and distribution of public power made him a utilities genius. Even his methods of distributing stock ownership contributed to his reputation as a millionaire democrat who gave opportunities of wealth to little people rather than to the big banks and provided Chicago with an opera house and his workers with good medical care and social services. His advisory role during the war and his plans for state utility regulation had won him international fame, so that he was sought after by foreign governments when they needed to modernize their utility systems. Insull's utility empire in Chicago weathered the first shocks of the Crash and the early Depression years, but the need to shore up his pyramided investments with bank loans finally did him in. His fall—and it was a big one—did as much as any other story of the period to mark the image of the business leader of the twenties as a myth, a perceptual aberration characteristic of a decade of myth.

In many respects, Andrew Mellon and the policies he followed as secretary of the treasury reflected the more conservative aspect of what was nonetheless a new business phenomenon in the 1920s: the responsible innovator seeking to become involved in the formulation of public policy, not solely for the purpose of protecting the private sector or for personal gain but to expand the innovative power of a new technical system. Herbert Hoover, as secretary of commerce, reflected the more radical aspect. The distinction between the two would ultimately come to rest on the definition of the role to be played by government in supporting or regulating the innovative process. Both appealed to what each believed to be the dual responsibility of the managers of the industrial system: responsibility not simply to the inner moral standards all human beings were expected to obey but to industry as the driving engine of the social system. What seems at times their difficulty in distinguishing between personal morality and public responsibility may be due to a flaw in their perspective, but it was a flaw shared by many Americans in their approach to the relation between public interest and private concerns. The businessman pursuing just profits and the good citizen preserving a just society were not supposed to be in conflict.

The attitudes of men like Hoover and Mellon, Brookings and Young, added a new element to the progressive commitment to science, a positivistic faith in the utility of precise, mathematical data, organized to govern life, to predict the future, and to provide programs of reform. The new economists were no longer viewed as "radicals," as in the days of Veblen and Richard Ely; now they functioned at Brookings and the National Bureau of Economic Research. They reflected a wide range of ideological positions, but they agreed on the importance of collecting, analyzing, and distributing information to provide those responsible for making decisions with the data on which, from their point of view, public and private policymaking had to rest. The war experience had reinforced beliefs that the new generation of professional economists had held for more than two decades. Economic knowledge *was* governmental power. The difference now was that the leaders of the country, in business and in government, were beginning to accept the economists' statements not as

the meanderings or threats of ivory-tower intellectuals but as the prescriptions of a new class of technicians. They sought their advice and, in turn,
supported their research.

It is possible to view Hoover's faith in academic economics as naïve, but the
faith came naturally to a professional engineer, accustomed to calculating
stresses and temperatures, and the social scientists shared his faith and
aspired to make their new science as accurate and objective as his. William
F. Ogburn had had the words of Lord Kelvin cut in stone on the outer wall of
the new Social Science Research Building at the University of Chicago. "If
you cannot measure," the message read, "your knowledge . . . is meager . . .
and unsatisfactory." While some saw this as a grim slogan, others took it as the
open sesame to a utopia in which full knowledge would be achieved, to the
benefit of all mankind.

The relationship between the new business leaders and the new social
scientists was fundamental to the development of the "New Era" and to
understanding its relation to the prewar past. The old industrial leaders had
helped build the new universities; but their interest in new knowledge had
been limited to the traditional fields, like medicine, political economy, law,
and business administration. To the extent that they worried about curricu-
lum at all, they periodically focused attention on moral issues in the teaching
of the young and the possible influence of what they called "radicalism." The
new business leaders were increasingly inclined to see the industrial utility of
a wide range of scientific inquiry. As the war experience had already suggested, psychology, the various fields that investigated foreign affairs—an-
thropology, sociology, history, and political science—and the burgeoning
field of administration all promised to improve the knowledge and skills of the
new managers.

For the more advanced of the new managers, Taylor's teachings were
carried a step beyond the implications many had seen in his writings. A kind of
social Taylorism emerged among men like the Boston department-store
magnate Edward A. Filene, who not only provided his workers with medical
and social services but gave them a voice in management. A promoter of credit
unions around the country, Filene sought practical and effective ways of
implementing industrial democracy. Henry S. Dennison, the manufacturer
of ingenious little mechanisms for improving managerial efficiency—paper
clips, gummed reinforcements for repairing the holes in loose-leaf sheets,
labels of various sizes and shapes, and attractive little boxes to keep them in
and organize them efficiently—was also a disciple of Taylorism. More important, he, like Filene and others in the growing school of industrial managers,
saw the need to involve government in what they were openly calling "planning." Planning, the cooperative alternative to regulation, was a term more
acceptable to businessmen accustomed to thinking of government as an

enemy. While many in the business community still considered such ideas "socialist" or worse, others were quick to pick up bits and pieces of the programs suggested to them. If research would improve production and marketing, keep factory workers happier and more productive, and maintain profits, then research was obviously a good thing.

Part of the argument of the new managers, however, involved at least an implicit acceptance of the position Veblen had been arguing in economics—specifically, that the basic purpose of the new systems of production was not profit but the health of the entire system. An efficient industrial system would produce profits for everyone. This was the message Tom Swift was preaching. It decried greed and regarded wealth as incidental to the adventure of industrial management.

In virtually every respect one can name, Herbert Clark Hoover appeared to be the ideal figure to lead the nation in the culminating presidency of the decade. His career in mining engineering had provided him with a background in natural-resources exploitation that combined science and technology with the popular myths of the American West. He was a self-made man, an international traveler. In fact, all the elements of his boyhood and youth could have furnished the plot for a boys' tale by Stratemeyer. Later, psychological analysts would find his status as an orphan raised by relatives a potential source of personality problems, but at the turn of the century that fitted well with the Victorian conception of hardship overcome, of inner strength triumphing over tragic circumstances. The zeal with which Hoover turned to public service after he had "made his fortune" also marked him as a characteristic philanthropist of his generation. Andrew Carnegie had regarded service as the duty of the self-made man, but he did not become personally involved in the extensive philanthropies he funded. By contrast, Hoover turned to war-relief work in 1914 as a welcome responsibility and thus began a career that was to take him to heights of popular acclaim by the end of the war. One of his wartime neighbors in Washington, D.C., Franklin D. Roosevelt, thought him the ideal candidate for the presidency, early in 1920—as a Democrat, of course. At that time Hoover's political affiliations were unclear.

Hoover's lack of partisan commitment was also characteristic of what might be called post-Progressive progressivism. What the new political analysts saw as the people's disinclination to vote during the 1920s was also a restatement of the progressives' rejection of partisan political organizations. The Progressive party of 1912 had been an antiparty movement in many respects, and the role played by regular party organizations in the 1920s confirmed the progressives' antiparty attitudes. The rise of political independence on the part of voters and their new willingness to shift party allegiances were both part of a transformation of party politics from rural and regional to urban and national.

Shifts in urban voting patterns, as urban immigrants adopted political commitments of their own, seemed to suggest that major partisan realignments were under way.

From 1920 until he ran for the presidency in 1928, Hoover was secretary of the Commerce Department, a position that, until he took it over, had been one of the least conspicuous cabinet offices, a part-time job. Hoover's expansion of the department, his effort to make it a central government advisory system for American business, was a remarkable feat, although not one that pleased those in Congress and elsewhere who did not like to see business that well represented in the executive branch. Hoover's statements in the twenties follow a remarkably consistent pattern. Science, he argued, produced innovation. The adoption of innovation by industry increased production. Increased production produced profits. Profits would be passed on to labor, on the one hand, and to science on the other, to provide greater consumption, more innovation, and the continuous development and expansion of the system. It was a marvelous social machine; but, as Hoover discovered in the twenties, when he tried to sell it to industry, the button to start it was always out of his reach. The presidency ought to have provided him with that, but the onset of the Depression seemed to move it farther away. Yet he remained convinced for the rest of his life that in time he *could* have reached it.

A letter that Roosevelt circulated on the eve of the election of 1928 suggests that by then the promise of Hoover's business progressivism had begun to fade, even though the Crash was more than a year away. Hoover, Roosevelt wrote to many of his progressive friends, was now a captive of the business and banking community and could no longer be considered one of the progressives. Roosevelt was going to vote for Al Smith. To be sure, Roosevelt's partisan commitments were clear: he was, after all, Smith's hand-picked candidate to succeed him as governor of New York. But the language he used in describing Hoover, his one-time friend, was strong.

Hoover's arguments during the campaign spell out the dilemma he was going to face as president, and far more clearly than he ever seemed to realize. Government authority over the nation's economic development might be necessary, but it was dangerous. Business, he insisted, was a centralized, authoritarian, and, in effect, nondemocratic system for making decisions and applying them. Democratic government required community cooperation, committees, and consent; it was, in effect, the exact opposite of business management. For government to go into business required it to become authoritarian, hence nondemocratic. Hoover did not reverse the equation and suggest that businessmen in government necessarily became authoritarian; but that was part of his problem. He did not become an industrial authoritarian in the presidency. He continued to insist that such behavior required "regimentation," the term he used to describe the operation of socialism and fascism. Yet the elements of his argument are precisely those used to define the need for dictatorship in industrial crises. Indeed, as conditions worsened, Hoover seemed to reject power, to seek no authority, and, ultimately, to provide no leadership. A door closed on the era of silent efficiency and left him stranded in a new and clamorous age.

The fact was that Hoover had not been able to persuade industry in the twenties to adopt his outlook. His talk of the utility of labor organization had brought cold responses from the many industrial groups to which he preached. His efforts to generate industrial cooperation through the development of trade associations had trapped him between critics of industry, who were concerned about the antitrust implications of such associations, and management people, who were willing now to use government regulation as a way of getting around antitrust attacks by having government agencies fix rates and prices. Hoover saw the opposition clearly but, as was his wont, ended up becoming the enemy of both. He wanted trade associations, but he did not want government to give them legal authority. He wanted farm organizations to manage prices and production, but they were not to use governmental authority to do it. He wanted local communities to provide supportive services for citizens in need, but not with federal assistance, lest that dry up the traditional springs of local self-help. He saw the needs, but the solutions terrified him; for they implied that the revolutionary changes taking place elsewhere in the world could now be threatening to happen here.

As the New Era's leader, Hoover effectively embodied all of the paradoxes Americans were destined to encounter during that era's search for effective government. The old order's candidate for the new order, Hoover accepted the technological changes and the new concepts of industrial management that had transformed the old class societies of Europe into the new mass societies; but he saw no threat to his beloved American individualism in that transformation here, unless outside forces, foreign ideological influences, produced such a threat. Early in his presidency he sought the advice of William F. Ogburn, whose sociology, Hoover believed, was one of the new sciences American society needed. Even Hoover seemed to know that something like "cultural lag" was the issue; yet he, like many of his contemporaries, seemed in themselves to exemplify the existence of the problem, not the solution.

The sense of a breakdown in values was part of the experience of the twenties, as it had been for earlier generations of Americans coping with the relation between past ideals and the realities of social change. But the issue was dramatized in the twenties by Prohibition and the socially disruptive and threatening conditions produced by what was intended as a great leap forward in the improvement of popular morality. By the end of the decade it was clear that, whatever its intention, the actual consequences of the Eighteenth Amendment were now part of a social history that looked rather different from what had been anticipated, either by its original defenders or by its critics.

Successful reform of this kind required public acceptance of the prohibited action as a crime, and to achieve this was not easy. The drinking of alcohol was a traditional social custom particularly among many of the cultures brought here by the immigrant populations, including the Anglo-Saxons. Institutions in which drinking took place included not only the bars and saloons the reformers had long sought to close but fine restaurants and family-style beer gardens. Local police, particularly in large cities, were accustomed to accepting alcohol as part of normal daily life, and the bars and saloons that went with it were sources of useful information and of occasional gifts and off-hours conviviality. That saloons were often adjacent to political clubs and party offices was an acknowledged convenience for everyone concerned. The corruption that existed was part of a system of urban control that was not going to be easy to eradicate.

Relationships among the various enforcement groups—local, state, and federal—made jurisdiction an intriguing problem. The automobile made the roadhouse a helpful solution if state police were more willing to look the other way than city police might be. State boundaries served a similar purpose if the state "across the river" took a more lenient attitude toward enforcement or did not share its neighbor's hostility toward gambling, an increasingly popular pastime, which often accompanied the enjoyment of roadhouse drinks. For wealthier patrons in coastal cities, luxuriously appointed ships, anchored just outside the famous "three-mile zone"—the limit of federal jurisdiction— served their purposes.

Although federal officials had been concerned about the growth of national crime even before Prohibition, the public popularity of alcohol gave whatever system had existed before the war an unprecedented opportunity for growth. The fact that the production and distribution of alcohol was now an industry totally outside police protection, even where it was tacitly sanctioned, added elements of violence and warfare that contrasted sharply with the elegant and theatrical trappings the "speak-easy" provided as background for socially acceptable entertainment. "Bootleggers" and "rum-runners" may well have been illegal professionals, but they were clearly professionals, and they supplied businesses that were engaged in what were otherwise perfectly legal activities: food preparation and service, the provision of linen and tableware, music and entertainment. The interpenetration of businesses and professions made enforcement difficult.

The association of prostitution with saloons had always been one of the factors reformers had used in their arguments, saying that "good women" did not frequent such establishments. The new establishments—except for the ones explicitly designated as being for "gentlemen only"—made no such sexual differentiation. Women were not expected to sit at the bar itself, but they were welcomed as guests at tables when accompanied by men. The new illegality thus brought with it a new, if limited, liberation.

The popularity of the new illegality made enforcement a game if not a joke. "Raids" took on a sporting atmosphere, particularly in popular literature and the movies. The portrayal of citizen prohibition enforcers as blue-nosed Puritans and the police as either heavies or fools implied a certain innocent view of alcohol as something needed for relaxation or socializing. Even the occasional violence associated with it was approached with ambivalence and served as the subject for adventure. In detective stories like Dashiell Hammett's *Red Harvest*, for example, the characters enjoyed alcohol at all times of the day and in quantities that forty years later would quite clearly have labeled them "problem drinkers." But alcoholism in the twenties and thirties, and indeed for almost three decades thereafter, was defined primarily by the observable social behavior of the drinker, not by the quantity of alcohol consumed or by physiological dependence on a substance that would only much later—and then very reluctantly—be classified as a drug. Drunken behavior and drinking were morally separable.

Along with drinking, as a bonus in this new era of social adventure, went cigarettes. Men had smoked pipes and cigars, not cigarettes, which, in Europe at least, were manufactured primarily for women. While in some circles smoking by women was still regarded as a sure sign of debasement, the "modern" woman of the twenties could smoke a cigarette offered her by her male companion if she were indoors, preferably seated at a dinner table. She did not walk with a cigarette in her hand, and certainly not on the street. The popularization of cigarette-smoking by men was aided by such movie heroes as Rudolph Valentino and Gary Cooper. In addition to the fact that the porcelain features of either man would have looked strange if adorned by a cigar or a pipe, the cigarette could also serve as a visible instrument of seduction when it was exchanged between hero and heroine, the curling smoke a part of the intimate screen closeup. Cigarettes were already being advertised as health items, good for relaxation and thought. One brand claimed that there was "not a cough in a carload."

Such elegance masked, very lightly at times, a sense of the attractiveness of danger that faded in and out of the scenes of literature and entertainment in the twenties like the sounds on the early radios. Radio, even in its early, primitive form, proved itself capable of dramatizing grotesque incidents, which, while part of daily life in any era, would previously have depended on a longer, slower process of myth-making. In February 1925 an amateur cave explorer stumbled into a sandstone pit in a limestone cave in the cave country of southern Kentucky. Pinned by a rockslide, he was interviewed by a Louisville newsman who had crawled through the shifting sand himself, adding his own sense of terror to that of the buried victim, whose frightened prayers and entreaties he reported. The slow death-struggle of Floyd Collins was described to a national audience of crystal-radio-set owners while coal miners and the Army Corps of Engineers launched a massive rescue mission, using all the latest equipment. The cave site in Edmonson County was suddenly filled with tourists, who wanted to witness either the rescue or the martyrdom of the simple Christian, whose fundamentalist conceptions of death so closely matched their own. Food concessionaires and souvenir salesmen materialized to sell their wares to the instant throngs. During the seventeen days it took Collins to die, a phonograph record company executive, vacationing in Florida, managed to commission a ballad by one of the leading radio hillbilly artists, and "The Death of Floyd Collins" became a national best-selling phonograph record, perhaps the first instant folksong. Collins's brother went into vaudeville. The event remained in American folklore for years. It combined a religious horror tale and a peasant hucksterism that were reminiscent of the Middle Ages.

The ability to dramatize events—including catastrophes—for a popular audience was part of the ballad tradition. Such events were intended to evoke religious terror and to call for the kind of redemption the sermons of evangelist Billy Sunday assured the temporarily fallen would be theirs if only they would repent. The Collins ballad joined a literature of mining and railroad catastrophes that suggested the traditional dangers of work and sought to sustain a morality built on the age-old fear of death. Yet society, trapped between the older values of agrarian society and the newer industrial ideologies, celebrated heroes similarly trapped: Floyd Collins, dying alone while every available kind of modern technology was being used to rescue him and to broadcast his plight, or Charles Lindbergh successfully flying the North Atlantic, again alone, while audiences waited to learn what had befallen him. The hero lived or died alone, but radio audiences of thousands cheered or wept in sympathy as he did so.

The decade is thus an era marked by the paradoxes of major historical transitions. The beliefs of generations who considered themselves rural or urban, Victorian or modern, isolationist or internationalist, individualist or collectivist, competed for the attention of the uncommitted young, whether they were small-towners, first-generation immigrants moving from ethnic enclaves to suburbs, or middle-class city-dwellers seeking to adopt the trappings of upward mobility that once were reserved to the wealthy elite.

Similar transitional eras had occurred at earlier stages of American history. What gives the decade of the twenties its particular cast is the rapid development of the new communications media, which made people conscious that their society was in transition. Since profit was the fundamental aim of the communications industry, the ideas communicated had to appeal to wide audiences, who would buy tickets to the movies on a regular basis or purchase one radio sponsor's product rather than another. That in turn meant that subject matter, from news to serial drama, had to reflect a middle level of taste and intelligence. Those who controlled the radio and, particularly, the movie industry did not often reflect the literary and artistic tone of the growing intellectual elite, but their products are a rich source of information on American taste. The chaotic variety of films produced in America contrasted sharply with those seen in other countries, where stricter government control provided films suited to different levels of taste and judgment. That method, however, was destined to have its own disturbing consequences, when state control of communications in societies like Fascist Italy and Nazi Germany came to govern more than taste.

In 1928 the "roaring twenties," the "incredible era," was coming to an end. The Crash that ended it was not foreseen during the election of 1928, although those who watched the stock market climb were worried. Looking backward was, in a sense, too easy. It was a rich decade, in more respects than the obvious material wealth that seemed to promise endless opportunity; but the stock-market crash seemed to carry everything down with it.

5

Defining the Great Depression

Hoover's inaugural parade in March 1929 was described to the nation by radio network "announcers," as they were called, stationed atop office buildings on the parade route. For days before the event, newspaper advertisements had anticipated the spectacle, urging readers to buy radio sets so that they could be part of it. Primitive television images flickered on experimental sets in Baltimore. Banners carried a medallion showing the profiles of Hoover and George Washington side by side. Washington's early career as a land surveyor suggested to presidential publicists that he, too, had been an engineer; Hoover was then called "the first engineer since George Washington" to become president. On the eve of the presidential campaign Hoover had been photographed visiting scenes of flood devastation in the South, an act that reflected his compassion for the displaced and bereft but also seemed to imply the promise of his technical skills as an engineer: an ability to control nature's destructive habits.

A technological aura lingered during the early months of Hoover's presidency as newspapers carried canned White House reports of his efficiency. He was the first president to have a telephone placed directly on the Oval Office desk rather than in a small room nearby. A row of buttons summoned secretaries to his presence. News releases commented on his early arrival in his office, the speed with which he could change from ceremonial costume to street clothes. Taylorist concepts of time and motion colored descriptions of his day and of Mrs. Hoover's elaborate system of hand signals, which silently guided the service of formal dinners.

Congressmen became gradually aware that this president had a "staff" instead of the usual secretary or two, no more; and when they found themselves encountering different faces each time they visited the White House, rather than the president himself, they bridled at requests that they fund the four assistants. They were not aware of the need for assistant presidents, so Hoover paid for them himself. It was a small disgruntlement, but it rankled all the parties concerned. Hoover didn't think Congress appreciated the managerial demands of the presidency. Congressmen didn't like intermediaries standing between themselves and their chief executive.

Magazine articles discussed visits with him and his highly organized day. He spoke little but did a great deal, according to such accounts, delegating authority to subordinates, whose actions he supervised without commanding. He relaxed with exercise games like "medicine ball" and enjoyed small dinners with friends and associates. His silent effectiveness had a certain appeal, initially. It seemed to take the edge off a concern voiced by many who had watched him closely during the war years that he was dictatorial and threatening. Yet he did not seem to enjoy public informality and generally appeared politely uncomfortable under public scrutiny. He allowed himself to be photographed in fishing garb but refused photographers access to his family. He built a retreat for himself in nearby Virginia. Hoover's hideaway was the kind of primitive campgrounds that wealthy Californians were accustomed to using as proof of their commitment to nature, and he often went there to escape from public Washington. One of the rare photographs of him enjoying play shows him throwing out the first ball of the baseball season. Surrounded by stony-faced cabinet members—and their wives—Hoover pitches enthusiastically, the boyish smile suggesting his recollection of a country childhood. It is a momentary relaxation of the stiffness that would, by the end of his term, be interpreted as a barrier.

When Hoover became president, he was aware of the precarious state of the economy. Having observed national and international economic conditions from his eight years in the cabinet, he also had a reasonably sophisticated sense of what the problems were. American agriculture had been in a continuous state of depression. The prevailing wisdom tied that depression to lower prices on world markets and to international tariff wars, as other nations sought to protect themselves from "dumping" by countries willing to sell agricultural surpluses at lower prices while they supported prices at home. At the center of the problem was the availability of gold as payment for purchases. The three factors—agricultural surpluses, protective tariffs, and hard currency—were the points of an old international triangle now complicated by the growing number of new industrial and technological products and, perhaps most important of all, by the international debt settlement that had followed the Versailles Treaty.

The debt settlement was the trickiest because it involved two things: the highly questionable $33 billion in reparations payments the Allies had levied against Germany, and the debts the Allies owed the United States for the costs not only of the war but of the postwar reconstruction of Europe. The amount of debt agreed on in the initial settlement, including interest payments, came to an astronomical total of more than $22 billion. The United States had never before been so deeply involved in international economics; it had now, in effect, become banker to the rest of the world. The British had at first called for a general cancellation of all debts it owed in return for its cancellation of the debts owed to it by its other Allies, but Woodrow Wilson had rejected this. That rejection set the stage for a decade of conflict; it also reflected an American political problem. Americans, as individual citizens, had contributed very largely to financing the war by buying war bonds, and the private banking system had also played a significant role in supplying loans for both war goods and reconstruction costs. Congress could scarcely be sympathetic to the idea of cancellation. Moreover, American presidents did not have the kind of control of banking policy that British and French prime ministers had. German reparations complicated the matter further still, for it became clear that the payments on the Allies' debts to the United States would have to come from the money the Germans paid to the Allies.

The impossibility of the structure became increasingly clear throughout the 1920s, and Americans headed a series of conferences designed to scale the obligations down to more reasonable proportions. A system of private bank loans to Germany was finally instituted to enable Germany to pay its reparations so that other countries could pay their debts. It was a gigantic international chain letter, premised on a much more stable international economy than existed at the time. The problem was compounded of the Allies' unwillingness to give up the punitive reparations they believed they deserved, the Europeans' anger against the United States for demanding payment for debts incurred in a war that Europeans had carried the brunt of, and an American public opinion that agreed with Calvin Coolidge when he said, "They hired the money, didn't they?"

Such a remark may sound naïve to us now, but it must be understood in its context: the novelty of international engagement for Americans and the utter uncertainty with which the United States assumed its new status as a world power. Although Hoover may come through as a prescient internationalist, in advance of his times, even his insights have to be placed in the context of his contempt for European politics. His enormous compassion for Europeans did not extend to their rulers, and he had little respect for most of their forms of government. Like many of his contemporaries, including Woodrow Wilson, he held a fairly fixed set of beliefs about what kinds of government were *really* democratic, and he mistrusted all the rest. His economic insights—and he had many more than he was credited with having—must be placed against the background of his basic mistrust of politicians of any nationality, including his own. Economics for him was definitely not a political matter.

The fact that there appeared to be no acceptable political solution to the economic problems caused by the international debts and reparations has to be the beginning point for any approach to the domestic issues of Hoover's administration. Hoover saw these problems as the chief burden of his presidency, and few other Americans did. This need not make him into a latter-day hero, now that we can see more clearly what he saw. As the nation's political leader he was faced with the task of finding a political solution; but as an engineer and businessman, convinced that politics could solve few if any of the technical problems central to either profession, he approached his task from a perspective that made dubious any prospect of success.

His initial step as president in 1929 was to call a special session of Congress to deal with the agricultural crisis. The experience of the previous eight years should have taught him that, unlike industry, and certainly unlike labor, the farmers exerted a potent and direct influence in congressional politics. The history of that influence went back to the beginnings of populism in the period after the Civil War. By the 1920s it had succeeded in entering directly into traditional politics; thus the farm bloc could not easily be labeled a radical fringe or a special-interest group or "trust." Efforts on the part of Coolidge and Hoover to identify farm politics as special-interest politics had little or no real effect on public attitudes toward agriculture. Unlike bankers, who could be perceived as a lobbying force, farmers were still romanticized as America's yeomanry and were accepted as political participants.

Twice during the 1920s the farm bloc in Congress had succeeded in passing legislation designed to protect the domestic price of agricultural products by having the federal government purchase them for sale abroad at the lower world price. While the difference between the world price and the domestic price was to be covered by an equalization fee that producers would be charged, the result was supposed to be a higher domestic price for the producer. Coolidge vetoed both of the McNary-Haugen bills, one in 1924, the other in 1928, on the grounds that they were special-interest legislation and unconstitutional.

Hoover recognized the international implications of such legislation. He also saw the connection between depressed agricultural sales abroad and the protective tariffs favored by American industry. The world economy, he correctly perceived, was now dependent on American capital. By using the tariff to inhibit American purchases of foreign goods, Americans were limiting the power of foreigners to purchase agricultural products. While no free-trade advocate himself, he nonetheless saw prohibitive tariffs as a danger both to the international economy and to American agriculture.

His problem lay in the fact that the farm bloc did not see the tight relation between agricultural prices and tariffs on industrial goods. By the same token, spokesmen for industry did not see agricultural prices as their problem; in their search for protection, they did not feel it necessary to worry about the farmers. Hoover's insistence on dealing with the two issues together was part of his systematic approach, but it was a political blunder.

By calling the special session, Hoover hoped to use the initial momentum of his administration to push his agenda through, but as the spring deepened into the customarily hot and muggy Washington summer, the effort seemed to wilt. Members of his own party worked their way through the sluggish prose of the president's public statements, wondering just exactly what he wanted, looking for leadership, bridling over veiled threats that Hoover would veto anything that smacked of federal control of prices or production. The tariff issue was pushed aside, though Hoover did get the voluntary system of farm production controls he had wanted. It looked like a partial victory, but that sense dissipated when it became clear that voluntary limits on production simply would not work.

Hoover's sense of his relation to Congress was not clear to the congressmen of either party. His popularity in his own party did not run high. Some feared his drive for power. Others were familiar with his disdain for the party regulars and their persistent demand for jobs for constituents. The conservative elements in the Democratic party regarded him as a progressive, while the progressive elements in the Democratic party not only continued to believe in Smith but suspected that Hoover had to some extent encouraged the intense anti-Catholic hostility that had marked the campaign of 1928. Hoover's long administrative career in Washington had given him an odd role to play, that of a committed nonpartisan who had nonetheless been a highly visible actor in the partisan battles of the entire decade.

Nonetheless, the fact that Hoover came to the presidency from such a close-in position in the Harding and Coolidge administrations provided him with an extraordinary opportunity to plan the management of the office most Washingtonians knew he had coveted for a long time. He had played an important advisory role in all of the major policy decisions of the era and had been generous with newspaper and magazine writers who wanted his opinions on a wide range of subjects. They respected his wishes when he asked not to be quoted, and they looked to the staff members of his rather large entourage for additional leads to his points of view. He could speak about the problems of bureaucracy, a term he used with all of its pejorative connotations, and he maintained contacts with experts in all of the essential fields. His appointment of a former Stanford University president, Ray Lyman Wilbur, to head the Department of the Interior was a step toward a major reorganization of American government. The Interior Department, Hoover believed, could take charge of two essential policymaking functions he wanted Washington to perform in the realm of domestic affairs. Just as State and Treasury advised on foreign policy and the economy, respectively, and as Commerce, under his direction, had advised on business, Interior could set up a system for advising on social and welfare policies and on matters involved in what were generally called "public works," a field increasingly dominated by the government's management of waterpower resources.

This idea, and the appointment of Wilbur to implement it, point once again to the political problems of the Hoover administration, even before the Crash had marked his presidency. Ever since its creation in 1849 the Department of the Interior had been the government's central means of control over the nation's natural resources. From parceling out the free land of the West to overseeing government property in most of its nonmilitary forms, Interior had governed the distribution of resources in the expanding nation. It was thus vulnerable to corruption, especially since wealthy Americans competed for the same land that spelled homesteading opportunities for adventuresome Americans of modest means. The minerals found on government lands in the West were obvious sources of wealth, but so were the rights of homesteaders and settlers. Next to the Post Office and the jobs the postmaster general had at his disposal, the Department of the Interior was the department of government most closely tied to political favoritism. Perhaps it was even more closely tied; for the constituents who demanded favors from congressmen, who would in turn appeal to the Department of the Interior, were asking for something more than jobs. They were looking for opportunity from the land itself, for the ownership that would make them independent.

Wilbur was a college president, a Californian who, like Hoover, had long associated himself with nonpartisan reform. Like Hoover, he suspected politics and politicians, and, yet again like Hoover, he now held one of the nation's most political positions. Both men reflected the era's most significant question: whether an industrialized society and its resources could be managed efficiently through a political system its managers considered corrupt and wasteful. That was the essential progressive dilemma. Unwilling to believe that corruption was an inherent element in American politics rather than the aberration they persisted in calling it, they looked for reforms that would keep their vision of the political system intact. Yet generations of newcomers had been drawn into politics by politicians who gave them jobs in return for their votes. Such corruption, if that's what it was, had provided these Americans with their first glimpse of opportunity. Reformers attacked their benefactors as "bosses," a term which, to the beneficiaries of patronage, had no worse implications than the term Hoover's followers affectionately applied to him. Long after his administration, the men who had worked for Hoover addressed him as "The Chief," and the recollection of respect and admiration formed a bond untouched by criticism and defeat.

Wilbur and Hoover both began to marshal the intellectual forces of the two communities that each was familiar with. As one of the nation's leaders in medical education, Wilbur was aware of the philanthropic agencies that had provided the nation with two decades of tremendous scientific progress in hospital care and medical research. Hoover had similar contacts in the fields of industrial research and engineering. He was well aware of the principle of using public works as a device for dealing with unemployment during periods of decline in the business cycle and had urged the advance planning of such projects. He admired Wesley Clair Mitchell's research in the economics of the business cycle and believed that refinements of it would lead to the intelligent use of public works, unemployment insurance, and other methods of balancing the normal and, as he believed, natural ebbs and flows of an industrial economy.

What distinguishes Hoover's approach from that of the later Keynesian economic planners was his conviction that such programs could be funded privately or by combined public and private resources. He appeared to object not to planning as such but to the *federal* government's funding of the projects that were planned. His acceptance of Congress's creation of the Reconstruction Finance Corporation, very late in his administration, was the farthest he was willing to go in that direction. The RFC could lend money to local financial institutions, which could in turn fund local contractors.

Hoover was very familiar with the planning movement that had begun to spread through the country in the mid-1920s, and he was sympathetic with its aims. Regional planners in New York and Chicago had begun to define new forms of urban organization. The concept of the "metropolitan region" had emerged as the way to describe the relation between the city as a political unit and the surrounding countryside that had grown increasingly dependent upon it. Programs to plan for such regions had brought together urban leaders, philanthropic funders, industrial organizers, social scientists, and newspaper and magazine publicists eager to obtain support from local citizens. Hoover had helped organize such regional groups and saw in them the base for the national program he hoped to promote as president.

The special session of Congress with which he began his administration left little doubt that Hoover's commitment to programs efficiently organized and managed might not be as compatible with congressional politics as he seemed to believe. It was difficult to describe the ten-year-old agricultural depression as critical, though it was obviously serious, and even Hoover himself was uncertain about the best way to approach one of the oldest political issues in presidential-congressional debates: the tariff. Again, the relation between the European war debts and the national and international economy was only beginning to seem critical. The afterglow of the nation's initial efforts to establish itself as the manager of world economics had not yet entirely faded. The essential interconnectedness of all of the issues seemed to impress no one.

Hoover was also conscious of another crisis, one that had been building for over a year. The Federal Reserve Board's refusal to raise interest rates when the decline in industrial production released funds for market speculation had generated an explosion of stock-market activity that would, Hoover knew, lead to a collapse. While few were prepared to predict the severity of it, the certainty of it was clear. Such things had happened before, for similar reasons. What was new, as Hoover saw it, was the heightened impact of the international situation and the transformations produced by the war and its economic settlement. Raising interest rates would, as some of the managers of the Federal Reserve System saw it, imperil the Bank of England by draining its gold reserves. If the British abandoned the gold standard (as they were ultimately forced to do), the United States' commitment to gold would be threatened. Hoover's belief that some kind of fundamental renegotiation of the war debts had to be undertaken if gold were to be preserved as the medium of international exchange was thus clear even before the stock market crashed in October. The factor that was destined to provide the sharpest contrast between Hoover and Roosevelt—economic internationalism versus domestic economic controls—was there at the very beginning. The fact was that international affairs had no political clout in Congress and even less resonance in American public opinion. Whatever one says about Hoover's lack of political skills, especially in dealing with Congress, the fact remains that it would have been difficult to find a political constituency for an international solution to the crisis, either to prevent it from happening, to lessen its impact, or to deal with it after it had reached the proportions of a national disaster.

Hoover saw the instability of international currency as the cause of the Crash, and he believed that the ensuing Depression would be cured by restabilizing it. Restructuring the debts was the key to that restabilization. If Hoover saw any weaknesses in the domestic economy, he did not appear to consider them fundamental. Yet, there is little indication that he saw America's role in the establishment of the debt structure as critical either. For Hoover the Crash and the Depression were the result of European events that affected an American economy he believed to be basically healthy. That conviction seriously limits whatever one can say about the intellectual depth of Hoover's international insight.

The great stock-market Crash of 1929 began on the 24th of October, when thirteen million shares were traded. On the 29th, sixteen million shares changed hands. By the 13th of November, $30 billion in market value had been wiped out. Hoover, along with most knowledgeable Americans, including New York's governor, Franklin Roosevelt, looked on all this as a necessary adjustment provoked by unprecedented speculation. It was paper empires that toppled—or so it seemed initially. But the Crash brought the European economies down with it. The Great Depression began. The problem of interpreting the events began, too, and it remains as unresolved for historians today as it was at that time. The array of possible positions can be spelled out, but it is the choices one makes among them that ultimately determine how one makes historical judgments about the decade from 1929 to 1939.

According to one position, the Crash and the Depression were essentially unrelated. If the Crash did not necessarily trigger the Depression, then Hoover's initial interpretation of the events was correct. That is, the Crash was no different from previous panics. The ultimate economic readjustments would take place in time, just as they had in the past. No major restructuring of the economic system was required; in fact, the less action government took, the better. By taking the actions it took, the New Deal, according to the extensions to be made from this argument, prolonged the Depression or at best did very little to affect its course.

The alternative argument insists that the Crash was different from previous panics, for various reasons, and therefore that the Depression was integrally related to it. Such arguments had developed by 1931, and they clearly influenced Roosevelt's thinking by 1932. The industrial system was described as stagnant or overbuilt, and reactions to that took a variety of forms, ranging from a Turnerian concern about the consequences of life without a frontier to the antiindustrialism reflected in *I'll Take My Stand*, a collection of essays by twelve southern agrarians.

More radical positions suggested that industrial capitalism had come to the end of an era, that the old individualism no longer worked, that centralized planning was imperative. This was not antiindustrialism; it was superindustrialism. From this point of view, the Crash was also a product of urbanization, and it was seen as the first genuinely national depression, one that affected the entire society, not simply a few segments of it, as the panics had in an earlier, more diversified, America. From this perspective the New Deal can be criticized for not doing enough.

Still another position sees the international origins of the Depression and its relation to World War I. As early as 1919, in his book *The Economic Consequences of the Peace*, the English economist John Maynard Keynes had predicted that a general economic collapse would result from the Versailles settlement. In his opinion the United States alone had the power and leadership to effect the necessary restructuring of the world economy. Oddly enough, his view of the international causes of the Depression was not the same as Hoover's. Keynes's argument can be extended to say that the failure of the United States to lead the world away from Versailles was the root of the collapse. Hoover's internationalism was the reverse, in a sense. By the end of his presidency he was still committed to a punitive view toward Europe; he argued that the United States was the victim of the failure of Europe to properly liquidate the economic effects of its war. The United States might, out of a combination of generosity and self-interest, attempt to salvage the world economic system by helping to stabilize gold; but it would not revise its position on the war-debts issue, or consider the relation between that issue and the reparations payments, or in fact do much beyond the one-year moratorium on payment of interallied debts, established in 1931. In short, Hoover's internationalism contained the same hostility to foreigners—the basic American xenophobia—that characterized the traditional isolationist. He very much wanted to maintain gold as the international monetary standard, and he announced the willingness of the United States to take part in an international conference assembled for that purpose. In that sense, Hoover's understanding of the international causes of the Depression did not bring him into conflict with general American attitudes toward Europe. The only essential difference was that, for him, a somewhat greater degree of American benevolence could be considered politically permissible.

Preoccupied as it was with international economics, Hoover's view of the Depression appeared to grow increasingly abstract as unemployed Americans exhausted the limited public resources available to them locally. So profound a crisis cut across class lines. Traditional relief agencies—the Salvation Army and the Red Cross, other local public charities and religious groups—were geared to short-term activities directed to segments of the population labeled "unfortunates," not to continuing support of what was rapidly becoming not only a major portion of the labor force but a significant number of the nation's small businessmen as well. Drawing on methods Wilson had used during the war, Hoover exhorted national leadership groups to organize support for local agencies. He knew that such philanthropic groups had proliferated during the twenties, and he called for their further expansion. Yet even their resources were being stretched to reach classes of citizens they had never before been required to help and for whom "charity" was as unfamiliar as extended unemployment. These unemployed citizens had supported charity, not asked for it, and the experience wounded and damaged their sense of themselves. Comic strips like *Little Orphan Annie, Annie Rooney,* and *Apple Mary* (later *Mary Worth*) described the plight of the dispossessed middle classes, who moved from security, even affluence, to poverty and back again in roller-coaster sequences that gave readers a sense of hope that their discomfort was temporary. In the movies, children were used to evoke a similarly comforting sense of innocence betrayed.

What seemed to change during the Hoover administration was the people's perception of the Depression. In the beginning it was seen as a temporary condition, affecting some members of society, but it came to be seen as a permanent condition, affecting all. Hoover clearly did not see it as permanent, but by 1932 the depth of discontent made his emphasis on international causes seem much more abstract and distant that it had seemed in 1929. Pressured by a public urgency he could not control, Hoover agreed to increase government involvement in public-works projects and to revive the wartime agencies for lending money to selected industries. He finally approved both the creation of the Federal Stabilization Board for planning public works and the Reconstruction Finance Corporation for making the necessary loans; but his initial reluctance to take these steps lost him the credit he ultimately deserved.

Hoover also emphasized the need to support positive psychological attitudes toward the nation's economy. Prominent entertainment and business personalities were urged to tour the country and to appear on radio programs designed to spur public confidence in business. The wartime experience with bond sales was again the model. As in the campaigns to get communities to help their own citizens, the initial response was useful and supportive; but the voluntary system ground to a halt when local communities diverted school money to *feed* children rather than to teach them. Hoover's urgings began to sound unreal.

Yet localism had once worked. Most Americans—even the distressed— were not inclined to see Washington or the president as the cause of their difficulties or as the source of their salvation—certainly not at first. Hoover's insistence on local management of the crisis reflected general attitudes. "Hard times" described a condition that his generation, at all levels, still assumed to be part of a natural process, an aspect of fate no one could seriously question. If radicals here and there thought otherwise or if some farmers toyed with the idea of a managed system capable of meeting their needs, they did not represent a majority. Middle-class entrepreneurs, still inclined to be suspicious of government control, were ashamed to have to seek "relief" or to "go on the dole." Moreover, organized labor was just as worried about the ultimate effects of federal intervention as industrialists were, and farmers, though they sought various forms of federal support for prices, were still convinced that federal controls on production would threaten their freedoms.

The drama of New Deal legislation, particularly at the beginning, sheds a false light on the years that preceded the New Deal, for it seems to imply that Congress passed the new laws in response to a public that demanded massive federal intervention after the Hoover years of inactivity. Emphasis on the Crash distorts our view of a crisis that grew slowly. Confidence in Hoover and the government ebbed gradually, and it never completely disappeared, as is evidenced by the fact that over fifteen million Americans voted for Hoover in 1932. (Twenty-three million voters gave Roosevelt his landslide victory.)

It is important to be conscious of the American sense of Washington and the federal government in the years before the New Deal transformed it. The popular view of the economy as a natural system, influenced by only a few specific government policies, like those respecting tariffs and currency regulation, changed in the years after 1933. Despite the efforts of progressives to make the federal government responsive to social change and capable of influencing it, the absence of an American consensus on what constituted social justice, let alone social equality, had always restricted the power of

Washington to do anything more than call attention to problems; even that power was limited by the unwillingness of the national administration to offend regions of the country where local custom made inequity the norm. Hoover had appointed a committee to study social changes in recent decades, but he had intended its report to supply government with a factual account of national conditions, not with a blueprint for rebuilding American society.

Hoover had been elected to manage the old system of government in new ways, not to transform it. It appeared for a brief time that his successor had been given greater power to transform the system, but Congress quickly moved in to reassert its control, limiting the powers Roosevelt requested and, in the aftermath of the New Deal, recovering them. Much more slowly than the drama of the Depression crisis allows us to see, government economic policy became the responsibility of the nation's chief manager, the president; but every new president would have to define that responsibility for himself, persuade Congress to give it to him, and convince the public that it was appropriate. The shift in focus from Congress to the president and the expansion of economic machinery to control the economy mark changes wrought by the New Deal on popular expectations about the role the federal government should play; but no future president or Congress could be sure just what actions those popular expectations could be made to support.

The crisis of 1931–32 was worldwide, a vortex into which Americans found themselves drawn as victims, not as responsible agents. Whatever insights anyone may have had into the causes did not include a politically acceptable agenda. As many historians willing to give Hoover his due have pointed out, he did more than any president before him to cope with the national aspects of the crisis. But for a mind committed to research as the basis for experimentation, the increasing number of proposals for action, for the use of untried methods, was fearsome. Like a doctor contemplating a critically ill patient, the president had to measure the danger of drastic, untried courses of treatment against some conception of just how ill the patient was. Hoover did not believe the economy was dangerously ill, let alone moribund. He blamed the drama of election politics itself for much of the crisis; it made the business community uncertain of what a new administration would do (and it was becoming increasingly clear that there would *be* a new administration). That fact severely limited his power to persuade, let alone to act. Efforts to convince the banking community to aid banks that were in trouble—a method previous presidents had used during banking crises—did not work for Hoover. The Reconstruction Finance Corporation did not work for him either. Whether Hoover's administration of the new instruments was more conservative than Congress intended remains an open question; the congressional debates and the suggestions of intent before 1933 provide no real answers. Congressional "radicals," led by Fiorello LaGuardia and Robert F. Wagner of New York, did not yet wield any considerable influence.

In fact, Hoover's most remarkable misperception was his growing conviction that radicalism underlay the opposition to his arguments. As had been the case at the beginning of the decade, the news media, many of whose owners shared Hoover's fear of radicalism, dramatized periodic outbursts of radical activity far out of proportion to the actual power of the radical movement, which was minuscule. There was, finally, an incident that seemed to confirm their fears. The Bonus Army of 1932, a march on Washington, consisted initially of no more than a thousand ex-servicemen. Its purpose was to pressure Congress into authorizing a cash bonus, to make good on a promise made to the veterans in 1924 and one that Congress in fact had tried to keep ever since, only to have the legislation vetoed by every president from Harding to Franklin Roosevelt. The ranks of the servicemen camped on the Anacostia Flats ultimately swelled to 17,000. At that point Hoover sent in federal troops, equipped with tanks and led by Douglas MacArthur, to disperse them. Two veterans and two policemen were killed in the ensuing battle. The action was excessive on Hoover's part, to say the least.

Moreover, the Democratic platform contained nothing that foretold the New Deal programs, let alone radical actions. It called for drastic cuts in government spending, a balanced budget, participation in an international monetary conference, aid to farmers *if* constitutional means to do it could be found, old-age insurance *if* it could be handled by state legislation, and a sound currency—all measures perfectly consistent with the previous administration's policies. Yet Hoover persisted in seeing Roosevelt's intentions as radical.

Hoover's growing tendency to see ideological conflict as the heart of the problem seems extreme now only because we know what actually did happen. In 1933, however, world events seemed to portend the kind of ideological crisis Hoover feared. William Randolph Hearst funded a movie entitled *Gabriel over the White House* in which a politician became a temporary dictator. Miraculously saved from death in an accident, the former political hack underwent a conversion and became a benevolent tyrant. His brief assertion of total authority was necessary to realign the nation's political system. Miraculous also was the heart attack that finally got him out of the White House—a *deus ex machina* that no one looking at events in Italy and Germany could find reassuring.

The Depression of the 1930s was a worldwide event. Like the world wars that preceded and ended it, the Depression period reflected the complexities of an international industrialism that appeared to turn the nineteenth century's dreams of legal and constitutional stability into a nightmare. Concepts of world order based on independent national states working "in concert" through the World Court and, later, through the League of Nations had generated an optimism that made perpetual peace a real possibility in the minds of many thoughtful people on both sides of the Atlantic. The Nobel

Prize for International Peace, Andrew Carnegie's Endowment for International Peace, and Wilson's designation of the war as a war to end all wars dramatized various aspects of the same ideal. The establishment of the League in a permanent location in Switzerland—the exemplary peaceful state, which had escaped the misfortunes of industrialization—promised a stability the world had not known since the Congress of Vienna in 1815.

Yet, the conference at Versailles had not been the same. World leaders seemed more concerned with self-interest than with concert, and the portrayal of Wilson as the hero of the new movement did not last the decade. By the end of the twenties he had become the martyred saint and, to some in Europe, the villain. For American internationalists, Wilson had been either the dupe of European greed or the victim of American politics, depending on where you stood on the Senate's rejection of the Versailles Treaty and the subsequent refusal to join the League. For Europeans, particularly for Germans, Wilson had failed to produce what he had promised. He had come to represent the pointlessness of American intervention and the unreliability of the United States as an ally.

The crumbling of the League had been part of the twenties, as had the continuing economic imbalance produced by the Versailles Treaty. Revolutions or threats of revolution against traditional forms of government, which reflected the economic order of a simpler day, produced a growing sense that the political and economic methods used by constitutional democracies to maintain order—parliamentary systems, upper-middle-class leadership, and political parties with competing programs—were not working. The short-lived parliamentary democracy that Wilson and others had heralded as Russia's replacement for its czarist monarchy had produced the world's first Marxist system, feared by leaders on both sides of the Atlantic for more than a generation. In Italy and then, a decade later, in Germany, forms of government called "fascist" replaced constitutional parliamentary systems with a single national party, which, like the Communist party in the new Soviet Union, represented the whole state, not competing groups within the state, and its leaders functioned as the embodiment of nationalism, their power derived from their unassailable control over the party apparatus and their adoration by the public.

The Depression was, for Europeans, the worst of the series of economic crises they had suffered since the 1870s. Americans had been affected both economically and socially by these European upheavals, but the effects had been cushioned by the westward settlement, the diversity of economic opportunities in various regions of the vast continent, and the speed and diversity of economic growth. Indeed, the economy had absorbed incredible numbers of Europeans, displaced by the more extreme economic conditions there, and Americans complained only in hard times, when they had to compete for jobs with the newcomers. Not until the end of the century had American urbanization reached the point where traditional nativist opposition to immigrants could be organized successfully. American economic crises were short-lived by comparison with European ones, and their impact was unevenly distributed across the nation. Even in the twenties, when agriculture remained in or at the edge of crisis and employment in some industries—coal being the chief example—was considerably softer than in others, the nation still perceived itself as prosperous.

The fact that Americans and their leaders were not initially inclined to see the Crash and the Depression in cataclysmic terms is thus part of a historical experience that differentiated them from Europeans. Easily within living memory there had been two depressions, the immediate postwar one and the earlier, more dramatic, one of the late 1890s. Both had been cited as models of the cyclical nature of the economic order. Since the system would right itself, there was no need for dramatic government intervention, let alone for a significant transformation of the form of government itself. Americans had no need to look for revolutionary solutions to problems that would, in time, solve themselves.

Nonetheless, by 1932 it was clear that something in the national mood had begun to change. This Depression was coming to be perceived as different in a sense that was only slowly defined. At least two aspects of that redefinition are important. The first is that the Depression came to be understood as national, affecting everyone in some way. This does not mean that the federal government was being asked to do something about it, at least initially; it means simply that everyone felt that something had to be done because everyone was being affected. Part of that perception can be traced to newsreel and radio descriptions of life among the unemployed. *Time* selected colorful examples of unrest on the nation's farms, of the suicides of bankrupt stockbrokers, and of veterans selling apples on streetcorners.

A second aspect of the new perception suggests a more profound change in attitude. This depression, it seemed, would not go away by itself. The cycle, in some critical respects, had stopped moving. According to theories that had begun to circulate as early as 1930, the halting of the cycle could be dealt with in several ways. One could accept the permanent ending of the cyclical process either by dismantling the national industrial system on which it rested and returning to a more regionally controlled mixture of agriculture and local industry—the change recommended by the agrarians who wrote *I'll Take My Stand*—or one could move toward a planned and controlled industrial system, as the proponents of Technocracy and Production for Use were beginning to suggest. The Technocrats were latter-day Taylorites, but the kind of industrial planning they called for Taylor would have found extreme. Production for Use bore resemblances to Veblen's promotion of industrial production governed by consumer needs rather than the drive for profit. Such ideas did not gain any major national constituencies; for the most part, they circulated among small groups of intellectuals.

In some respects, the most remarkable new conception was the one that stressed the need to get the cycle moving again by the sheer force of popular will. The war experience suggested that the public could be persuaded to be patriotic and hardworking and to sacrifice self-interest for the common good. Hoover, and ultimately Roosevelt, were convinced that the public could be persuaded to push the business cycle back into motion by cooperative attitudes. They could persuade one another to produce more, to buy more, to invest more, to save less, and, above all, to stop fearing the future. Fear, according to such arguments, was what had paralyzed the cyclical process. One could restore prosperity by having confidence in the economy. Psychological attitudes, it was argued, had produced the speculative fever that had led to the Crash; now psychological attitudes were preventing the recovery. For Americans who had for generations blamed economic catastrophes on government decisions about specific matters, like the currency or tariffs, the notion that a mass psychology was the source of national troubles was new.

Between them, the idea of the Depression as a national experience and the idea of the Depression as a psychological aberration helped make the Great Depression great. Americans as a whole people were being encouraged to blame themselves, if not for causing it, then for failing to end it. The Depression of the '30s rapidly became a historical—indeed, a legendary—experience. The fear that it would never end, that it represented a significant departure from the past, built rapidly; and, as the subsequent record of the New Deal suggests, this depression would not go away by itself.

The World War I experience had compelled the nation's policymakers to accept the validity of the argument that progressives and labor statisticians had been making for several decades, namely, that any kind of national policy on labor conditions would have to rest on more carefully collected employment statistics. How to measure the scope of the agricultural depression had been part of the political debates of the twenties, and precise measurements of the relation between agricultural prices at home and abroad and of the relation between industrial prices and agricultural prices had joined currency values as a way of gauging economic conditions.

Yet, in 1930, the Department of Labor was receiving employment statistics from only twelve of the forty-eight states, and these figures represented only 12 percent of American industry. Moreover, uniform standards of reporting had not been established. The Bureau of Labor Statistics was using relatively sophisticated sampling methods, but only a few expert observers were willing to agree that the results were accurate. Political leaders, unwilling to accept the new concept of statistical sampling, played with numbers they believed were reliable—or at least politically useful. The public judged of its own condition by personal experience. If you and your neighbors were out of work, you were unemployed as only that generation of Americans knew unemployment: the empty, vulnerable state of being caught without income, insurance, or savings. Americans had always been poor savers. Those who had put some money away now listened to news of bank closings and raced to retrieve their savings before disaster struck them. This resulted in the famous "runs on the banks," some of which reached panic proportions.

Unemployment figures, reported in millions of unemployed, were suspect. Official statistics, showing percentages of the civilian labor force unemployed, still included the category "fourteen-year-old-workers," but they are the most reliable we have. According to them, 3.2 percent of the labor force was unemployed in 1929. That percentage rose rapidly between 1930, when it was 8.7 percent, and 1933, when it peaked at 24.9 percent. The lowest percentage the New Deal was able to achieve was 14.3 percent in 1937; but the sharp economic decline of that year returned the figure to 19 percent in the following year. By 1941, when the country was preparing for war, the number of unemployed was still 9.9 percent of the civilian labor force.

The use of statistical data to influence attitudes became part of the politics of the Depression. A 1 percent improvement in employment conditions in the spring of 1930 encouraged Hoover to begin predicting the end of the Depression. He knew that the figure was unreliable, but he thought that the prediction would alleviate the psychological depression he believed was paralyzing the nation. Throughout his presidency, he issued predictions deliberately designed to bolster public confidence. Small improvements were taken as signs of breezes that would lift the economic kite if only people could be persuaded to run with them. Roosevelt continued the process, though he tried to get better information.

The influencing of attitudes was not the only purpose behind efforts to improve data-gathering. As early as February 1931 Congress had given Hoover a planning agency, responsible for planning government-financed public works. This agency was to determine in advance what projects would be useful. Only the president could initiate the actual building of roads or bridges, and his decision to do so was to be triggered by certain statistical "indicators," primarily unemployment figures, on which the president and Congress would agree. The mechanism itself represented the federal government's first experiment in countercyclical planning, a process that ultimately became central to the New Deal and in the later period, when Keynesian economic methods were adopted. The belief that accurate data should control the spigot that turned government spending on and off was as important an innovation as the discovery of the economic impact of psychological attitudes.

Such innovations placed demands on Hoover that may have been greater than those faced by any of his predecessors. While there are suggestions that the public's attitude toward economic conditions had affected previous presidential careers—most notably that of Grover Cleveland and the abortive presidential attempts of William Jennings Bryan—the pressures on Hoover were, by a comparison with the past, extraordinary. He was certainly not as committed to laissez-faire economics as his critics painted him, but the mechanisms being urged upon him had never before been used by a peacetime president. His slowness to adopt them subjected him to criticism, but so did his adoption of them. He reluctantly revived the mechanisms that had proved useful during the war effort. As the Depression deepened, he faced problems that threatened to push him even farther into the use of government control.

The relief of poverty, the heart of the old tradition of local charity, local religious organizations, and state and local public institutions for the poor, the orphaned, and the sick, was clearly becoming a national problem. Hunger, illness, the loss of home and family security were assuming epidemic proportions as banks closed, small businesses went bankrupt, and mortgages on farms and homes were foreclosed. With the sole and troublesome exception of the pensions it paid to the veterans of the nation's wars, the federal government was expending no direct funds to individuals; that is, there was no national relief of poverty. Traditions as fundamental as the old commitment to local responsibility as "the wellspring of charity" and as complex as the constitutional separation of church and state stood in the way. Hoover, faced with innovations that threatened his entire view of the limits of American government, as well as his own belief in the causes of the Depression, found himself staring across a historical abyss.

By the winter of 1931–32 neither new statistics nor the persuasive efforts of stage and radio stars like Will Rogers (on behalf of the Red Cross) were sufficient to sustain the belief that prosperity was, as some were saying, "just around the corner." Hoover's increasing glumness, his rumored emotional outbursts at critics and criticisms, and, above all, his seeming slowness to seek further legislative support for relief seemed to mark a growing desperation. Progressive social critics like Charles Beard and John Dewey moved even further to the left than they had been in 1912; by 1931 they began to suggest that the American government in its present form did not have the means to cope with what clearly seemed unprecedented historical change.

Hoover continued to see the international economy as the basic source of his difficulties. He had proposed a moratorium on international debt payments in June 1931, and the step had been approved on all sides, with a great deal of hope; but its purpose, to halt the collapse of the European banks, had not been achieved. He faced the prospect of default when the one-year moratorium came to an end; but by then the American banking system was moving toward its own catastrophe.

The virtual collapse of rural banking in 1931–32 under the weight of declining farm prices provided a continuing drama of discontent. Farmers gathered together to protect one another from forced sales of their land, livestock, machinery, and homes. Incidents made headlines when crowds threatened bidders at local auctions and dragged judges from their benches to prevent foreclosures. The radicalism portrayed seemed inspired by simple self-protection, not by ideology, although there were many who interpreted such events as harbingers of revolution. Communist organizers, who thought they saw in agriculture an American proletariat ready to march, welcomed the instances of violence or threatened violence. By 1933 over a third of all American banks, rural as well as urban, had suspended operations. The national banking system was being drained by withdrawals of foreign capital in response to the European crisis, and all American banks—from the small rural ones, which were traditionally a source of some instability, to the nation's largest and most solid—were in serious trouble.

It is difficult to describe the banking crisis of 1932–33 to readers habituated to Federal Deposit Insurance. Generations of Americans had grown accustomed to suspecting the safety of banks. Many regarded the Postal Savings System, set up during the Taft administration, as the only safe place to put their money, and they accepted its 2 percent interest long after this had become a pittance by comparison with other savings rates. The term "panic" accurately describes what occurred in the wake of rumors that a bank might be about to fail. Depositors raced to bank windows to withdraw their funds, only to discover that others, terrified by the same rumors, had beat them to it. Unable to meet demands for cash in such volume, given the fact that their reserves were not properly expected to cover all of their recorded deposits, banks confirmed their depositors' fears by closing their doors. Normally such events were self-correcting—as the panic subsided, the healthy banks reopened; but the events of 1932–33 seemed to be suggesting something much more dire.

Beginning in October 1932, when the governor of Nevada declared a twelve-day bank holiday to stop the run on the Nevada banks, the alarm spread across the country like an uncontrollable fever. By February 1933, when the run on Detroit banks reached catastrophic proportions, it was clear that an unprecedented national crisis was brewing. Hoover pleaded with Roosevelt for help, and Roosevelt refused. The governor of Michigan declared a bank holiday on the 14th. Hoover, as president, could presumably have done the same thing on a national scale had he chosen to, but he insisted that support from the incoming president was essential. The national economy seemed like a house of cards in a high wind.

Hoover continued to look to voluntary organizations, made up of prominent and concerned citizens, to produce some kind of supportive consensus on banking, on industrial government, and on relief. At his request, former wartime industrial leaders toured the country to drum up public support and to provide him with information and advice. Such steps encouraged those who heard about them and even provided some temporary moral support to banks and industrial employers; but nothing seemed to work for long.

In the long run, this kind of wartime volunteerism was not going to be sufficient. Nor were efforts to inspire media support of the administration. Hoover, once the darling of magazine editors eager to provide their readers with a glimpse of the industrial hero in action, had become a pariah. White House attempts to place articles favorable to him and in support of his policies were met with diffidence. Hoover's outbursts of annoyance with the press had not helped. His policies had not caused the Depression, and it is difficult to see what he could have done to prevent it. Once it began, his gradually escalating efforts to cope with it pushed the federal government further into economic intervention than it had ever gone before. Yet it was not enough to inspire the confidence in his leadership that was the sine qua non of political survival. Even so, his defeat was more than a political event. Hoover was ultimately made to bear responsibility for the national catastrophe the Depression had become.

In one sense, Hoover's style of leadership was completely out of place. He was essentially a managerial technician and proud of it. He sought facts—facts to organize and analyze. His wartime successes had occurred when he had selected specific projects to direct, individuals to manage, materials to organize and control. He had worked in a similar way during his years as secretary of commerce; there, too, he avoided assignments with histories of political dispute that would have taxed his skills. Commerce was ideal, in a way, because it was too new to have much history behind it; he could build it virtually from scratch. Agriculture and Interior would certainly not have allowed him such leeway, and he refused them when they were offered to him.   221018

Critics who suggested that he was not a politician were partly right. He avoided some political engagements, but only some—chiefly, those he could not control. He could maneuver behind the scenes, and very effectively; but his public skills were limited by his unwillingness to make rhetorical statements, which he considered part of the politics he detested. He set great store by precise verbal statements and took public criticism much harder than most experienced politicians were inclined to. Again, unlike many political leaders he refused to sell programs in advance of his own private conviction that they would work. He was, in that sense, an engineer, not a scientist. From his point of view, experimentation was a public danger. No responsible engineer would use real people to test the stresses on a bridge or the safety of machinery in a mine.

Yet the Depression had come to be perceived as a novel event, a historic event, and it did not respond to the analytic factors and scientific methods he had believed economists were on the verge of perfecting. The fact that he himself apparently did not perceive this depression as an anomaly made no difference. The public in general, and his critics in particular, were gradually being pressed to understand the Depression as an unprecedented crisis requiring unprecedented experiments. Hoover could not accept that, so he set about acquiring the new information he thought would provide him with the answers.

The government ought not to frame a public-works policy, he believed, until it had first surveyed the existing plans for public works in the state and local governments around the nation. Many new buildings were needed, and old buildings were in need of repair everywhere, he and his advisers reasoned; but the work had been put off because of the Depression. If the states and localities could be encouraged to go ahead, now with federal support, work projects would be provided for the unemployed and there would be some assurance that the buildings were in fact needed and not simply make-work projects. Federal support would thus be for projects communities had already determined to begin for themselves, not for projects imposed on them by the federal government.

Similarly, the government could not have a proper relief policy until it had exact information on the amount of relief already being provided by private and local relief agencies. If the government was going to provide support for these already existing efforts, it would have to know precisely what was being done so that it not interfere with or accidentally suppress local initiatives. Local organizations knew their local communities and their own needs. The federal government did not.

Much of Hoover's work from 1931 on was devoted to this kind of requisitioning of information, most of it being assembled in Washington for the first time. It looked like foot-dragging, and when it did result, finally, in presidential action, Hoover appeared to be pushed and shoved into positions he had at first rejected. The fact that his successor inherited a wealth of plans and program ideas based on the hardest data researchers had been able to collect did not help Hoover's reputation. No one was ever destined to know exactly what he would have done with his data; we know what Roosevelt did with it.

After the congressional elections of 1930 saddled Hoover with a Congress under at least partial Democratic control (the Republicans lost eight seats in the Senate and control of the House), he seemed to withdraw. He did not call a special session, despite the urgings of those who thought the emergency serious enough, partly because he felt that he could operate more effectively as an executive manager than with Congress in session. At least the political storms might be fewer and less intense.

His public statements grew more complex and turgid. Photographers seemed always to catch him in a dour mood, looking down or to the side, and never with more than the slight smile he occasionally managed. He had never been a laughing, jocular figure; but reporters described him now as irascible and curt—characteristics that those who dealt with him closely had always noted. Hoover hadn't really changed; but his manner became more noticeable against the background of the Depression.

Hoover himself continued to insist, long after his presidency was over, that conditions had begun to improve by early 1932. He argued that the uncertainty of the election itself, plus his successor's refusal to join him in efforts to stabilize conditions during the long period separating the election in November from the inauguration in March, was chiefly responsible for the dramatic intensity of the economic crisis. It remains difficult to see a clear argument either for or against this view.

The election of 1932 brought Roosevelt to power in a landslide victory that was more a repudiation of Hoover, in the minds of many, than an overwhelming endorsement of Roosevelt. Few could have predicted the heroic stature that Roosevelt was destined to achieve. He had had to battle for the Democratic party nomination, for many of the professionals felt more secure in supporting other candidates. Hoover's growing unpopularity had made the Democratic nomination an attractive prize. Few presidents have been so effectively and dramatically stamped by events for which they were forced to take responsibility. The makeshift shacks near railyards, which had housed the traditionally itinerant tramps for generations of "hard times," were labeled "Hoovervilles." The newspapers with which the homeless, who slept on park benches, were reputed to cover themselves were known as "Hoover blankets." A magazine cover design depicted Hoover as a round, blank face with slits for eyes and tightly shut lips.

Roosevelt's four years as governor of New York had established him as a good vote-getter, but they had only begun to identify him as a crisis manager. Nor did his presidential campaign provide the assurance many were looking for. He wavered, promised a New Deal, agreed with the call for a balanced budget, called for aggressive actions he could not describe. A speech he made late in the campaign before the Commonwealth Club of San Francisco seemed to echo both Frederick Jackson Turner and the neo-agrarians: the frontier, he said, was closed, and with it the opportunities held out by free land; moreover, the industrial system was overbuilt and hence incapable of the expansion needed for new jobs.

The ultimate uncertainty about Roosevelt—whether a man confined to a wheelchair could function as president—was more often a subject for gossip than discussion. Newspaper photographers operated under tacit agreement not to show him being lifted from one vehicle to another. He was shown standing rather than walking, and then with a cane and the arm of an aide rather than on the crutches that were his effective means of locomotion outside a wheelchair. Yet visually he projected a sense of energy and command. His face and head were mobile. The upper part of his body showed the effects of a decade spent maneuvering himself from place to place with shoulders and arms. Photographs from Warm Springs, Georgia, the retreat where he had helped build a spa for fellow polio victims, depicted a fatherly water athlete, a jolly Neptune, romping with the children who were the disease's most familiar victims.

The growing sense of danger that accompanied the campaign was heightened by Hoover's insistence that something revolutionary would come from his opponent's election. The bank closings provided an ugly obbligato to such fears. After the November election, the transition to new leadership could not occur until March 4, the inauguration date set by the Constitution. The result was a sense of limbo that grew more threatening by the week as the uncertainty, which would have been characteristic of any presidential transition, intensified. One by one the banks fell like stones in a slow-motion movie of a rockslide, and the news reports of angry bands of farmers and roving groups of unemployed fed the mood of crisis. Hoover's seeming inaction as president became paralysis when he was a lame duck. Roosevelt's smiling but totally noncommittal attitude assured those willing to be satisfied by the simple assurance that he was going to be president on the fourth of March. Between the fall election and the spring inauguration stretched a winter that had to be crossed like a barren field of ice.

Despite the complex negotiations between Hoover and Roosevelt during the long interregnum, the impasse that finally developed was caused, ultimately, by Roosevelt's belief that any action he took before the inauguration would compromise him politically and by Hoover's belief that without Roosevelt's concurrence he was powerless to act. That that concurrence, even on Hoover's own view, would have committed Roosevelt to Hoover's policies is an additional factor. In many crucial instances, particularly with regard to the banking crisis, the actions that Roosevelt ultimately took were based on policies Hoover's advisers had been pressing, and this fact must also be added to a picture that remains unclear. American banking came to a grinding halt between mid-February and 4 March 1933, a visible, frightening, and ultimately half-comic thing that simply did not have to happen but for the necessity of changing presidencies. Roosevelt was aware that the drama of the banking crisis would be far more useful to him politically than any aid he could give his predecessor would be useful to the banking system. Hoover's overblown belief that Roosevelt had known exactly what he was doing only sharpened the hatred he felt as he watched the man he now considered a demagogue—in his terms a "gesticulator"—ride a wave of public hunger for dramatic action that Hoover considered a product of pure artifice, of politics.

Support for Hoover's point came, in a sense, in the initial banking "reforms" themselves. Using provisions of a World War I piece of war emergency legislation, the Trading with the Enemy Act of 1917—something Hoover had considered using but had been advised would not be legal—Roosevelt stopped the outflow of gold and declared a four-day national bank holiday. He issued his proclamation on 5 March, the day after his inauguration; the holiday was to run from the 6th through the 9th. On the 9th, Congress quickly passed legislation confirming all of the emergency steps Roosevelt had taken since the 4th, including the embargo on shipments of gold and silver abroad. The act provided for supervised reopenings of banks in the Federal Reserve System and various supportive measures for national banks; but given the fact that Federal Reserve and national banks accounted for a relatively small part of the nation's banking system, given the limits of the reforms, and given the brevity of the closings if the purpose was to determine the banks' stability, it is difficult to see the action as amounting to much. What had to be restored was public confidence that the reopened banks, regardless of where they stood in the banking system, were sound.

It would be difficult to find an event in the annals of modern political leadership that compares with Roosevelt's coming to office. From the richly intoned religious metaphors and ringing promises of his inaugural address to the warm and supportive simplicity of his Fireside Chat lessons on banking, he stirred energies and soothed fears. Public psychology and popular attitudes were instruments he played with consummate skill, and the new media, which carried his voice and photographed his smile, his gestures, the long cigarette-holder held at a jaunty and confident angle, were tools he used to represent feelings that gave words, facts, and numbers a meaning and a utility that later analysts might well find puzzling. The truths Americans needed in that first week of March 1933 did not depend on the sciences Hoover had sought to invoke but on gut reactions that had to be produced before history could be put back into motion.

On Sunday evening, 12 March, Roosevelt entered American living rooms via the radio set and quietly, patiently, and in a genially schoolmasterish fashion assured Americans that their banking system was being made sound. They responded by lining up at the banks—to return their money, not to continue to withdraw it; and, until the moment the doors opened, no one could be sure which would happen. The sequence of events that had begun the winter's economic drama had come to an end in the triumph of a successful projection of leadership. Without vindicating Hoover of personal blame for his failure to take effective action, one can still say that, after four years of steady decline, it would have been nearly impossible for him to summon support for actions that even he was finally willing to consider. At the same time, Roosevelt's consciousness of the utility of dramatization and his remarkable skills in achieving it gave force to actions that in other hands might not have been effective. Later analysts of New Deal policies would continue to see occasions for criticizing Roosevelt's unwillingness—or failure—to use the drama of the moment to its fullest, to nationalize banking and credit and achieve direct presidential control over the economy. The assumption that such steps would in fact have been possible in the long run, even if one could argue that the seeming collapse of the nation's entire banking system ought to have provided sufficient crisis to justify such action, raises again the problem of public perception of the nature of the crisis itself. Roosevelt's decision seems to have rested on his understanding of the oddly orchestrated nature of the event, unprecedented though it may have been. Without the constitutional power to affect it as president-elect, he could choose to allow it to play itself out, seeing the advantage to be gained by doing nothing.

While Roosevelt clearly did not use the banking crisis to produce an economic revolution—and was criticized, even at the time, for not doing so—he did use it to bring about a fundamental change in the nature of presidential leadership. He allowed himself to become a media event, above the realities of the crisis, more startlingly visible than presidents were accustomed to being. He thus began a new presidency as none before had begun his, and none since. For Americans a new era of mass politics had begun.

The opening of the New Deal came as a moment of redemption in an era replete with redeemers, in the United States as well as abroad. The attack on liberalism and liberal democratic forms of government had grown throughout the twenties and now, in the thirties, threatened to become universal. Even nations relatively new to industrialization—Japan, for example—moved toward a repudiation of the liberalism Western democracy had sought to commit them to. China, rocked by rebellions for two decades, edged toward what seemed an inevitable choice between extremes, left and right. Strong leaders, men no longer on horseback but astride the postwar engines of industrial power, looked to ways not only of managing systems efficiently but of exercising control over the attitudes and emotions of the mass populations required for running the systems.

The tradition of commitment to classic liberalism did not prevent a nation from embracing the new type of leadership. Germany provided the extreme test, raising for intellectuals throughout the world the question of how the homeland of Goethe and Schiller could have produced Hitler. Even in England, which for Americans was the model of imperturbable historical liberalism, the thought of emergency leadership was raised. The brief monarchy of Edward VIII was going to involve a curious threat of constitutional crisis, for the king, who had been a very popular prince of Wales throughout the twenties, surveyed the Depression casualties and intoned, some thought ominously, "Something must be done." That he was watching Hitler's Germany with more interest than apprehension was also clear. His abdication in 1936 to marry "the woman I love" relieved those who thought they saw beneath the popular and romantic exterior a threat to use the potential of monarchical leadership as it had not been used in more than a generation.

As the thirties worried on, other nations would exhibit similar moves toward centralized effectiveness in one form or another, in keeping with their various national traditions. Nor did "the age of the antidemocratic revolutions" necessarily bypass the United States, as both critics and defenders of the New Deal were inclined to argue. Many saw this tendency reflected, if not in Roosevelt, then in the leadership of Huey Long of Louisiana. The Long of the early thirties is, in a sense, a different historical figure from the Long of

Robert Penn Warren's novel about him, *All the King's Men*, or the much later biography by T. Harry Williams. At the peak of his career in the Senate, before and for a time even after his assassination in 1935, Long's militant populism, his Share Our Wealth program, and his seeming hunger for power were viewed as threats by conservatives and liberals alike, who saw him not as a traditional American democrat but as a radical extremist.

Father Coughlin, the Michigan priest, used his magazine and his radio program to broadcast criticisms that demanded fundamental changes in the nature of American government and greater government provision for public well-being. A more intellectually ambitious effort to develop an indigenous fascism, led by Lawrence Dennis, never quite got off the ground, but it too reflected a significant mood. Various centralized industrial plans, that of Gerard Swope of General Electric being the best known, called for acknowledgment of the end of liberal capitalism and the need for something else in the management of the industrial order. The crisis was real enough.

Roosevelt's position on the issue of revolutionary change was a shifting one. His inaugural address suggested the need for broader constitutional, perhaps unconstitutional, powers, but the New Deal itself provides no single focal point from which to view his conception of the purpose of government in times of crisis, except, perhaps, the need to relieve the crisis as quickly as possible. What is useful, however, is to see Roosevelt moving to control new forces with new methods in a fashion that reveals his response to the problem of leadership in his times.

If the difficulty of adjusting mass society to technology had been one of the causes of the crisis of the thirties, the willingness to use new technology as the means to resolve that crisis, or, more important, to create the necessary illusion of resolution, is what makes more general comparisons of the American and European experiences useful. A remarkable number of the successful world leaders of the thirties were unusually gifted managers of the new media. Their success as radio personalities is notable, as is their conscious presentation of themselves as figures to be photographed in motion. All in all, the need for access to a mass audience on a continuing and supportive basis marks the leadership of the thirties much more strikingly than does the effectiveness of their programs, which is still being debated. Yet the effectiveness of the programs was closely related to the public's attitude toward its leader. In country after country the programs and policies of a given administration were identified in an almost mystical fashion with the personality of the man who led the country out of its crisis. Some of the leading figures of the period seemed instinctively to sense the public's need, not only to project all the complexities of the technocratic state onto the leader, but to believe that his love for them and theirs for him was the effective instrument of their salvation.

The perceived relation between the need for tightly organized programs to deal with industrial change—planning had become a worldwide term, capable of supporting virtually any revolutionary ideology—and the extremely visible, heroic leadership needed to sustain the public in making the sacrifices required by the transition to the modern industrial state would ultimately produce the same historical transformations wherever the transition occurred. In Italy, Germany, the Soviet Union, and the United States, the emphasis on public works as a device for coping with unemployment tended to produce monumental government buildings, vastly extended highway systems, and massive electrification projects. Social programs, from housing to aid for the aged and indigent, were part of most plans, as were methods of organizing industry for purposes of the greatest employment rather than efficient production or profit. Ideology could be used to promote or defend such ideas, but the need to reemploy the unemployed and to find a place in the industrial process for those being pressed out of agricultural employment transcended ideological interests. Unemployment had ceased to be an acceptable, let alone a justifiable, condition and was therefore available for use by political leaders promoting radical ideas on both the right and the left. While no two states, or regimes within states, were inclined to give equal emphasis to all methods of reemployment, the sameness of some of the results is striking. Even Hoover seemed to favor the eclectically classic style of government buildings that were his era's contribution to the Washington landscape. A similar bureaucratic classicism marks structures built at this time in Rome, Moscow, and Berlin.

The abilities of leaders to marshal public opinion behind them led some of the new regimes not only to invoke press censorship, an old method of control, but to establish official propaganda agencies, close to the seats of executive management. Even leaders who still defended freedom of the press, as some no longer did, recognized the need to use the press to influence public attitudes. The exploitation of radio and movies as a means of bypassing traditional legislative leadership and political organizations, of bringing the executive leader directly before his public, took varying forms, depending on the conditions that brought the leader to power. But they all had the effect of putting the leader in direct contact with his audience, in the family living room or, far larger than life, on the screens of darkened movie theaters. Facial expressions and physical gestures communicated with audiences as individuals, not as members of a crowd. Such living portraiture could show the leader informally—patting a child on the head or smiling toward the camera as he entered or left a building—or formally—saluting the flag, reviewing a line of troops, or delivering an address to an assembly. It was all in motion, alive and immediate.

By later standards, Franklin Roosevelt's press conferences were tightly controlled. Transcripts were kept in the White House, and reporters could not even consult them, let alone publish their contents. Previous presidents had allowed themselves to be observed from a distance—had issued formal statements, answered prearranged questions, or sat for a rare special interview. Roosevelt opened up a new conception of communication from the White House. In this he was not, like some later presidents, a target of reportorial attack or a lawyer in an adversary proceeding but rather a teacher in a classroom of students, genially fielding queries, joking with his audience, admonishing them, and guiding them at times like a conductor orchestrating sounds his musicians had no idea they were producing for him. The scene was one of openness—the reporters stood about his desk in the Oval Office, watching him as he sat playing with the trinkets and gifts that cluttered the top of his desk—but he managed the news. He answered the questions he chose to answer, posed the questions he needed to answer, refused permission for quotation when that seemed appropriate to him, talked only for background at times, and, when necessary, introduced subjects he wanted the public to hear about. They were there on sufferance, not as a matter of professional right or presidential obligation. Reporters accustomed to wandering the halls of Congress or searching out favorites among the top bureaucratic echelons learned to look to the White House, to the Oval Office itself, for the kind of news they wanted. And he gave them news in forms they could use. He was anecdotal and teasing, delightfully and bitingly quotable when he chose to be.

Movies helped to popularize the regime's symbols and to rally the masses to action. Newsreels carried footage of parades, complete with flags and slogans, from New York and other major cities to every movie theater in the country; parades like this were actually organized to support New Deal recovery efforts. Government action became part of the nation's entertainment. While Americans were somewhat slower than Germans to see the utility of visual "documentaries" for organizing public opinion, the *March of Time* movie shorts adapted the magazine's pace and style to film and established a method of reporting that the government itself picked up, later in the New Deal, when it began to use movies to inform the public about its programs and to influence public attitudes toward them.

The emotional and psychological reactions to the worldwide crisis of the 1930s had been building for a long time. Reformers everywhere had watched with misgiving as workers crowded into the centers of the big cities. Even in ethnically homogeneous countries the growing armies of urban workers constituted a dangerously displaced group—displaced not only from traditional local systems of support and protection but from traditional standards of intellectual and social behavior. The reforms that had expanded democratic suffrage throughout the Western world were giving such workers political power. The reformers who had fought to extend the right to vote claimed that otherwise the working classes would rebel and seize it for themselves. They believed, or at least hoped, that the power of the vote would be exercised rationally or, in any event, in keeping with some agreed-on concept of the national interest.

Now there were consequences they had not foreseen. Industrialization and now the depression not only quickened the pace of internal migration but increased its risks. As workers crowded into the cities, where they had no roots, the loss of traditional family and local ties resulted in special hardship for children and old people. That the government should be responsible for the welfare of these groups seemed obvious.

The transfer of social responsibility from local and private groups to the centralized state was more acceptable to Europeans, long accustomed to political parties of the left, ranging from social democratic to revolutionary. President Hoover expressed the attitudes of the American middle class when he opposed federal intervention and looked for ways of maintaining control of relief by local communities and private organizations. He cited experiments, like one initiated in Wisconsin, as proof that unemployment insurance could be privately funded by local insurance companies and effectively regulated by state government. He also believed that private insurance could provide pensions for the elderly. He recognized the importance of government advice, even pressure, but he objected to the federal government's direct intervention.

Nor was he alone in his concern for the future of local communities and their fundamental role in sustaining an American culture. Sociologist Robert Park and his colleagues at the University of Chicago lamented the decline of neighborhood solidarity and worried about the effects of migratory labor on community stability. The hobo or tramp again served as a useful symbol, however ambivalent their attitude toward him had become. He was a "free spirit," the descendant in some respects of the lone pioneer, the trapper, and the forest wanderer. But his freedom offered no stability to a society without frontier forests, and his wandering threatened the stability of the communities through which he now moved. (The idea of the irresponsibility of the wanderer and his effect on small-town life was destined to play a role in movies and drama for several decades to come.)

The role the state should play in training the young had long been a subject of debate among Western educational theorists. By the 1930s the central topic of debate was use of the schools to initiate or prevent social change. "Civic education" was what political scientists called the effort then being made in several nations to teach citizenship and patriotism to schoolchildren. A professor of education at Columbia University, George Counts, observed the process in the Soviet Union and urged its virtues on his American colleagues. One of them, Harold Rugg, the author of one of the era's most popular series of social-studies textbooks, joined Counts in arguing that children could be taught a greater respect for their collective responsibilities toward one another. "Collectivism," the term used by many to designate their new sense of Depression needs, had to limit, if not replace, "individualism." Rugg's texts ultimately came under criticism for their apparent radicalism, but in the 1930s his views fitted in with the idea that there was a need to change—not in revolutionary directions, he would have insisted, but in directions capable of bringing public beliefs into line with the realities of an industrialized society. The old progressive idea was that the school should Americanize the child; Counts's view was that the school should create a new social being for a new industrial order.

A similar idea was manifest in the Chicago World's Fair, which opened in 1933. Bravely entitled "A Century of Progress," its exhibits were carefully planned to educate the public to serve technology, to appreciate its needs, to give industry its affection and respect. To be sure, all modern fairs aim to introduce new industrial developments to the public, but there was an edge of desperation in the Chicago fair's insistence that the public accept and serve technology. The Art Deco design of the buildings, destined to be satirized magnificently by Charlie Chaplin in *Modern Times* (1936), show human bodies entwined with machinery, a necessary if not very natural mating of forces.

Reformers in the 1930s were particularly worried about teen-agers and young adults. They hoped that the young could be taught social commitments their parents had rejected. The schoolroom and the museum exhibit halls could become the staging ground for changes that could come about rationally and peacefully, under the guidance of the nation's educational and technological elite. Otherwise the young might pose a threat to society not unlike that posed by hoboes. If the labor force could not absorb those who had completed the compulsory years of public education, the young could become unmanageable. Programs to train them for specific jobs, to organize them into work forces, so that they would spend their energy in performing useful public services instead of banding together on city streets, were part of reform movements in many countries in the thirties. One of Roosevelt's earliest and most original programs for the New Deal, the Civilian Conservation Corps, was designed to do many of the same things that German and Soviet youth movements were doing: it would provide young men with the discipline of outdoor life and a commitment to the land, under military direction; it would remove them from the ranks of the urban unemployed; and it would use the solidarity of the group to build a commitment to national order.

Roosevelt's genial simplicity in his Fireside Chats, however much it may have blurred the complexities of economic processes, provided a similarly paternalistic kind of mass communication and education. The president was news now, not simply at election time or in the wake of some crisis, but each day as he assumed a national leadership role unlike that of any of his predecessors. Leaders like Hoover, who found public exposure embarrassing and unpleasant, would find that they could not avoid it without jeopardizing the one thing they most needed: the continuing faith of the public. Presidential withdrawal and silence would henceforth be commented on as news. The radio and the movie industries needed news. Magazines and newspapers had to compete, not only with one another, but with radio and film and, in the near future, with television. Leaders who knew how to capitalize on the revolution in the media could make it an essential ingredient in their success even while they sensed the risks and sought to contain them. It was a ride on a tiger, but the popular will demanded that they appear, at least, to enjoy it.

In a moment of crisis so severe that crumbling institutional structures seemed capable of carrying social and moral values along with them, a leadership based on respect, even admiration, was insufficient. What was needed was a leader whose love of the masses he led was so clear that it could generate love as its response and, along with love, a confidence that did not depend on rational judgments of programs or on technical and complex economic analyses. Roosevelt himself launched the New Deal. His personality, which combined a sense of patrician responsibility with an extraordinary power to manipulate others for his own purposes, sustained it.

6

Half Way to Waterloo

U SE OF THE TERM "The Hundred Days" to characterize the initial legislative program of the New Deal involves several historical ironies. In its original use—to mark the period from Napoleon's return from Elba to his defeat in the Battle of Waterloo—the term described a crusade that failed. Those committed to Napoleon as a heroic leader may have wept at his defeat, but they did not lose their commitment to him. Those who considered him a dangerous threat to the stability of modern government may have rejoiced in his defeat, but they did not lose their fear that his ideas might still transform the world.

Anyone attempting to interpret the legislation that opened the New Deal faces a similar irony. New Deal legislation was subject to constitutional challenges from the beginning, and a significant part of the earliest legislation did not survive. Much of the rest of it was either temporary, intended as short-term relief, or experimental, subject to later revision. Thus the aura of triumph that surrounds the coming of the New Deal must be balanced against the failures and defeats of much of its initial program. One can find at least the threat of Waterloo in the triumphal return of reform if one looks for it. Among historians who have written of the period one can find those who are still committed to the heroism of the New Deal's Hundred Days and those who are relieved by its failures.

By 4 March 1933–inauguration day—a sense of crisis had built like the head of steam in a calliope, and Washington, D.C., was in a state of anticipation not unlike that of a crowd waiting for a circus parade. Newcomers to the public-service professions and newly elected congressmen filled the hotels, the halls of Congress, and the outer offices of an executive branch emptied of its top management echelons. That peculiarly sweeping revolution that accompanies changes of administration in American government had removed the federal bureaucrats not protected by civil service. Newly arrived job-seekers jostled one another, exuding new ideas with a naïve enthusiasm that refused to yield to the somewhat jaundiced views of the professional bureaucrats who remained on the scene, but, this time around, the professionals had reason to wonder what was in store.

The Seventy-third Congress elbowed out the lame-duck Seventy-second and prepared to meet on 9 March, five days after the inauguration of the president. The New Deal's Hundred Days was the last such period in American history to be dramatized by the convoking of a special session in what would, under ordinary circumstances, have been the long recess that followed the establishment of a new administration. Traditionally, presidents had been given a relaxed period of time, stretching from early spring to the following December, in which to prepare programs for presentation to Congress. The Twentieth Amendment, ending lame-duck sessions and beginning new congresses and new presidencies in January, had been ratified in February 1933. Depression fear had spurred passage and ratification of the amendment, but the problems caused by the long hiatus between election and inauguration had been recognized for some time. Presidential campaigns that evoked a sense of new programs, new leadership, and transformations in the ways of conducting the nation's business could not benefit from the traditionally languid transition, indeed, could not benefit from the energies built up by the campaign. To be sure, not since the election of 1860 had the country faced such a sense of uncertainty in a presidential transition; but the programmatic politics of the progressive era had long since raised the issue.

Both Wilson and Hoover had tried the tactic of the special session, with mixed results. Neither had had a crisis environment to give point to such a session, however, and Roosevelt did. Roosevelt's successors would all puzzle over the problem of how to create an aura of innovation in a system in which innovation was always more a matter of style than of reality; and the Hundred Days would always serve as a model.

Roosevelt's call for national planning to cope with the industrial crisis, like the image of the Hundred Days, presents another dilemma for historians of the New Deal, for what "national planning" meant was never spelled out. No one could be sure how much "planning" was publicly acceptable or politically possible. The term had a certain intellectual and academic attractiveness, but it could also be associated with alien ideologies. Moreover, the whole process of presidential electioneering made it almost unworkable as a concept. Candidates for the presidency could not waste precious campaign time planning programs for presidencies they might never win. They planned for the nominating convention by assembling staffs of experts whose energies were directed toward one end: the nomination. They planned election campaigns, adding where necessary yet another collection of technicians whose efforts were focused on victory at the polls. In the interim between victory and the new job, the president-elect could begin the search for ways to articulate—or artfully to gloss over—the promises contained in the party platform and the hints and suggestions of program sprinkled throughout the often contradictory pronouncements of the campaign.

Roosevelt's "Brain Trust," the group of advisers assembled for him by one of his aides, Samuel Rosenman, consisted largely of academicians interested in economic and industrial planning. A. A. Berle, Jr., Raymond Moley, and Rexford Guy Tugwell were by no means in agreement about the state of the economy or about ways for dealing with it. How many of their arguments Roosevelt understood or even listened to is an open question, but in using these men as his initial administrative cadre he established a new linkage between the academic community and the bureaucracy. Its most serious weakness was and would remain the braintrusters' difficulty in coping with the congressional and popular suspicion that was so evident in the name attached to them. That they were "brains" suggested that they were an elite, and the word "trust" evoked complicated fears of oligarchy.

The suspicion was most sharply focused on Roosevelt's "professors," but it extended to the whole idea of planning itself. Planning threatened the tradition of local control; it also threatened the power of interest groups, who were accustomed to getting things done by lobbying members of Congress. It could easily be attacked as radical by those who did not, or would not, acknowledge a basic dilemma of American national government. That Americans governed themselves was no patriotic cliché. They expected government to respond to the cacophonous sound of individual interests as though it reflected a harmonious general will. Government could respond to that only by doing as little as possible, but that option the crisis had, for the moment, removed.

The two pieces of legislation most closely associated with the Hundred Days—the Agricultural Adjustment Act of 12 May and the National Industrial Recovery Act of 16 June—were both later declared unconstitutional by the Supreme Court, the latter by a unanimous vote. The AAA was designed to raise farm prices by introducing crop controls—to produce scarcity—and by fixing the prices of farm products at a rate called the "parity price." Parity was determined by a formula that defined the purchasing power of the farmers' dollar as 100 cents in the base period 1909–14 for corn, cotton, wheat, rice, hogs, and dairy products; the period 1919–29 was used for tobacco. The farmer who *voluntarily* limited production received a subsidy payment, funded by a tax on the processors of particular products.

Both the tax and the production controls were declared unconstitutional by the Supreme Court in *U.S. v. Butler* in 1936, but even before this there was serious question whether the plan was really doing what it was intended to do and whether, indeed, it made any sense at all to create scarcity and raise prices in a period of high unemployment, poverty, and hunger. Nonetheless, the essential historical principle—that agricultural production, though still private enterprise, represented a vital public need and hence required special public support through government intervention—was established.

The AAA also guaranteed farm mortgages and greater power to the president to control gold and manipulate the currency. The control of gold, like the establishment of agricultural prices, had been emergency measures during the war, and the emergency state of the Depression was now equated with the wartime emergency. The Court's action in 1936 did not end the revolution. The second AAA in 1938 modified the objectionable provisions of the first but did so in ways that could be interpreted as an even franker recognition of government intervention. The original act's provision for a processing tax, for example, was intended as a way of making those who processed the agricultural products pay for the cost of the system of supports. The flour-millers, the owners of cotton gins, and others whose contribution to the system of agricultural production consisted in preparing the products for market—the "middlemen" whom farmers had traditionally accused of usurping their profits—were to give the system at least the illusion of being self-financing; but it didn't work. The Supreme Court attacked the tax as unconstitutional. It was replaced in the later legislation by direct payments out of the Treasury. It was more constitutional, apparently, for the public to pick up the tab directly.

The National Industrial Recovery Act (the NIRA) was hailed as the first major step toward a government-supported system of industrial planning. The National Recovery Administration (the NRA) established under the act gave each industry the opportunity to set up codes to fix prices, set wages and hours, determine the appropriate number of employees to be hired by each member of the industry, and decide other details of production and distribution appropriate to the industry in question. The code-making bodies were to consist of representatives from the affected industry, not only from management but from the laborers who worked in it and from the consumers who used its products. Once approved by the president, the codes were to have the support of the courts; that is, they were to have the effect of laws passed by Congress. The spirit of voluntarism was to be maintained by making the signing of the code voluntary on the part of the businessman. If he signed the code, his factory or store could display the Blue Eagle, the symbol of the NRA, which showed the bird with its wings spread above the slogan "We do our part." As a flag to be flown over the factory, a decal to be pasted on store windows, or a stamp to be attached to merchandise, the symbol was intended to indicate that a business was complying with the national need as defined by the code. People were urged to boycott businesses and merchandise that did not display the sign, and firms that did display it were required to meet the standards set by the code or be subject to prosecution.

The existing trade associations were to function as forums for discussing problems common to the members of a given industry and for setting up practices that would make the industry more effective without running afoul of the antitrust laws. Such associations served, in many instances, as the nuclei of the code-making bodies. The inclusion of labor unions, who were struggling to get both government and industry to acknowledge their right to exist, along with groups representing the interests of consumers, was an innovation that quickly lost its significance as the more experienced industrial managers took control. One section of the act, section 7A, did give labor the right to bargain collectively, but later interpretations of the language of 7A meant that labor would play a limited role. The framers of the legislation also liberalized the bankruptcy process, an indication of their consciousness that small businesses would not benefit from codes that required them to hire more people at higher wages and for fewer hours. Some businesses, large and small, began raising prices hurriedly, before the codes could go into effect, a practice known as "chiseling in advance." The government, on its side, issued hastily contrived "blanket codes" in order to get something in place until carefully worked out codes could be devised for each industry. What critics feared would be a highly organized national program of industrial control turned into an emergency system of price and wage management aimed at reemployment of the unemployed—at any cost. Within months that cost was clear. The largest industries were able to use the NRA in ways that smaller businesses could not. In the short run, however, the obvious weaknesses of the NRA were overshadowed by the political importance of reemployment as an end in itself.

By 1935, when the Court issued its ruling against the NIRA, arguing that the delegation of rule-making powers to the code-making bodies was an unconstitutional delegation of legislative responsibility, it was attacking a system that had few supporters in any camp, liberal or conservative. The killing of the NIRA was far less of a problem than the Court's effort to limit the government's effort to seek admittedly novel solutions to the economic crisis. It was in the *Schechter* case (*Schechter Poultry Co. v. U.S.* [1935]) that the Court ruled against the delegation of legislative authority to the executive. But the *Schechter* rule, even though it formed the basis of the Court's argument against the NIRA, did not remain much of a principle. Successive congresses would continue to delegate to boards and courts the power to make the kind of administrative rules the growing activities of the federal government seemed to require. Congress's later enactment of bits and pieces of the NIRA in other forms of price, wage, and hours legislation was not nearly so important as its acceptance of the principle of delegating greater authority to the federal government to guide American life. Ending the NRA could not alter a direction determined by the conditions of modern industrial life. In the next chapter we will see that that delegation was accomplished initially by decentralizing much of the decision-making process, allowing state and local governments to observe "guidelines" in their execution of federal programs. The reins were loose and at times nonexistent. More than forty years would pass before federal administrators would dare to enter the political sanctuaries of the cities and the states to demand strict accountability to the federal government in return for federal funding of local programs.

More than the AAA, the NIRA suggested a comprehensive system of planning; but the federal administrators of the act did not move in that direction even at the beginning, and it was apparently the president's intention that they should not. Title I of the NIRA had established the NRA. Title II called for a comprehensive public-works program, to be run by a Public Works Administration. Roosevelt separated the industrial program of Title I from the public-works program. He put General Hugh Johnson in charge of the NRA; management of the PWA went to Harold Ickes, an undersecretary in the Interior Department. A single administrator for both programs would have had powers of control over the economy that no other figure had ever held, including the president. Moreoever, Roosevelt thought that Ickes, an old progressive, would keep pork-barrel politics and local corruption out of the Public Works Administration and would insist on high standards of efficiency and quality at the construction sites. This lofty perspective was not suited to an emergency situation. Roosevelt seemed to know that but to prefer it, though it limited the use of the comprehensive powers inherent in the original legislation. In the end, a more political program of public works was instituted under relief administrator Harry Hopkins, the president's confidant and aide, a man whose background in urban philanthropy and traditional relief organizations gave him a very realistic view of the useful relationship between local politics and public works. The pork-barrel had its uses.

The NIRA was the result of a remarkable set of compromises. As a piece of legislation, it was a blend of planning positions that had been debated for two decades. As an administrative program, it met the political demands of presidential management of the economy and, more important, the traditional public-works politics of Congress and the states. Its importance as a historical event is that it was the first significant American attempt to meet the critical needs of the industrialized world of the thirties. Given the limited ability of legislatures to manage an industrial system and the revolutionary pressures that could be felt by governments that failed to meet the demands of powerful masses and the traditions of public order, the need for centralized direction was obvious. Events abroad had already demonstrated the extent to which powerful leaders could appeal to the masses.

In Europe, more than in the United States, the organizational instruments for centralized control were already in place: strong unions, centralized banking systems capable of working closely with government, and at least the framework for the cartelized industry the American antitrust laws had sought to inhibit. The New Deal would ultimately move the United States closer to adopting such organizational instruments, but they were not yet there for Roosevelt to use. Nor were they yet acceptable to the public. Americans had traditionally disapproved of central banking, labor unions, and industrial centralization in the "trusts," and the New Deal responded to that attitude. As the arguments of New Dealers shuttled between praise for the potential of the American industrial system, so recently demonstrated during World War I, and the traditional populist suspicions and hostilities exacerbated by the Depression, they accurately represented the uncertain state of the American mind on economic matters. The NRA was designed to produce clear victories for no one; therefore, it could be argued, it was designed to fail. On the other hand, the NRA was designed to give the majorities in all groups the sense that it embodied the search for public order at a time when that order appeared to be under severe threat; viewed in that light, the NRA was a major success.

The Hundred Days provided at least one incontestable success. The Tennessee Valley Authority is one of the few innovations of the Hundred Days that is still part of the American scene, its hydroelectric dams still delivering electrical power. Yet even its apparent continuity suggests the limits of the New Deal reforms. The social reordering many of its advocates thought would result from bringing a technological revolution to one of the nation's most backward areas was not fully realized; the TVA became, essentially, a regional public utility, committed to local conceptions of social and economic order, not to the grand national model envisaged by some of its planners, including the president.

Electricity had come to be the ideal target of what leaders of Hoover's and Roosevelt's generation regarded as effective planning. In the 1920s electricity and telephone companies had begun to plan for the future by setting up five- and six-year plans that would enable them to respond quickly to increased demand. Such plans inevitably intersected with public programs of planning for transportation, sanitation, and community development, and the effort to find useful ways of providing for cooperation between the public and private sectors had engaged the era's more progressive governors. As governor of New York, Franklin Roosevelt had thought it essential to make local government more effective by modernizing the way towns and cities provided services and giving state government a more centralized role to play both in regulating such services and in establishing relationships with neighboring states. The fact that power lines crossed state boundaries made it clear that the old political boundaries were no longer realistic dividing lines, that they might even inhibit the delivery of needed services. Like the rivers that flowed in and among the states, serving different communities in its different ways, electric lines made old barriers obsolete.

The TVA started with a dam and two munitions plants on the Tennessee

River at Muscle Shoals, Alabama, built during World War I with government funds. Postwar efforts to dispose of the facilities, useful in peacetime for producing not only electricity but nitrogen fertilizer, ran head-on into a dispute between the private utilities and the advocates of greater public control of all utilities. What is particularly interesting about this debate is that it tells us how people of that time tried to deal with the puzzle of interstate management and control. Like air transportation and radio, electricity could not be a locally controlled industry. Transmission lines crossed state boundaries with ease. Some kind of federal involvement seemed appropriate, but no one was sure what it would be.

At the same time, however, the Tennessee River ran through a region of river valleys inhabited by what was virtually an American peasantry. For generations they had witnessed the destruction of the land. Poor farming practices by cotton and tobacco growers had depleted the soil's nutrients, lumber exploiters had denuded the hillsides, and coal operators had dug up what remained. Short of a massive redirection of the lives of the old communities, hard hit now by the Depression—the final blow—it was hard to justify the economic utility, at least in immediate terms, of increased electrical output.

Roosevelt's commitment to a vision of new lives for the poor people of the Tennessee valleys seems clear from some of his comments, but it is, once again, a vision lacking structure or detail; he left it to others to complete the picture. The battles among the first generation of administrators left little doubt that the Tennessee Valley Authority would simply build dams to provide electricity. The lines that crisscrossed the region would increase the available resources, but what changes that would make in the lives of the people below would be influenced by the traditions of southern life. There was, in short, no agreement on a plan to redirect the lives of the valley people.

The idea of planning could be respected, even romanticized, by readers of popular articles about the new idea (the articles usually dealt with the idea alone, not with specific plans or with the special interests being subjected to planning). It was an idea that was very much in the air. The Depression had made everyone think about abstract economic problems, about the problems posed by technological change, about the revolution that progressives of all persuasions had been calling for. And plans were made. There was industrial planning, agricultural planning, water-resource and land-use planning, and urban planning, but none reflected a unified or comprehensive plan, either overall or within each category. Conflicting interests and competitive demands stood in the way.

The framers of the National Industrical Recovery Act and the Agricultural Adjustment Act did, however, intend them to provide comprehensive planning systems, each to include as many group interests as possible under a single umbrella. The industrial codes were intended to meet the needs of industry, labor, and consumers not only within a particular industry, covered by a particular code, but generally. The provisions of the agricultural agreements were to apply to commodities as different in their production and marketing as corn, cotton, and tobacco and to producers as different as small farmers, sharecroppers, and hired agricultural laborers. One can admire the ambition and reflect on the intelligence of the aims of the planners without concluding that their plans constituted a tyrannical threat or, on the contrary, that they were potential triumphs, aborted by a conspiracy.

The New Deal did not really seek the one weapon essential to all of the European theories of planning: direct administrative control of the economic order itself and all of its resources. By leaving that control in the hands of private industry and seeking to manipulate its use through political means, Roosevelt followed traditional American practices. If he seemed to be changing the scope of government activity, he was still using familiar methods. It was difficult even for him to call it planning.

The ambivalence historians have expressed toward the NRA and the AAA in many ways epitomizes the ambivalence historians have come to feel toward the New Deal as a whole. As part of the drama of the Hundred Days, both programs can be taken to represent what Roosevelt himself so unequivocally represented: the power of the national government in control during a national emergency. Yet historical accounts of the great programs of the early New Deal are forced to call into question their effectiveness and to point out the degree to which the ordinary people involved in industry, the labor movement, small business, and family-farm agriculture had to look elsewhere for help. The NRA and AAA came all too quickly under the control of the major industrial and agricultural interests, and the government, appearing to acquiesce in mute helplessness, was forced to supply relief to those pushed out of the system. By 1935 the programs the New Deal was devising to help those who had not benefited from the earlier efforts appeared to be either repudiations of the original national programs of the Hundred Days or obvious acknowledgments of their limited effectiveness.

At the same time, to call the national programs failures seems also to overlook significant parts of the historical experience. Such comprehensive programs seemed, at the outset, the only approach capable of promising effective crisis management. The public needed that promise. As in the case of the bank crisis, however, the mechanisms for giving the federal government control over a centralized, nationalized industrial system simply did not exist. A skilled federal bureaucracy was not available, and, even had it been, it is doubtful that a managerial army would have been acceptable to most Americans, accustomed as they were to looking on active government as a threat. To argue that new machinery for managing the country would have been accepted requires one to argue that the Depression itself had created an acceptance of a national industrial state that had not existed before and convictions strong enough to obliterate memories of wartime controls and strong enough also to produce a major intellectual reversal of regionalism and localism, both of which had experienced a vigorous rebirth in the 1920s.

It may make more sense to argue that the New Deal's initial commitment to a centrally managed state rested on the emergency alone. Hugh Johnson, the NRA administrator, tried, briefly, to reawaken the old wartime nationalist fervor by torchlight parades and by ringing speeches, calling for national solidarity. The historical nationalism to which Hitler and Mussolini appealed when they recalled old dreams of empire was, for Americans, a frontier individuality that had served altogether different purposes. The United States and American public opinion were not prepared for the revolutionary reordering a national crusade would have required. The heated language from both left and right in the years from 1931 to 1933 did not reflect middle-American opinion. Middle America was solidly behind the establishment of some sense of continuity, and control of American economic life by a strong central government was not part of the usable past. As one looks back at the events of the period, this much becomes very clear: as the sense of emergency diminished, the fear of strong national government increased. The fears provoked by the economic emergency had produced a call for government aid; but when that aid reduced the emergency, it became itself a source of fear. Even though rejection of strong central government was an old American tradition, in the context of the thirties the threat intensified when the continued existence of democracy itself came to rest on the question no one seemed able to answer: How strong a government was necessary for coping with conditions that some perceived to be historically new?

Roosevelt's continuing use of the wartime analogy to describe what he saw as the role of government in the emergency suggests at least part of the problem he faced. War was a temporary emergency with a short-range goal. Under such circumstances an increase in government power could be justified not only by the presumably unprecedented conditions but by the promise that the power would not be permanent, that it would exist only for the state of the emergency. Yet many of his advisers and many thoughtful observers believed what some of Roosevelt's campaign statements had already suggested, that there was need for a more permanent change in the role of government. The term "planning" had become a kind of verbal signal, so that, despite its many possible definitions, it summed up a need for more managerial control—something the progressives had long been calling for. The social-science technicians and the various sympathetic leaders from banking and industry whom Roosevelt selected as his circle of advisers held widely varying positions on many subjects. Any introduction of the term "planning" in their discussions tended to polarize their views. In the thirties, planning could mean the application of rationality and available scientific knowledge to the course of human events, a conception certainly consistent with Jeffersonian ideas, or it could mean the imposition of goals and methods by a managerial elite committed to its own identification of social purposes.

Roosevelt and his experts tried to employ the full range of planning ideas available to them. The inconsistencies and contradictions that emerged from programs that appeared to work at cross-purposes was attributed to "pragmatism" or "experiment," terms that gave the impression, at least, that scientific techniques were being employed. Thus, one agency could work to get land out of production in order to control surpluses, while another searched for techniques with which to make unproductive land more productive, and still another worked to move populations from unproductive land to more productive land. The country was large, its farmlands were diverse, and its people were committed to living where they wanted to live, not where the government sent them. The basic emphasis of all the plans was, however, the same: find everyone work to do—work that satisfied the need to be employed. For Thorstein Veblen the need to work was a human instinct, and for Veblenians in the New Deal the need to satisfy that instinct was far more important than the technical needs of a modern industrial system.

The working relationships between Roosevelt and his experts were ad hoc, personal, and basically political; they were in no sense professionally structured. In the aftermath, and even within the thirties, when the social scientists and public administrators had begun to absorb the experiences the crisis had forced upon them, the early efforts to be objective experts would look amateurish and crude. Roosevelt's theoretical naïveté and the experts' inexperience, particularly when both were working in the shadow of a worldwide crisis, were contributing factors. Even within their own community there were few, if any, clearly acknowledged leaders whose advice had been tested. The presumed discrediting of business leadership did not affect the president; there was no shift of power from Wall Street to the academy. Roosevelt was free to seek advice wherever it seemed appropriate. If the conservative Lewis Douglas, the liberal William O. Douglas, the banker Joseph P. Kennedy, the friend and neighbor Henry Morgenthau, Jr., Hoover's economist Wesley Clair Mitchell, and the Brain Trust gave Roosevelt conflicting advice, they did so from platforms of opinion and constituencies he did not have to reconcile or push to logical agreement. His advisers were experts from backgrounds he and his generation could treat as equal in worth if they chose to. But the edge was usually given to experience, and the newly established experts simply didn't have it. Roosevelt looked to academics for ideas, but his programs seem more traceable to the experienced political leaders and the community of managers with whom he had always worked.

The essential innovations of the New Deal tended to be hidden in the way the new plans were implemented. Since it was this that in fact transformed the way government worked, what is important to look at is not the programs that failed but the practices that succeeded. Chief among them was the growing tendency of Congress to imbed in loosely constructed legislation the compromises a growing bureaucracy would have to face up to and work with. Despite the fact that observers of the American legal system had long been disturbed by this increasing delegation of rule-making authority to administrative agencies, and despite the Supreme Court's concern with delegation in the *Schechter* decision, the New Deal in effect legitimated its expansion. The administrative state had arrived. Henceforth, what Congress would not decide, administrators of programs would have to decide for it, and a reorganized system of administrative courts would have to come into being to support the new system and make room for it in legal practice.

In a special sense the most innovative programs of the New Deal were those popularly considered to be the most temporary, namely, the various relief measures. Throughout American history the problem of poverty was something local communities were supposed to deal with as they saw fit. In the post–World War I years the issue had been defined nationally in terms of unemployment figures, along with a growing sense that the federal government could do something about the problem. But the definition itself implied the conviction that unemployment was a temporary condition and that poverty was a temporary consequence of that condition. The idea of permanently irreducible unemployment, like that of hard-core poverty, had no real place in the American work ethic. The very word "relief" suggested the temporary nature of programs designed to deal with the problem.

The New Deal decision to let the federal government provide relief for the unemployed thus raised complex issues that did not have to be dealt with as long as the temporary nature of the programs could be assumed. That assumption may have seemed a bit strange in the context of discussions about the nature of the Depression itself—that it carried the threat of permanent stagnation—but it was still sufficient to counter criticisms voiced by the many who shared Hoover's fears of federal intervention in the management of traditionally local concerns. At the same time, it seems clear from opinion-sampling conducted in the late thirties, as well as from attitudes that have continued to be part of the middle-class ethos, that federal relief, like latter-day welfare programs, was never accepted as normal.

The title of the act that created the Civilian Conservation Corps gives one a glimpse of the factors that had to be combined to make such an innovation acceptable. The Civilian Conservation Corps Reforestation Relief Act of 1933 ultimately employed over two million young men between the ages of eighteen and twenty-five. It housed them in camps run by the army (a "civilian corps") for the purpose of restoring the nation's forests, landscaping its highways, maintaining and improving the national parks, aiding in flood-control projects, working with farmers to stem soil erosion, and—of course—staying out of the industrial labor force. Old-line conservationists were pleased. If local communities near the CCC camps were not inclined to see the amateur foresters as happy Boy Scouts when they surged into town for week-end entertainment, they could be mollified by the local improvements the boys were creating and by the fact that it was all a relief measure, temporary by definition.

The complex and confusing relation between public works and relief, embodied in the seemingly endless combat between Secretary of the Interior Harold Ickes and Relief Administrator Harry Hopkins, illustrates the problems that stood in the way of systematic planning. Ickes, as Public Works administrator, was in charge of funding large-scale projects—roads, public buildings, bridges, dams, and the like. Local construction companies were to do the actual work. Ickes' progressive background led him to seek out plans and programs that would assure the best use of resources, and his ideas more often than not ran counter to local political interests and local perceptions of needs and opportunities. Moreover, the PWA's efforts to meet criteria set by planning and public-works engineers made it too slow a way to deal with an emergency—if that was, indeed, what it was intended to do. The Army Corps of Engineers, the nation's traditional manager of highway-building and dam construction, was far more sensitive to congressional pressures than Ickes was willing to be, a fact that led to frequent squabbles between the secretaries of War and Interior; the relation between water power and agriculture also assured the involvement of Secretary of Agriculture Henry A. Wallace.

The Federal Emergency Relief Administration, created by the Federal Emergency Relief Act of 1933 and headed by Harry Hopkins, tried to meet local needs through state and local governments with outright grants of one dollar for every three the local agencies were willing to spend. Certainly from Ickes' perspective, Hopkins was playing directly into the hands of "pork-barrel" politicians by meeting the need for reemployment head-on and in accordance with local leadership's perceptions of needs. If the process was politically useful to the administration, and if the activities it supported looked to critics like the useless spending of public money they had long associated with local patronage and corruption, the system still managed to distribute jobs to some of the needy.

The relationship between Ickes and Hopkins reflects with remarkable accuracy the planning dilemma of the thirties. There was, on the one hand, a sense of urgency, a consciousness that failure to meet the widespread need would lead to a national catastrophe. There was, on the other hand, an awareness of the dangers involved in a hasty and ill-considered selection of projects to be funded and in the lack of any system for assessing results. The federal government had engaged in such funding in the past. Federal assistance in the development of the railroads was the most significant example, and few in either government or industry were inclined to transfer that method wholesale to all of American industry. Some kind of new systematic relationship between private industry and the federal government seemed to be required in order to assure a measure of responsibility to the public; but the call for a partnership between a government beset by a national emergency and an industrial system already bankrupt seemed a pitiful echo of the old-line progressives' optimistic call for a happy partnership between government and industry. Over-all planning was the only answer.

But over-all planning embodied a threat of its own. Ickes' planning board was perceived as a danger by those who saw government planning as the route to fascism. Italy, Germany, and the Soviet Union had all identified the planning of the industrial system as the major issue and had moved to take control. Some saw the PWA and NRA as steps in the direction of such control, but a look at what Hopkins was doing disposes of that idea. "Politics as usual" was as important to presidential management as it had ever been. The Congress of 1933 was no more the rubber stamp of presidential control than it had ever been. Roosevelt was pushing to its limits a legislative body that was far less radical than he was willing to be. It was unwilling to give up any more authority than the emergency required, and that only for so long as the emergency lasted. The power that Roosevelt spoke of in his inaugural address—"I shall ask the Congress for the one remaining instrument to meet the crisis—broad Executive power to wage a war against the emergency, as great as the power that would be given me if we were in fact invaded by a foreign foe"—was still less threatening than the solutions that others were recommending.

World leaders during the Depression promised miracles to mass publics who appeared to believe that miracles were all that was left. Hoover had refused to promise miracles. Forced by his failures into actions he would have preferred not to take, he listened in fear to friends like Joseph P. Kennedy, who insisted that he would willingly give up half of what he had if he could be assured that he could keep the other half. Hoover was Kennedy's friend; but Roosevelt became Kennedy's savior, and Kennedy knew it. Yet Roosevelt appeared unwilling to take advantage of the moment of crisis, at least to those who saw in that moment a greater opportunity than he seemed willing to utilize. Later critics, too, were inclined to share this sense of disappointment. It was characteristic of Roosevelt's presidency that he never went as far as his detractors feared or his followers hoped. Like all miracle workers, he seemed to perceive that his real triumph lay in the ability to succeed by promising feats he could avoid having to perform.

It is thus difficult to see the Hundred Days as the beginning of a revolution. One can, by an act of historical imagination, see it more as the end of one, the aborting, perhaps, of a revolution on the edge of happening. The fact remains that, throughout his long presidency, Roosevelt retained for his critics the image of a tyrant about to be, a potential dictator, always on the threshold of power but never crossing it. He never denied that he would, if pressed, take the power the public seemed willing to offer him by its unprecedented election of him to four terms in the White House. The threat was there for those who chose to perceive it, but his willingness to use the power fully never was. Presidents since Roosevelt have sought—and received—far greater presidential power than he would have considered possible, even assuming that he would have considered it appropriate.

The historical recollection of the Hundred Days is built on an image of success few would have been willing to credit in the autumn of 1933, when the approach of winter and the end of the summer business revival signaled a hard season ahead. Architects of the New Deal's first phase worried at the prospect of a return to the crisis days of the previous winter, perhaps to even worse conditions than the ones that had brought them to power in the first place. The levels of unemployment were declining, but not fast enough, and winters were always hard. Yet Americans were going back to work. The government programs were providing support for those still unemployed. Additional emergency relief legislation was pushed through to help offset the slowness with which the PWA projects were getting under way. The Civil Works Administration provided make-work projects for those who could not find employment of any kind. The repeal of Prohibition, proposed the previous February and declared ratified early in December, provided a measure of cheer and a promise of increased tax revenues. Even more than the legislation of the Hundred Days, the efforts of the first regular session of the New Deal Congress were made in response to immediate emergency circumstances, not to anything that could be designated as "planning."

This is a point worth making in view of the tendency to see in the accomplishments of the first two years of the New Deal a program coherent enough to be designated the "First New Deal." To be sure, much of the legislation did deal with large national issues by means of large overall programs; but the apparent single-mindedness of the organizational principles seems more attributable to the need to act quickly in response to pressure than to any deliberate effort to create an effective national system. The crisis atmosphere and the threat of future crisis induced a speed that helped generate the illusion of a "program." What seems clearest about the first phase of New Deal legislation is its need to use the largest structures capable of having an effect. That the New Dealers turned to big industry and farming was less a product of logic, progressive or nationalist, than of the need to stimulate the largest units of production and employment in the shortest possible time. The knowledge that some people would lose out, at least initially and for a time, was clear in the provisions of the programs and in the administration of them. The legislation that followed was in large part clean-up and corrective in nature, enacted in response to experience with earlier programs and new perceptions of need. One should thus speak less of a program than of the actions of practical politicians sensitive to the need for action.

The desire to view the New Deal as a program or a succession of programs based on distinguishable intellectual positions is itself a New Deal phe-nomenon. The labels First New Deal and Second New Deal are products of the sense of program. So is the search for the influence of progressivism. The New Deal period was the first time that program-minded academics had moved into positions as managers in a governmental system controlled in fact by the political process. Products of the burgeoning social-science community of the 1920s, these academics brought an extraordinarily voluble expertise to government, and they published their beliefs and their experiences in a huge body of literature. Their reports, criticisms, plans, and programs gave a sense of structure that is not always easy to find in the actual legislative products of the New Deal. Their ideas were not irrelevant, but whatever intellectual structure the New Deal had stood halfway between the programmatic order that would become associated with the presidency in later decades and the traditional control exercised by Congress through its power to pass laws and authorize the expenditure of money.

Historians who suggest that the White House was transformed into a center of ideas in the New Deal years thus distort both the role of the New Deal intellectuals and the power of the presidency. They create a sense of structure that crumbles when it is confronted by the political realities of those years. They also set up Roosevelt as a hero who barely succeeds, or fails, or is forced to wait until a war finally salvages his program. One can get a clearer image of him by not overstating his commitment to ideas in the first place, by not glorifying his politics as pragmatism, and, above all, by not exaggerating either his power or his desire for power. Franklin Roosevelt is best under-stood as a career politician of an unusually talented order, one who both understood and enjoyed the process of political management. Unlike Hoover and many of the progressives, he saw both party politics and legislative politics not as impediments to action but as vehicles for action. That concep-tion of the professional politician, generally unacceptable to a public opinion that tends to regard all professional politicians as inherently dishonest manip-ulators, was concealed in Roosevelt's case, as in many others, by the fact that his money and social standing gave his career the image of an avocation or public service rather than what it in fact was: his lifetime occupation. From 1911, when he entered the New York State Senate, until his death he gave little serious attention to anything else.

The role of intellectuals in the New Deal was, then, the special role that intellectuals play for expert political professionals, whose skill in the end depends on recognizing the specific political utility of any idea and then reshaping it to the needs of the political process itself. The belief that such reshapings may be even better than logically constructed programs is central to the American profession of politics and central as well to a conflict that began in the New Deal and is with us still: the conflict between the specialist's understanding of the theories underlying economic and social behavior and the political leader's understanding of the limits and possibilities of politics. The special kinds of knowledge required for managing a complex economic and social system may not in fact have been available to American social scientists or to social scientists in Europe or the Soviet Union, where plans and planning seemed far in advance of American efforts. Yet the belief that such knowledge existed or had to be found had been given a new urgency by the intransigency of the Depression crisis. Whether such knowledge could be used in ways that would be consistent with the intuitive processes of American democratic politics was the issue the New Deal brought to the fore. The Roosevelt presidency managed to raise the issue but to keep it within bounds that most Americans thought safe. At the same time, the fact that Roosevelt's enemies increasingly raised the specter of dictatorship against his presidency suggests at least an element of recognition that what was going on in the United States bore some relation to the problems that were being faced elsewhere in the world.

The common use of the term "pragmatic" to describe the Roosevelt presidency also involves a misconstruction of the Roosevelt leadership—and the misuse of a philosophic term as well. Pragmatism refers to a rigorous and philosophically complex concept of experimentalism. It cannot possibly be applied to the New Deal. The Roosevelt method was political, not scientific. He himself distinguished between the two when he counseled his social-science advisers to keep their proposals scientific and let him provide the politics. The separation of science from politics made possible the compromises that were characteristic of New Deal programs. Designed to meet regional or interest-group demands, they contained compromises that no scientific method could justify. Roosevelt's relationships with the southern leadership that necessarily controlled congresses dominated by the Democratic party illustrate the kind of potential conflict he had to fight to keep under control. Senator Huey Long of Louisiana and Senators Carter Glass and, later, Harry Byrd of Virginia, together with their counterparts in the House of Representatives, saw national programs as threats to their regional independence. Where social programs were concerned, this was particularly true, since social programs on a national scale would either have to include blacks or find ways of excluding them that could be soothed in various ways, including Roosevelt's use of his wife as ambassador to the Negro community. Roosevelt depended on the South, not only because its votes could kill his domestic legislation but because the southern tradition of free trade, and a willingness to look on military interests as attractive, both socially and economically, were his most dependable bases for foreign-policy support in an isolationist era. The political negotiations that made it possible to bring reform out of such traditions can be labeled brilliant or shrewd but not pragmatic and certainly not experimental.

It is nonetheless inaccurate in some fundamental respects to deal with

Roosevelt only in political terms. His career as governor of New York gave striking evidence of his concern with the essential administrative problems of his era. The issues his New Deal Planning Board would raise in connection with land use, water resources, public power, and, most important, the need for government reorganization to provide more effective distribution of public resources and services to citizens can all be found in the programs he urged on the New York legislature even before the onset of the Depression. A closer look at his presidential administrative practices, once the immediate emergency of the early New Deal had subsided, shows a much greater concern with effective communication among offices concerned with the same or similar problems and a much greater sensitivity to the avoidance of duplication of responsibilities than the customary picture of the happy "pragmatist," manipulating his subordinates and forcing their confrontations with one another, reveals to us.

What most distinguishes Roosevelt from Hoover with respect to the relation between politics and administration is the fact that Roosevelt accepted the conflict between the two and did not regard as roadblocks to government the political victories his opponents scored against his administrative policies. Hoover's seeming insistence on seeing politics and administration as mutually exclusive was a classic case of the progressive problem writ as large as it can be written in American politics: at the level of presidential management itself. After all, as one political scientist reminded his colleagues many years later, the original distinction was between politics *and* administration, not politics *or* administration. This was something that Roosevelt understood. If Hoover even understood it, he rejected it completely.

Finally, it has been all too easy to exaggerate the power that Roosevelt actually wielded. His personality made him a popular leader, but his power over Congress was always limited. As early as March 1934 he was unable to get the votes to sustain his veto of the Independent Offices Appropriations Act, by which Congress restored the cuts the Economy Act of 1933 had made and raised government salaries and veterans' allowances by a total of $358 million. Whether the inherent conservatism some critics have seen in Roosevelt was the result of an intellectual commitment or a realistic appraisal of his limited congressional support is a question that needs more serious consideration than it has received.

At the same time, the creation of new administrative agencies, whose responsibilities for distributing and managing the nation's resources were so complex that Congress could no longer directly oversee them, gave the administrative branch of the government its greatest infusion of potential power in peacetime history. The relief agencies moved the federal government into the cities and into city politics on an unprecedented scale, and the National Housing Act of 1934 gave the federal government its first real opportunity to influence the social and economic organization of the cities.

The enlarged sphere of the bureaucracy created opportunities for the exercise of greater executive authority, but Roosevelt did not discover a way to use it effectively, and later presidents have not succeeded where he failed.

The creation of the Federal Housing Administration by the National Housing Act of 1934 gave the nation a publicly funded system for subsidizing mortgages and also for enforcing standards of construction—the quality of the housing itself. While modern public housing, one of the New Deal's most important innovations, was still several years away, the 1934 legislation opened the way to federal intervention in the quality of urban life itself. It also marked the reversal of the trend toward antiurban points of view that had become evident in the years before and after World War I, both here and abroad.

Fear of cities and a rejection of them as good places to live were by no means a new phenomenon, nor were they connected essentially with industrialization. There were cities before there was big industry; and industry was not confined to the cities. But industrialization and urbanization combined raised questions that social scientists and enlightened industrialists had tried to answer. What was the best way to house the labor force so that it would be healthy and happy? What was the best social organization for the masses of working people required by giant manufacturing concerns?

Throughout the twenties the effort to build middle-class suburbs outside the cities had, for a variety of reasons, replaced the older progressive effort to improve the urban tenements. The virtues of country living provided one reason. The fact that suburban land was cheaper than city property provided another. Even so, the movement, spearheaded by the Rockefeller Foundation, to build middle- and lower-income homes outside the central cities was a genuine attempt to improve living conditions for American workers, both black and white. The movement was perhaps antiurban only in its implications, but its effects on urban residential patterns were certainly deleterious.

The Depression crisis had a significant impact on attitudes toward the city, not only here but in other countries as well. The concept of the overbuilt industrial system was extended to include the overbuilt city, and in the United States in particular a large array of new intellectual concepts was available to explain the phenomenon and to suggest solutions.

The antiurbanism of the early New Deal illustrates some of the confusions surrounding the role of ideas in modern reform. Social scientists in the early thirties had constructed for themselves what was, in effect, a sequence of syllogisms to support their own conviction that urban growth had destroyed traditional community values. One syllogism went like this: If immigration was the chief source of population growth during the last century, and if immigration is now legally ended, then population growth is now over. A second one went as follows: If economic stagnation and more effective birth control lead to decline in the size of families, and if economic stagnation is a permanent condition of contemporary industrial society, then family limitation is a permanent condition too. A third went like this: If cities are the result of population expansion, and if the population is entering a period of decline, then cities are bound to decline. The thinking was circular; for the fact that they viewed cities as unhealthy social agglomerations encouraged demographers in the early thirties to envision depopulated cities by 1960, and that vision of depopulation encouraged them in their small-town, antiindustrial commitments. It also required planning for an antiurban society.

Roosevelt requested the American ambassador in Rome to find out more about Mussolini's experiments with deurbanization, and one of his first official acts was to appoint a cabinet committee to discuss the possibility of a similar American effort. In the initial years of the New Deal, particularly after the creation of the Resettlement Administration in 1935, the attempt to establish a new kind of suburban community, one that combined agriculture and industry, was a favorite conception among New Deal Veblenians like Rexford Tugwell. His Greenbelt idea, which led to the building of several new towns—Greenbelt, Maryland, near Washington, D.C., Greenhills, near Cincinnati, and Greendale, near Milwaukee—illustrates the early commitment to deurbanization and its relation to the Depression idea that the industrial system was overbuilt.

Deurbanization was a revolutionary idea, consistent with a view of the Depression as a new and continuing emergency requiring new ideas. As that view declined and a new quest for normalcy emerged, the more traditional conception of urban housing emerged with it. By 1940 American social theory had also developed conceptions of urban sociology to go along with the reemergence of the city as a valid way of life. The New York World's Fair of 1939, like the earlier Chicago fair, offered panoramic visions of the technological city. The "crisis" of industrialism had ended, at least for the time being; it was being replaced by a new crisis—the war—for which industrialism would be vital.

It remains difficult to explain the ending of the initial sense of crisis, since there were recurrent economic and political crises between 1935 and 1940. Yet the sense of an emergency based on a critical change in the nature of Western industrialism lost ground rapidly after the initial phase of the New Deal, the Hundred Days. And if one sees the Hundred Days as something considerably less than a period of revolutionary legislation, the puzzle of explanation becomes even more complex. One is left with Roosevelt—with the confidence, the smile, the patrician voice, and the uneasy promise of continuity. The nation's first modern experience with mass politics, charismatic leadership, and a political opportunism that responded to the pressures of as many constituencies as could make their power felt, had begun. The effort to shape that experience by the use of rational programs had also begun, and historians would struggle with that for more than a generation.

7

The Limits of Reform

THE DRAMATIC SHIFTS and reversals of mood that occurred in the years between 1935 and 1937 provide some of the high and low points of New Deal history. If the first phase of the New Deal had been marked by a sense of emergency and threatened paralysis, the second phase was all motion, not all of it in clearly marked directions. For observers at the time, and for historians ever since, the disputes that arose, and the sharpening of ideological conflict that accompanied them, make the period one of the most exciting in twentieth-century political history and one of the most difficult to analyze.

The Congress elected in 1934 was, of all the New Deal legislatures, the one most committed to the ideals of social justice and economic reform that Roosevelt had been enunciating. The legislative program of 1935—which took shape in the initial hundred days of what some historians would begin to call the Second New Deal—produced some of the most liberal, even radical, ideas of the period. Putting aside characterization of the actual legislation for the moment, one can agree that the ideas involved in social security, control of public utilities, and, most of all, a tax on the nation's wealthy generated a level of debate that differed markedly from that of the previous two years, when the emphasis was all on getting people back to work at any cost.

At the same time, the hostility of the Supreme Court, its willingness to oppose the New Deal head-on by attacking its major programs, even by questioning the constitutional authority of the government to manage the depressed economy, was unmistakably clear by May 1935. The battle that ensued between Roosevelt and the Court was perhaps the classic instance of such confrontation in American history. The Court had confronted other branches of government before, but not since the eve of the Civil War had national conditions been so volatile.

The presidential election campaign of 1936 was one of the most ideologically charged in modern American history. A highly articulate third-party opposition (the Union party) aroused a level of angry rhetoric not often found in national election campaigns. Business opposition to the New Deal had grown, but that was not abnormal or unexpected. What was new and threatening was the movement to organize northern blue-collar workers and southern poor whites. That campaign produced clear echoes of the kind of strident demagoguery that had occurred in Europe.

The media helped to intensify this mood by providing national exposure to volatile political figures who once would have been little known outside their own regional constituencies. It was difficult to judge how far the accents of Louisiana Senator Huey Long would resonate, say, among farmers who had now become members of the unemployed labor force in the cities or how far the radio voice of Father Coughlin would carry its appeal to Catholic workers. The tone and methods of such leaders were familiar from third-party oppositions in the past; what was new was the nation-wide scope of their effort and, with it, the possibility that national coalitions, appealing to traditionally Democratic voters, might be formed. When Long cooperated with the *March of Time* by allowing it to film his activities, the resulting footage offended urban liberals, as *Time* intended that it should; but the program also helped Long reach an even wider audience of potential supporters. Finally, even the elderly were represented as a political interest group for the first time.

All of this turmoil seemed to threaten the sense of stability and orderly continuity that Roosevelt had been working to achieve. The possibility that he might not win the election had for months created a profound uneasiness among even highly placed Democrats and, conversely, had caused high hopes among Republicans. As the attacks on him intensified, Roosevelt joined the ideological debate himself.

In the event, Roosevelt won the election of 1936 by an unprecedented landslide. He carried every state but Maine and Vermont and brought with him a two-thirds majority of Democrats in both houses of Congress—a majority no president since has commanded. Yet, within the year, he suffered a stunning series of legislative defeats. Moreover, the opinion polls suggested that these setbacks were approved by the same public that had reelected him by such an overwhelming margin. A severe economic downturn in the summer of 1937 concluded the roller-coaster ride of New Deal popularity, returning the nation, many feared, to conditions not much better than what they were when it all began.

As one examines each of the phases of the period, it is difficult to match the rhetoric and the reality. The most radical legislation of the second New Deal was strongly rooted in past reforms, which greatly modified its radical intentions. Roosevelt ultimately was able to celebrate what he considered his victory over the Supreme Court, despite the defeat of his effort to win through the so-called Court-packing legislation, but it is hard to see which side won if one examines some of the implications of the dispute. Finally, although Roosevelt's 1936 election victory, following a campaign fraught with demagogic challenges on all sides, looked like the greatest triumph of one-man leadership in American history, the fears that it aroused found no confirmation in the years that followed. If the people gave Roosevelt the blank check that even he thought he had received, they stopped payment on it long before it got to the bank.

Half way through his first term, on 4 January 1935, Roosevelt delivered his annual message to the new Congress, assembled the day before—the first Congress to meet on that date under the provisions of the Twentieth Amendment. The elections of the previous November had brought in a more liberal Congress than the one produced by the landslide of 1932. It is therefore not surprising that Roosevelt's 1935 message to Congress was liberal in tone. Some of the reform proposals it contained may have been intended to defuse the discontents that Long, Coughlin, and others were even then beginning to exploit, but it has generally been interpreted as a response to liberal criticisms of the early New Deal's emphasis on industrial recovery and thus as announcing a new departure, a new program—the Second New Deal. However, the three goals he announced were not new, for they had been in place during the previous two years of his government. The first, security of livelihood through better use of natural resources, was one of the goals of the programs initiated by the planning board Harold Ickes had set up in the Public Works Administration. The second, security against unemployment, old age, illness, and dependency, had been in the forefront of discussions not only in the Depression years but even back in the progressive period. Early in his first term Roosevelt had appointed a committee to study ways to help the unemployed, the aged, the ill, and the weak, and its report was now ready. The third, slum clearance and better housing, simply extended programs already initiated by the First New Deal.

A new tone, however, suffused the president's message, and it was echoed in later discussions of the programs he was now proposing. The First New Deal had indeed emphasized industrial recovery. If social justice was discussed, it was seen as a consequence of the recovery of the industrial system. A kind of Taylorism predominated, if not in the language, then certainly in the actual consequences of the programs. In the area of housing, for example, the emphasis on mortgage support and the tentative suggestions of quality control still spoke to the aim of preserving a middle class that was seen as hard-hit, but only temporarily so, by economic conditions. There were still echoes of the Better Homes movement of the 1920s, but with the federal government supporting private investment. By contrast, the new tone of the 1935 message and its direct reference to slum clearance suggest a transfer of concern from the middle to the lower classes. Roosevelt was now proposing that the federal government should spend vast sums on housing for the poor. This was the kind of project that private investors would never undertake and that even the wealthiest philanthropist would underwrite only in the best of times—and then on a small, experimental, scale.

With regard to unemployment, the new tone of the message is again clear. Many American policymakers had been seeking some kind of unemployment-insurance program since the end of the war. Hoover felt that such a program could be privately managed, and several states had begun discussions along that line. The Employment Act of 1931 had involved debates over the appropriate degree of federal involvement; in the end, the government's role was limited to providing informational services to the states. By adding to their program such formerly local concerns as old age, health, and dependency, Roosevelt and his advisers were now taking the important step of attaching the concept of federal responsibility for other social ills to the by then more acceptable idea of federal responsibility for the unemployed.

New concepts of social justice were similarly linked to the familiar concept of government conservation of natural resources. One branch of the conservation movement had always argued that more efficient use and management of nature was the key to industrial progress. The more radical branch espoused what later came to be known as "ecology"; they argued against the industrial invasion of nature and what they saw as the predatory destructiveness of technological expansion. Conservation as a political movement had succeeded only because the moderates—the proponents of a balance between industrial use and preservation of nature—had won out. Now electric power and waterways were the new battleground. As he had in the case of TVA, Roosevelt sought to link the idea of social justice to the more acceptable concern for industrial efficiency. He knew that appropriate language was important. "Conservation" was a loaded term. Even Hoover had substituted "wood use" in an effort to avoid awakening old battles. "Natural resources" was a more acceptable term, and, if one could argue that human beings were also "natural resources," one had achieved a rhetorical success that might have implications for the future.

This rhetorical linkage of old and new, the attaching of concepts some might consider revolutionary to ideas that few would question—a hallmark of the methodology of the Second New Deal—has confused many historians. Some have looked on it as a subterfuge, a concealment of conservative intentions by liberal language. Others have seen it as part of the slow process of educating the public to accept interventionist government. Those who associate the Second New Deal with Brandeisian theories of government are on the right track, but only because Louis Brandeis's thought exhibits the same characteristics; for Brandeis, an admirer of the Greek city-state, sought to modernize democracy by limiting and controlling the growth of the federal government. Of the two basic strands of progressivism, Theodore Roosevelt's New Nationalism and the Brandeis-Wilson New Freedom, the nationalist position had always been the more revolutionary of the two. Both Wilson and Brandeis had made a national conception of social justice palatable by attaching it to an image of the small-town agrarian past rather than to a revolutionary future. Veblen had at least implied much the same point of view. The New Deal inherited both the old dream and the new reality.

Historians who use the term "the Second Hundred Days," like those who try to describe a Second New Deal, imply that Roosevelt had a clearly defined program or change in program. Yet the "program" resists easy definition. What is clear is that the pressure of extremes resulted in a desire on the part of the administration to find a middle course and to communicate that course to a constituency grown uncertain after listening to so many competing voices. Later scholars, sifting through the programs, would wonder just what the hubbub had been all about, but the fact of hubbub was undeniable. The public was growing accustomed to a level and pace of legislative activity that was unprecedented. It seemed now to be the norm.

The legislative energy of 1935 began in April and reached its peak in August. The opening sally exhibits all the characteristics that give the programs their special distinction. The Emergency Relief Appropriation Act of 8 April created the controversial WPA—the Works Progress Administration—under the direction of Harry L. Hopkins. It was designed to make jobs for people who might otherwise not be employed; that is, its purpose was not to revive industry or to spur investment. In its eight years of existence it built 650,000 miles of highways, roads, and streets, 125,000 public buildings, 8,000 parks, and more than 840 airports, to name only a few of the 1,410,000 individual projects, which employed 8,500,000 people and spent $11 billion. From the point of view of the projects themselves, WPA could be said to be doing the same thing that Ickes' PWA was supposed to do; but there were differences, and these explain not only the persistent conflict between the two men but the essential nature of WPA and its relation to the tradition of public charity.

WPA actually employed people; that is, it did not rely on stimulating industry to create employment, which was the way that the PWA, at least in principle, was supposed to operate. Some 85 percent of the money the government spent on WPA went into wages and salaries rather than payments to local construction companies. This raised questions about competition between government and industry, about comparability of wages and hours, and, ultimately, about the rights of workers to hold jobs. To cope with such problems, the government resorted to tactics long familiar to those who had had experience with the older practices of local charities and local political patronage. To get a job, an individual had to certify his or her neediness—to subject him or herself to what many considered the indignity of a means test. Local political organizations exercised much greater influence on the distribution of WPA projects and jobs than they could with PWA projects. Such influence acknowledged the traditional relationship between public works and political patronage, the old corruption, which had long proved its efficiency in distributing money to the unemployed without asking questions about the utility of the work being performed.

Hopkins remained under persistent attack for his management of the WPA program. Part of the attack stemmed from the program's involvement in partisan politics. Hopkins was quoted as having said that the Democrats would "spend and spend and elect and elect and elect." But, like its relation to the older forms of charity, its connection to partisan politics was the traditional, even conservative, aspect of the WPA. What is interesting is that the WPA was increasingly attacked as a radical program, a label that stuck. To be sure, the WPA found jobs for left-wing writers and artists. Many were employed by the Federal Writers Project, whose Guide Book Series was viewed as radical despite the unmistakable tone of nationalist pride that pervaded it. The label was, more appropriately, applied to some of the work produced by the Federal Theatre Workshop. Then, in 1939, when workers struck against government cutbacks in WPA, the radicalism seemed, to many, clear-cut. Yet such criticism paled to insignificance in light of the numbers employed and the projects completed. The whole attitude toward the WPA may well be summed up by the fact that, throughout the period, those who worked for it were not included in the statistics of employment. No matter what they did, WPA workers were not "employed" if the work they did was paid for by the government.

The Resettlement Administration, established under the authority of the Emergency Relief Appropriation Act of 1935, placed Rexford G. Tugwell in charge of a program designed to gather in the impoverished farmers whom the AAA could not help, move them to more usable land, or make their land more usable by improving its quality and their use of it. The Rural Electrification Administration, also a product of the relief legislation, was intended to extend electricity into areas not served by private companies, in order to improve the quality of rural life. It was also intended to promote power cooperatives, and in fact the development of the cooperatives as independent local organizations ultimately dominated the REA programs.

Emergency relief also led to the establishment of the National Youth Administration, a program designed to employ persons between the ages of sixteen and twenty-five. The basic idea was to encourage young people to continue their education, to retrain those who needed it, and, above all, to keep the young out of the labor force until they were trained for careers that would be both satisfying and useful. Here, again, a traditional program of progressive social reform ultimately achieved a radical label; for when Aubrey

Williams, the administrator of the NYA, sought to extend aid to *all* youth, Negro as well as white, he came up against the hard core of opposition that inevitably limited all New Deal reform. The power of the southern Democrats made it impossible to avoid the connection between social reform and radical politics, on the one hand, and Negro rights and radical politics on the other. Efforts to include improvement of the condition of Negroes in social-reform programs either gave such programs a radical tinge or led to administrative subterfuges designed to make the exclusion of Negroes possible.

The position of the labor movement in the New Deal can to some extent serve as a test of whether the New Deal can fairly be described as radical or whether it was instead solidly committed to middle-class values and never moved farther to the left or the right than middle-class opinion would permit. American labor had never constituted a national political force, either as an independent political party or as a significant bloc in either of the major party organizations. The Populists had had trouble finding a place for the working-man within their party, and the Progressives had done only a little better. Rural-newspaper readers associated unions with urban violence. The urban progressives' approach to "labor" problems was usually limited to campaigns to abolish child labor, to improve factory conditions for women, and to establish safety controls for everyone, in about that order of importance.

Roosevelt remained personally aloof from the labor movement. His compassion for the workingman, "the forgotten man," was based on a patrician sense of charity, a respect for the dignity of individuals regardless of what Roosevelt's own generation would have called their "station in life." The phrase "a living wage" embodied a humanitarian principle; it meant simply the amount necessary to keep a family alive and well. Bargaining for wages and hours had to be understood initially in that context.

Roosevelt's generation of patrician reformers seemed to distinguish between the laboring man, for whom they had very profound sympathies, and organized labor, for which they did not. They judged individual behavior, their own as well as that of those who worked for them, by standard Victorian conceptions of duty, class responsibility, and social order. They limited democracy just as their British counterparts did and felt that individuals with aspirations could transcend class lines in ways that "agitators" could not. They did not believe that an adversary relationship between management and labor was either necessary or useful. Those who created the Department of Commerce and Labor in 1903 wanted the combination of the two functions in a single agency to symbolize their sense of unity and cooperation. Nor was the Wilson administration's separation of the two into separate departments in 1913 necessarily symbolic, since neither represented powerful constituencies.

Wilson's appointment of a Commission on Industrial Relations in 1915 was his response to the one kind of labor event that generated national concern: an episode of violence. In this instance, it was the so-called Ludlow Massacre, which occurred in 1914 during a strike against the Colorado Fuel and Iron Company. A Rockefeller holding, the company requested that the National Guard be called in to deal with the strikers, and that set off what was virtually a civil war. Eleven women and two children were killed. The Industrial Relations Commission heard eloquent testimony on behalf of labor from reformers, liberal ministers, newsmen eager to exploit a general hostility toward Rockefeller, and traditional advocates of the special needs of women and children in industry. Frederick Winslow Taylor took the stand to deny accusations that he was attempting to exploit labor by giving management more precise tools with which to measure work. He also testified that he had come to believe that a spirit of cooperation was essential to the creation of his factory utopia.

The various industry boards created during World War I contributed to the sense of a need for a national labor policy, but the emphasis was still on compassion rather than organization. The identification of labor organization with radicalism was strengthened in the public mind by newspaper editorials on the Industrial Workers of the World, the "Wobblies," who now were promoting strikes in eastern factories rather than western mines. Yet, by the end of the war, there was still no national consensus on labor organization itself, and the Depression brought only further confusion.

By selecting a woman, Frances Perkins, to head the Department of Labor Roosevelt was in a sense acknowledging the only consensus that as yet existed: the general concern about the employment of women and children. Yet it was a step forward, for Madam Perkins was a forceful reformer whose interest in promoting the cause of labor went back to her days as a social worker in New York City at the time of the Triangle disaster. She had pleaded labor's cause, and in office continued to do so, from a position far closer to that of Robert Wagner and Fiorello LaGuardia than that of Roosevelt. Roosevelt was quite satisfied with the NIRA and its mild Section 7a, and he was prepared to veto efforts to secure any further bargaining rights for unions. Faced with the Supreme Court's invalidation of the NIRA, however, he was forced to recognize the need for some form of federal protection of labor organization. Senator Wagner's proposals went beyond Roosevelt's intentions, but these were what he was handed. They had support in Congress and in the mind of Secretary Perkins, and Roosevelt signed them into law. The provision of a National Labor Relations Board, with power not only to determine collective-bargaining units and to supervise elections but to issue cease-and-desist orders against employers engaged in actions the bill defined as unfair marked a revolution in the history of the American labor movement. Nonetheless, in its initial form, the act still operated under the limitations of all federal legislation. Local unions, not nationally affiliated, and industries not engaged in interstate commerce were still governed by state legislation alone. The act was intended to spur the states to pass "little Wagner Acts" of their own.

The complex relation between national and local policy exemplified by the Wagner Act only begins to illustrate the problem of creating and enforcing a national policy. Union leadership reflected the diversity of labor organizations, industry to industry and state to state. The mining, steel, auto, and clothing industries, to name only the most obvious, had such varied structures and histories that no single policy could deal with them effectively. Roosevelt had no recognizable set of options, even had he been inclined to look for one. When the CIO began to organize the auto and steel industries, following the passage of the Wagner Act, the size of his difficulties became clear.

On the last day of December 1936 a group of workers in several of the General Motors plants at Flint, Michigan, took control of the plants, inaugurating what was for American industry a new kind of strike, the "sit-down strike." It was a remarkable tactic, and it provided newsreel drama for the forty-four days the sit-downs lasted. Workers, smiling and waving from factory windows, generated more sympathy than the slow motion of the picket line. The tactic spread to other industries, and its effectiveness began to threaten the kind of labor progress that Roosevelt seemed prepared to support. Strikers walking picket lines could inhibit the employment of "scab" labor, but strikers preventing access to the plant itself meant that part of the labor force could prevent all of the labor force from working. The Supreme Court declared the sit-down strike illegal in 1939.

The steel industry also resisted unionization, and violence was the result. The Memorial Day Massacre in May 1937 was the most dramatic incident. Ten people were killed and eighty-four injured when police fired on demonstrators at the Republic Steel plant in South Chicago. Not until World War II did the New Deal achieve a clear position with regard to labor's political role, and even then there was residual suspicion on the part of both management and labor. Labor reluctantly made Roosevelt its hero, and Roosevelt reluctantly accepted. The coming of the war perhaps did more than anything else to establish the New Deal as a promoter of union rights.

Roosevelt's own attitude seems never to have changed. He had begun his presidency with a campaign to return people to work. Union organization seemed a side issue compared to the search for jobs. If anything, it was a luxury that might be attended to after the primary aim had been achieved; and in his late years, as he searched for ways of defining the promise of the future for Americans, he still placed jobs, not union organization, on the list of new rights he wanted Americans to consider fundamental. The right was a right to work, not the right to agitate for the conditions under which one would work. Roosevelt's generation had never considered labor policies a part of the political system they managed. If he and his policies made it possible for labor to organize, it was a change about which he would continue to feel a certain uneasiness, and the labor leaders he dealt with always knew it.

Perhaps the best example of the complex nature of state and federal compromise is the Social Security Act of 1935, for it embodies all of the various conceptions of responsibility for the disadvantaged that had grown up through the Progressive Era. By 1935 a number of states had experimented with measures for providing pensions to widows and aid to the blind and disabled; but these were minimal where they existed, and they existed only in some localities. The state of Wisconsin had recently tried to work out a program of unemployment insurance, and other states were looking at that as a model. But then the Depression cut short those experiments. The need was too great.

Federal Social Security began with unemployment insurance. The system that was set up involved a complicated cooperation between the federal government and the states. The basic idea was to promote uniformity of plans among the states and to press states without plans to legislate programs of their own. A federal tax on payrolls of employers of eight or more workers (the tax was set at 1 percent in 1936, 2 percent in 1937, and 3 percent thereafter) was to provide each state with a fund that it would administer. A liberal tax credit for states instituting such programs, plus grants to cover the cost of administering the program, were further incentives.

In the area of aid to the indigent, the act authorized money grants to the states to support both traditional charity services, such as aid to needy children and the destitute blind, and the newer social services, such as public health, vocational rehabilitation, and maternity and infant care. The needy aged would be covered by a maximum federal contribution of $15 per month for each individual, again with support for administrative services. These sums, again, were to be in the form of matching grants, the state being required to make a contribution before the federal money would be forthcoming.

The only exclusively federal part of the program was the provision of old age and survivors' insurance. The tax, which was to begin in 1937, was to be levied in equal amounts on employer and employee. The first pension, which was not scheduled to be paid until January 1942, would range from a minimum of $10 per month to a maximum of $85. This, the most revolutionary, and national, part of the system, was perhaps the weakest response the government could have made to the pressures generated by the Townsend movement (Townsend had recommended a pension of $200 a month), and it is difficult to conceive that these small amounts could have been thought adequate to the immediate needs of the elderly even in 1935.

The Social Security Act of 1935 is primarily an act that sought, in the tradition of reform legislation, to organize local agencies in a more rational way. Such a goal was characteristic of much of the New Deal. The exclusion of certain occupations from coverage by the act—farm labor and household workers, for example—indicates the compromises that had to be made by a Congress under Democratic control. Southern states with large populations of impoverished Negroes would be unwilling—and in fact unable—to pay for coverage of their needs.

A national ambivalence toward pensions forced Roosevelt to shape his Social Security program into a form that would be widely acceptable. Americans had come to accept pensions for widows—usually women without careers, whose livelihood ended if their husband died. Pensions for persons in low-paying public services like school-teaching were also winning acceptance. But the idea that a man, employed throughout his life, should be compensated for having failed, as they would have seen it, to save for his later years—let alone expect to retire in good health to enjoy those years—was not part of the traditional work ethic. Thus Roosevelt's insistence on the individual-account system, despite the opposition of more sophisticated administrative specialists, who saw taxation and general funding as the only economically reasonable approach, spoke to the tradition of independent saving, however illusory it might be. Moreover, as he told one of his advisers, Luther Gulick, it would prevent any future Congress from taking the system away. That the individual-account system would withdraw money into savings at a time when economists believed that to be adverse to the economy, that it was far more costly to operate, and that the returns would bear little real relation to the actual contributions, all were arguments known and worried about at the time. But, for Roosevelt, politics remained the primary concern—politics and public education. If a consensus did not exist, it would have to be created. Social Security had to have a beginning point, and this was it, minimal or not.

The disputes among his advisers were never resolved. Those who saw the national welfare programs in Germany, England, and the Soviet Union as the wave of the future were committed to ideas of central control, uniformity, and efficiency that others found increasingly threatening. It was not only southerners who wanted to limit federal control in order to preserve special traditions. Some of the Wisconsin progressives who served on the advisory board and who helped manage the program in its formative years were concerned lest federal management destroy the necessary involvement of the states and of local communities in their own government, thereby inhibiting, even ending, an important tradition of participatory democracy.

The distinction between a central government's taxing all of its citizens to support wage-earners' survivors and temporarily unemployed persons, on the one hand, and a citizenry saving for the future with government aid, on the other, seemed illusory to those who saw something very dangerous in the government's new legal authority to force "saving" through taxation. Yet Social Security was attempting to combine the two positions. Keeping significant parts of the program in local governments seemed to provide some protection. It was at least a halfway point between European centralization and the frail voluntarism on which Hoover had tried to depend.

The minimal support the program provided was also a means of stopping short of full government responsibility at any level. If the federal program would spur the states to undertake supplementary measures, it might do the same for the citizens themselves, by encouraging private saving for the future. Pensions had not been a significant part of the private insurance business before the establishment of Social Security. It was clear to some in the insurance industry that the new program might change that. They had seen a boost in the purchase of small life-insurance policies as a result of the government's wartime insurance for servicemen, and some in the industry were prepared at least to experiment. The government's program would serve as a base on which private programs might be built. The ultimate result was a great increase in private pension plans, including union pensions. This rather awkward mix of public and private plans substituted for a national system; it worked unevenly and unequally, to be sure, but it remained within the control of those groups who believed that private control was the heart of democratic politics. Most Americans preferred to maintain a balance between the dangers of local corruption and private dishonesty, on the one hand, and the threatening federal government on the other. Like charity, self-government began at home, not in Washington.

This kind of ideological dispute between centralization and local control provided the background against which Roosevelt conducted his battle to restructure the Supreme Court. To depict it as a battle between nine reactionary old men and a young and liberal president served Roosevelt well, but it does not explain the fundamental miscalculation that led to his defeat. The popular image of the nine old men in monolithic opposition was inaccurate. The Court was split between supporters and opponents of aggressive government action, but the split was not necessarily between liberals and conservatives.

What the Court would do in response to Roosevelt's use of power had been an object of speculation from the beginning. Chief Justice Charles Evans Hughes had written a decision upholding a Minnesota law granting a moratorium on debt repayment, arguing that an emergency could evoke implicit powers of government. The emergency did not create new power; it made implicit power explicit. This decision gave hope to those who were looking to the use of emergency powers to achieve reforms. But Hughes had also provoked puzzlement and consternation by a series of decisions involving the joint resolution that abrogated the clauses in public and private contracts requiring that payment be made in gold.

One of Hughes's decisions argued that regulation of trading in gold was a regulation of currency and was hence within the government's legitimate powers. That looked good. A second Hughes decision defined gold certificates as currency, not as warehouse receipts for actual gold, and that looked even better. Gold certificates were not like wheat, cotton, or tobacco storage tickets to be turned in for the actual commodities they represented. But a third Hughes decision ended whatever satisfaction the first two had provided to proponents of government control. The abrogation of the gold clause,

Hughes and the Court majority agreed, was unconstitutional; but the man who had sued for the difference between the value of his gold certificate in gold and its value in post-abrogation dollars had no suit. He had, the Court insisted, suffered no damage. The compromise the Court appeared to have struck led Justice McReynolds to intone that "this is Nero at his worst." In a sense he was quite correct, for the decision seemed to argue that there was no judicial recourse against an unconstitutional action of Congress. That all three gold decisions were five-to-four decisions helped to fuel the sense of ideological split, and the feebleness of the logic in the third decision lent support to the view that the Court was politically obstructive.

An irascible Supreme Court was by no means Roosevelt's only judicial obstacle, though it was the one on which most commentary centered. New Deal legislation was moving into areas never before entered by federal lawmakers, and the precedents being set for state legislation in some of the key areas of labor and welfare and mortgage and banking policy were unclear. Cases moving through lower federal courts were meeting that uncertainty in the form of cautious judges not eager to be overruled by higher courts and possibly themselves unsympathetic to New Deal reforms. Vacancies on the federal bench had, after all, been filled by Republican presidents for the past twelve years, and not all of Wilson's appointees could be characterized as liberals (he had, to be sure, appointed Brandeis to the Supreme Court, but he had also appointed McReynolds). In discussing the Supreme Court's contribution to the crisis, therefore, one must also deal with the whole question of the federal judiciary at all levels and the degree to which the high Court's response reflected a wider judicial reluctance to certify the new reforms. Focusing on the "Nine Old Men" does not show us the whole picture.

The case in which the Supreme Court declared the NIRA unconstitutional, *Schechter Poultry Corp. v. U.S.* (May 1935), is far more complex than either its New Deal critics or its business defenders were inclined to admit. Because of its importance, the case provoked a unanimous decision, so the concurring judges necessarily included those Roosevelt looked to as his defenders, Brandeis and Cardozo, as well as Hughes and Stone. The act gave to NRA code-makers, elected by no constitutional process, the authority to make rules that, when signed by the president, had the effect of laws enforceable in the federal courts. This was unacceptable in a world in which legislatures were turning their power over to dictators willingly or were having it wrested from them by popular demand. Even where rule-making bodies already existed— for example, in the Interstate Commerce Commission—Congress had at least retained some control over the process of appointment. Once the pressure of circumstances forced the administration to agree to "blanket codes"—which were hastily drawn rules, subject to few, if any, controls—the situation had reached the point where delegation, as Cardozo put it, was "running riot." Nor could Roosevelt have expected much support from Brandeis, who continued his opposition to the very large units of business organization on which the NRA depended.

The *Schechter* case was in many ways the least appropriate case on which to rest the constitutionality of so major a piece of industrial legislation. For one thing, the A. L. A. Schechter Poultry Company, whose business practices had already raised many legal and health-code questions that had nothing to do with NRA, engaged in the ritual slaughtering of chickens in accordance with restrictions established by Jewish dietary laws, a process not easily compatible with the bureaucratic restrictions drawn up by the hastily assembled NRA code-makers. Koshering rules required the rabbi to certify that the chicken was free of conditions defined as unhealthy by religious law, not by the health codes used in the nonreligious sector of the industry. Jewish butchers therefore had to be able to select birds for slaughtering according to their own practices. The code, however, forbade the buyer of live chickens to select among the chickens in a given coop; it required that the first bird at hand be taken for slaughtering. The reason for the requirement was simply to protect chicken prices by making sure that less-desirable birds not be deliberately left over, to be sold later at cut-rate prices. The two bureaucracies, one ancient and one modern, were clearly at an impasse. Discussions of the details of the process in the Court hearings had already provided a fair amount of comedy for Court participants and observers alike; and since a criminal penalty had been involved, the proceedings took on Chaplinesque overtones of comic justice and bureaucratic stupidity. The Blue Eagle, as the inevitable jokes put it, was turned into a sick chicken.

In deciding the case, however, the Court also insisted that the Schechter Company was not engaged in interstate commerce, despite the fact that its chickens were sold outside New York. For three decades the courts had allowed the constitutionality of federal laws respecting various social conditions—child labor chief among them—to rest on the Interstate Commerce Clause. Now the progressives' tradition of using the Commerce Clause as one of the chief instruments of social and economic change was being abruptly ended. Whatever Roosevelt thought about the continuing utility of the NIRA, even its revision in more acceptable form now seemed doubtful.

Of all the New Deal constitutional issues, the one that appears to have been most easily forgotton is the *Schechter* rule and its opposition to the delegation of legislative authority. Critics of big government would try to revive it, but throughout the 1950s and '60s the pressure for greater and greater federal intervention in social and economic issues rendered the rule irrelevant, the constitutional issue moot. Federal administrators would ultimately have far more control over the making of rules than Roosevelt would have dreamed possible, even assuming that he would have wanted it, and far more than the Court, in *Schechter*, seemed to think constitutional. Congress and the courts came to accept rule-making, the power to decide how legislative intent would be carried out, as a form of governmental management, *Schechter* rule or no. If this was delegation by another name, few critics would remember it by the end of the era, even those who still lamented what they saw as the expansion of the power of the presidency in the New Deal.

It is also important to point out that *Schechter* was not simply an attack on the New Deal but the culminating moment in a legal debate that had been going on in the law journals since 1914. Felix Frankfurter had raised the issue in the 1920s when, as a Harvard law professor, he had questioned the increasing amount of delegation to administrative bureaucracies that followed in the wake of the creation of administrative commissions by legislatures. He and legal writers like A. A. Berle, Jr., another soon-to-be supporter of the New Deal, had lamented the need for what they saw as a new legal structure in American government. They accepted it as one of the consequences of increasing technological complexity, but they called for some kind of as yet undefined surveillance to protect the legislative base of American democracy. In the aftermath of the Supreme Court fight, the American legal profession seemed to take on a new role for itself as it sought to adjust its practices to the inevitable change. The emergence of the Washington lawyer as a new power in government followed the emergence of increased administrative government. Law firms responded to the need to help manage the relation between their clients and the rule-making bodies that constituted the new administrative state.

The Supreme Court fight is thus a much larger issue than it has appeared to be. That is, it was less a heroic battle, won or lost, than a statement of the real revolution of the New Deal. Few events of the New Deal, or even of modern American history, so remarkably typify the tensions of modern government as does Roosevelt's battle with the Court. At one extreme stands the venerable tradition of the Court, the Constitution, and the sanctity of the law; at the other stands the mass public, on whose support the fundamental legitimacy of government depends. The importance of the desires of that mass public was perceived only gradually, and, when it was first perceived, it was misunderstood: the landslide election of 1936 made it appear that the American people wanted a strong president.

Roosevelt's personal victory in the election of 1936 had been supported by an equally dramatic victory for his party in both houses of Congress. In addition to the generally more liberal cast produced by the off-year elections in 1934, the presidential-year election of 1936 had contributed sheer numbers: the Democrats controlled more than 70 percent of both houses. Not only did such numbers suggest a legislature controlled by the president; they also seemed to assure the presence of at least the two-thirds majority necessary to amend the Constitution. The future of the New Deal seemed clear, Supreme Court or no. The second term thus began on a wave of confidence firmly based on a view of political control that rested in turn on a perception of overwhelming public support. Anything that needed to be done could now be done. All the necessary authority was there, for the first time in American history. The New Deal appeared to be a genuine revolution. The fact that within a year that vision had disappeared was not within anyone's range of predictions in November 1936.

Roosevelt's victory in the election of 1936 is a good example of the historical event that, by obliterating the uncertainties that preceded it, appears, after the fact, to have been inevitable. Yet, from the autumn of 1935 on, many in the inner circle of Washington, impressed by the increasingly strident opposition emanating from groups on which the new political coalition had come to rest, were not so sure that Roosevelt would win, let alone by such a margin.

Senator Huey Long, former governor of Louisiana, had begun to make very effective use of the mass media to transmit a populism of his own. He called it "Share Our Wealth," and he was promising a homestead allowance of $6,000 and a minimum annual income of $2,500 to every American family. Before his assassination in September 1935 he had reorganized the Louisiana government in such a way as to give him virtual dictatorial control of the state. Roosevelt believed him to be one of the most dangerous men in America. Even after his death, the fear that his power reflected a profound opposition to the New Deal among southern Democrats, whose resurgent populism suggested that Roosevelt had not gone far enough, was sufficient to cause concern. Roosevelt's position on the Wealth Tax Act of 1935—legislation for which Long had far more radical ambitions—had been a mixture of support for liberal enthusiasts, who wanted far more than Roosevelt himself was willing to accept, and a shrewd understanding of the views of the business community, which he was still trying to court.

A Michigan priest, Father Charles E. Coughlin, had begun a radio program and a magazine to popularize a movement he called "Social Justice" and, increasingly, to attack the New Deal. His appeal to northern working-class ethnics and his overt anti-Semitism spoke to some of the classic fears that Populism had sought to provoke. He attacked banks, argued for an expansion of silver currency, and, like Long, appealed to a major constituency on which Democrats knew they would have to depend.

A retired Long Beach, California, doctor, Francis Townsend, organized the elderly to campaign for old-age security in the form of a monthly pension that the recipient would be required to spend by the end of each month. The source of the $200 he recommended was a tax scheme that made little sense to experts at the time, although the principle of a minimum or negative income was one that later generations would find attractive.

Novelist Upton Sinclair established an identifiably socialist alternative in his "End Poverty in California" movement (EPIC), which again threatened to draw liberal support away from the New Deal by recommending forms of state ownership that Roosevelt had rejected. Roosevelt viewed the movement as enough of a threat that he provided aid to Sinclair's conservative opponent.

Within the Democratic party, former New York Governor Alfred E. Smith supported a group of anti–New Deal Democrats and conservative businessmen that also couched its criticisms of the New Deal in ideological terms. The name of the group, the Liberty League, was adopted to underscore the idea that the New Deal posed a grave threat to the liberties guaranteed by the Constitution. Again, particularly in the light of the pressures being exerted by the more liberal Congress elected in 1934, Roosevelt saw an important constituency slipping away: the traditional business Democrats, whose money and power had been a basic source of support.

The Republicans had been badly beaten in 1932 and 1934, but Hoover remained, at least for Roosevelt, the symbol of a formidable opposition. Roosevelt was convinced that Hoover's skills as an administrative technician could be used against him effectively, that the public would be impressed with the kind of criticism Hoover would direct at the most likely targets: the administrative inefficiency of New Deal programs, their cost, the overlap and duplication, and the fact that some of the essential ones, like the NRA and AAA, could be attacked as unworkable and ineffective. Hoover, Roosevelt knew from friends who had spoken with the former president, was preparing his attack.

The attack, when it came, was not on inefficiency and ineptitude, waste and corruption, all the terms that progressives had traditionally used in criticizing big government. Hoover's *The Challenge to Liberty* appeared in 1935. Its criticisms of the New Deal were almost entirely ideological. Hoover surveyed the revolutions in Europe to find the sources of New Deal programs and to find what he persisted in calling "regimentation." The term was intended to connote a militaristic organization of management and the work force, a dictatorial control of the economic and social system that obliterated freedom of choice. When former friends like Wesley Mitchell tried to convince Hoover that at least some of the New Deal rested on ideas he had been working with himself, he rejected the notion.

Roosevelt's efforts to attract the old-line progressives had had mixed results, and when the Republican party nominated Alfred Landon, the governor of Kansas and a progressive, it was clearly attempting to attract them, too, to form a broader national constituency than Hoover had been able to achieve. Roosevelt needed the progressives because he wanted to make it plain that the conservative old guard in both parties was the enemy that had to be defeated. By nominating Landon, the Republicans had made that more difficult. Hoover, who had very much wanted the nomination, adopted an ideologically strident tone that made compromise with New Deal reforms impossible.

Thus, in the year that preceded the election of 1936, it was not easy for Roosevelt's supporters to feel sure of victory. A poll conducted by the *Literary Digest*, a popular weekly magazine, predicted a Landon landslide. Frightening voices on both the right and the left spoke out in harsh revolutionary terms when programs promised by the New Deal operated uncertainly, in fits and starts, or failed to materialize at all. A public unaccustomed to looking to presidents to solve every problem watched bemusedly as Roosevelt sought to project the image of a very accomplished sea captain, facing an unprecedented storm in an unfamiliar sea, commanding an inexperienced crew, who seemed determined to rebuild the vessel in the process of trying to salvage it. In the course of the campaign, Roosevelt's speeches took on an increasingly ideological tone; he appeared to be trying to increase the divisions he had once sought to heal.

The opposition set the tone of the campaign, and Roosevelt accepted it. He had worked successfully to moderate the pressures from the left in framing the legislation of the Second Hundred Days. Whether social security, taxation, and labor legislation could have gone further to the left than Roosevelt would allow them to is a moot point, although the contrast between his conservative legislative management and the radical language of his campaign makes judgment difficult. Yet, if one takes the campaign as the high point of the period, with the legislation of 1935 serving as the road to the peak, then one must acknowledge that the collapse that followed the 1936 election victory was remarkable. It also suggests that Roosevelt's initial reading of public opinion as cautious, if not conservative, was correct.

Part of Roosevelt's skill in the 1936 campaign lay in his remarkably shrewd selection of an enemy to attack: he ran against the Depression, and he blamed the Depression on Hoover and the Republican party. Landon's well-known progressivism became irrelevant, as did the radical criticisms of Coughlin and the successors of Long, to say nothing of the conservative Democrats—the Liberty Leaguers—led by Al Smith, who had broken with Roosevelt.

It was a masterful campaign but one that was, in some ways, destined to be very costly. Such phrases as "economic royalists" subjected the business community to an attack that even the progressives would not have dared launch, chiefly because they would have known how unfair it was to attack the business community as a single-minded monolith. Roosevelt's tactics, however necessary he may have thought them, increased the view that the New Deal and the nation's businessmen were permanent opponents. Both sides knew how untrue that was, and in practice they ignored it in their continuing relations. But the myth became part of the history of the New Deal. The result was that, for the next three decades of American politics, social and economic reform legislation would be burdened by an ideological conflict that bore little relation to the real need for social change. Not until popular attitudes toward radicalism shifted would the New Deal and Roosevelt be relieved of the burden; by then, paradoxically enough, they would be criticized for their inherent conservatism.

Roosevelt's assumption that the election victory had given him the power to deal decisively with the Supreme Court was based on a great many supportive letters from citizens. Cabinet advisers like Harold Ickes had also canvassed friends and associates and had come to the same conclusion. There would be sizable popular support for curbing the power of the Court. The opposition, they said, would emanate from that national minority that had never supported the New Deal in any case.

A number of options were available to the president. Constitutional amendment to limit the Court's power to oppose the president and the Congress was the most direct method but also the slowest. A constitutional convention to revise the basic document was a possibility but, from Roosevelt's perspective, the most dangerous. Who would come to such a national gathering? Not Madison, Hamilton, and Washington, certainly. More likely it would be Father Coughlin, the followers of Huey Long, and a rag-tag-and-bobtail collection of radicals from both the right and the left. Another, strictly behind-the-scenes, option was to press for congressional action to provide pensions for justices, thus encouraging them to retire. One had been suggested for Oliver Wendell Holmes when he retired in 1932 at the age of ninety, but, under the pressure of depression economies, nothing came of it. Holmes lived another three years, able to support himself, but still an example to his colleagues of the problems they faced in surviving long careers in public service. Two justices were known to be willing to retire, but Roosevelt could not publicly call on them to do so without embarrassing the Court by appearing to try to buy them off, even though this was certainly the least ideological solution.

Roosevelt's choice was legislative revision, a bill to reorganize the judiciary, and he submitted it to Congress on 5 February 1937. It included a number of provisions designed to speed up the entire process of judicial review by sending constitutional appeals more directly to the Supreme Court and allowing federal attorneys to enter lower courts to be heard before injunctions would be issued on grounds of unconstitutionality. It called for some increase in the number of judges at all levels of the judicial system and the assignment of district judges to expedite court business in congested areas. That part of the proposal did speak, in fact, to the problems that New Deal legislation had created for the entire court system. Thus far, it was not an attack on the judicial system itself but on its acknowledged inefficiency in face of the changes produced by the emergency. It was ideologically charged in one sense only. The emergency was raising a greater number of constitutional issues than the court system had ever had to handle. Judicial review was in danger of becoming more of a norm in the legal system than it had ever been before; in the past it had rarely been resorted to, for the justices were cautious about interfering in the legislative process. To that extent, constitutionality, and all of the complex historical issues contained in the problem of constitutionality, were being raised as they had not been since the eve of the Civil War. Even the judicial issues raised by progressivism had been confined largely to the constitutionality of state legislation. The possibility of a crisis of constitutional proportions within the federal system itself was not perceived as such until it was well under way. And then it was difficult to acknowledge.

What triggered the unexpected explosion was Roosevelt's decision to expand the membership of the Court itself. He asked for the authority to appoint a new justice for every justice aged seventy who chose not to retire, up to a maximum of six, thus expanding the Court from nine to a possible fifteen. Roosevelt's determination to justify his proposal on the grounds that the Court was overworked was unpopular with the justices; even those who had been searching for ways to support him were forced into a defensive posture. His failure to consult congressional leadership ahead of time was also costly; congressional leaders accustomed to helping with the compromises required by the emergency stepped back and reexamined their positions. Congressional dissidents, who had not yet found an issue to use in projecting their dissatisfaction, discovered that they now had what they wanted. The popular leader had become a dangerous leader.

Roosevelt's dealings with the public on the issue also suffered from what seemed a sudden disappearance of his customary skills. He waited a full month before seeking a public occasion for justifying his actions. The first was the dramatic Democratic Victory Dinner speech on 4 March 1937, the anniversary of his first inauguration. In his second inaugural address, delivered the previous January, he had suggested that the Court's interpretation of constitutionality was an obstacle to effective action, but he had proposed no remedy beyond pleading for more flexible views on the part of the justices; he had also reminded his audience that the year 1937 marked the one hundred fiftieth anniversary of the Constitution. That Constitution, he argued, "did not make our democracy impotent." Now, in March, he was ready to attack a bit more directly and even to toy with some of the fears, not only of his opponents, but of some in his partisan audience. He quoted a supposed conversation with a "distinguished member of Congress" who had come to see him about the problem of the judiciary. He spoke of a new "ambition in life," something greater than "having twice been elected president of the United States by very large majorities." His friend, he said, was now "sitting on the edge of his chair." "John," the President continued, "my ambition relates to January 20, 1941." Roosevelt coyly suggested that he "could feel just what horrid thoughts my friend was thinking." To relieve his friend's anxiety, he explained that he wished to turn over the White House to his successor with the assurance that he would preside over a "Nation which has thus proved that the democratic form and methods of national government can and will succeed." There would be no dictatorship, not even a third term. There need not even be a reshaping of the Constitution, only a new look at its functions and purposes.

Five days later, on the 9th, Roosevelt delivered a Fireside Chat on the subject. His approach was, oddly, less direct than that of his Victory Dinner speech. He chose to single out the gold-clause cases rather than the clearer obstructions of industrial and agricultural reform he had cited earlier. Having selected the gold issue as his focus, he proceeded to the historical metaphor many in his audience might have found resonant. "In effect, four Justices ruled that the right under a private contract to exact a pound of flesh was more sacred than the main objectives of the Constitution to establish an enduring Nation," he intoned, deliberately invoking the image of Shylock and seeming to recall, as well, William Jennings Bryan and the Cross of Gold. Louis Brandeis and Benjamin Cardozo, two of Roosevelt's strongest supporters on the Court, were Jewish; nonetheless, the utility of the metaphor, anti-Semitic overtones and all, was too tempting. The audience to which he wished to direct his statement appears to have been precisely the group to which Bryan appealed, at least to judge by the agrarian imagery on which the speech continued to build. The American Constitution was "a three-horse team" created by Americans "so that their field might be plowed."

The key to Roosevelt's position can be found in the persistent religious tone of his address. "I hope that you have reread the Constitution of the United States in these past few weeks," he urged. "Like the Bible, it ought to be read again and again." There it was. The Constitution is "an easy document to understand," he insisted, pushing his argument toward the expansive interpretation on which he wished to rest his case. Roosevelt's Constitution was the central document in the secular religion he saw as the spiritual foundation of American government. It was not the literal statement of an interpreted past nor a detailed map for the future. Nor was it to be, like the common law, a positivistic support of political pragmatism, though much of what followed in the debates looks a bit like that. Roosevelt's Constitution, like his Fireside Chats, functioned more like the Bible in the traditional family religious service, a part of daily life, the record of the past only in part, but the only sure support for the future. In that sense, the Constitution itself was not to be worshiped; it was to be used in worshiping the quality of life it was intended to promote.

It is worth pointing out that Roosevelt's approach fitted comfortably with a supportive campaign being launched elsewhere in government. The opening of the National Archives building provided a new official repository for the basic documents of American history. The Constitution and the Declaration of Independence, until then located in the Library of Congress, were now installed in cases made of marble and special protective glass, in which they were surrounded by a gas that would prevent their deterioration. The cases could be dropped into an underground vault in case of attack. Like the gold bars in the newly designed vaults at Fort Knox, Kentucky, the documents were to be treated as great national symbols. The strange paradoxes were all there. Government could devalue the dollar, prohibit gold-trading, and preserve, elaborately and expensively, the metal ingots on which the value of the currency was said to rest. Could one treat the Constitution similarly? Roosevelt obviously thought so. Yet the battle that ensued showed that Congress and the public wanted to preserve more than the Constitution. The Court's view of it had become the issue. Roosevelt's plan to change the Supreme Court was defeated.

Moreover, the damage was not contained, for the reaction to the so-called Court-packing plan spread to other issues. A bill to reorganize the executive branch of the federal government along lines recommended by a committee Roosevelt had appointed in 1936 had become caught up in the debate of 1937. Nearly all of the changes the committee proposed had been advanced by the progressives long ago, but they did in fact call for more effective presidential control of government. In defending them, Roosevelt again spoke of the survival of democracy and of more efficient management as the key to its survival; but in the context of the Court fight, the call for a stronger, more effective presidency raised the specter of dictatorship. The idea that in order to preserve democracy one would have to support a more authoritarian government was perceived as a threat. The defeat of the Court bill and the subsequent defeat of the first Executive Reorganization bill reflected the same fear of a strong presidency.

The Court broke the stalemate between itself and the president, but the series of actions by which it did so is not easily explained. The five-to-four decisions against the New Deal became five-to-four decisions in favor of New Deal legislation. In March 1937 Justice Owen Roberts, whose opposition to the New Deal had not been doctrinally consistent, began to vote in its favor. The logic of the Court's anti–New Deal positions should have led it to overthrow the National Labor Relations Act and the Social Security Act. Roberts' votes changed the direction. Years later new information suggested that Roberts' position had changed before the Court fight, not necessarily as a result of it. The change might, therefore, have been less the result of political pressure than of a gradual change of views in the light of the events of the emergency era. What one wag termed "the switch in time that saved nine" was only partly true. Roberts' switch may not have been as politically motivated as it seemed, and the Court's subsequent decisions with respect to the National Labor Relations Act and Social Security Act show that it was moving away from the strict interpretations it had been trying to establish. Only a change of mind can explain so important a shift. Roosevelt's assertion that he had lost the battle but won the war was also only partly true. The Court was now upholding the New Deal principle of greater government intervention, but the cost to Roosevelt's political control and popular support, while difficult to calculate precisely, was clearly heavy. New alliances had formed against him, made up of opponents who previously had had no platform of attack. They had it now.

Another step toward resolving the dispute with the Court had been quietly taken by passage of the Supreme Court Retirement Act on 1 March. On 18 May Willis Van Devanter announced his retirement, thereby creating the vacancy Roosevelt needed. In the coming years Roosevelt would fill a total of seven vacancies. His first appointee, Senator Hugo Black of Alabama, did not appear to be the preeminent jurist many New Deal ideologues had hoped for. Roosevelt's refusal to name Learned Hand, one of the outstanding judicial spokesmen of his generation, was based apparently on Hand's age and on Roosevelt's concern that, having emphasized the problem of age, he would be in danger of contradicting himself. Questions were raised about Black's brief membership in the Ku Klux Klan, but the issue died out.

The great ideological conflict, which reflected what was perhaps the most serious constitutional confrontation since the Civil War, was dissipated by a series of discrete political actions. The ideas those actions represented bore little or no relation to the wrenching theoretical issues the battle kept trying to resolve. Roosevelt's refusal to deal with the constitutional problem as a problem of ideological interpretation was in part responsible. He seemed explicitly to reject the contention that actions he and the Congress deemed useful and necessary could be raised to the level of principle the constitutional debate kept calling for.

The Supreme Court fight nonetheless crystallized and organized the previously fractionated opposition to the New Deal; it also provided the New Deal with the clearest example of the kind of triumph Roosevelt was capable of achieving. As the most radical language of Roosevelt's 1936 campaign had already suggested, he could castigate capitalists without rejecting capitalism; avoiding ideological language, he called instead for responsible group behavior. He managed the Court problem in essentially the same way. One vote was conversion enough.

To assert that Roosevelt saved American capitalism is thus to miss the point entirely. In the thirties most Americans perceived the government itself, not capitalist ideology, as the cause of their problems. That was the straightforward way the progressives had put the question, and it had not changed. Ineffective government—more specifically, ineffective leadership—seemed the real source of impending catastrophe. Yet for Americans, unlike Europeans, the form of government could not become an issue without generating reactions more likely to produce stalemate than revolution. Americans did not want a new constitution; they wanted the one they had to work. Roosevelt assured them that it would, and he provided the politics that proved him right.

The political programs and debates of the years from 1935 to 1937 thus pose for us the essential historical problem of the New Deal. This is most often put in the form of a question: Was the New Deal a revolutionary epoch in American history and, if it was, to what degree? The answers are by no means easy. The New Deal programs did initiate basic changes in American government. The most significant and lasting of them resulted from incremental reorganizations of more or less traditional programs already in existence at various levels of government, and most of these were the product of reform efforts that had started in the progressive period.

At the same time, the political arguments that took place all suggest considerably more revolutionary ferment than the programs themselves seem to reflect. Revolutionary changes were in fact taking place in various parts of the world. Dissidents in this country were suggesting the need for drastic changes here. The campaign of 1936 was carried on in a distinctly radical tone of voice. Above all, the Supreme Court of the United States was in fact declaring the major legislative programs of the New Deal to be in violation of the Constitution. Although few clearly wanted to put it this way, the accumulated decisions of the Court were acknowledgments of revolution. The Court had put the New Deal on trial and was delivering its verdict case by case. The New Deal was a revolution against the Constitution of 1787!

By 1938 the revolutionary phase of the New Deal was over. Roosevelt's efforts to influence the congressional elections in November proved nothing one way or the other. He did not succeed in defeating Walter George of Georgia or Millard Tydings of Maryland. John J. O'Connor of New York went down to defeat, but there were other reasons for that besides Roosevelt's influence. The Democrats lost seven Senate seats and eight seats in the House, giving the Republicans the first gains they had enjoyed since 1928. The Democrats remained in control of both houses. In Roosevelt's terms, it was a conservative control. His own popularity was still intact, but congressional support of his programs was being eroded by the dramatic economic recession that occurred in 1937 and by a growing fear of the power of the federal government. It was a fear fed by the Supreme Court fight and the battle over executive reorganization, although neither was clearly the cause of it. Amid declining industrial production and soaring unemployment, the call for more radical action was replaced by concern for what the supposed radical action of the New Deal had already done—or not done. Stalemate appeared to have arrived, and it was a stalemate that began to take on a life of its own.

The heroic use of presidential power, required by the recurring periods of international crisis and exercised by charismatic individuals, would be checked by congresses dedicated to meeting the needs of the folks back home, or at least those whose needs counted. The courts would step in from time to time, sometimes to fill the vacuum but increasingly to redress imbalances, even to govern.

In its last phase, the New Deal established a model of policymaking that became the norm in American political life for the next four decades.

8

Thermidor and the Third New Deal

THE DISTINCTIVE DIFFERENCES between Roosevelt's legislative programs of 1933 and 1935 have encouraged historians to take a systematic approach to the New Deal as a reform movement. Whether or not one accepts the definitions of a First New Deal and a Second New Deal, one can still see important differences between the initial emphasis on big industry and agriculture and the later concern with social reform.

This programmatic approach, however, makes analysis of the period after 1937 particularly difficult, and it tends to produce accounts that emphasize failure, impasse, and finally a preoccupation with the coming of the war. Yet from another perspective the period between 1937 and 1939 is as interesting and important as the preceding four years, and in many respects the politics of the period are a good deal closer to the kind of politics Americans since the New Deal have come to accept as normal. The radio, and his skill in using it, had given Roosevelt an independent source of political control that none of his predecessors had had. His talent in dealing with the press had helped make the White House the nation's number-one center for news. The White House beat had finally replaced the news offices on Capitol Hill as the plum job for professional news reporters. The president had become a figure to be imitated in comedy routines or played straight by the actors who mimed the leaders of the world in the *March of Time*'s radio dramatizations of weekly news events.

The traditional battle lines between presidents and congresses were redrawn by this transformation. Individual congressmen had no comparable access to nationwide audiences. Nor was Congress as a whole accustomed to seeing the president as the nation's chief policymaker. The competition for leadership between the White House and the Hill had always been played according to rules that depended on traditional political negotiation, patronage, party discipline, and the knowledge that presidential careers were limited by tradition to two terms, while congressional careers could last a lifetime. Roosevelt changed that, not simply by the fact that he served more than two terms but by the fact that, under his direction, the presidency assumed a position in the public's mind that shifted the balance of power.

In the years since the New Deal the American voter has come to accept the responsibility of electing presidents to make national policy and of selecting them on the basis of their popularity, while local constituencies elect congressmen to represent local interests and to join in protecting the country against the misuse of presidential authority. No other government in the world depends so much on the creation of conflict between the executive and legislative branches, and it is a conflict that cannot be resolved, as it can be in other democratic governments, by resignation of the executive or by elections called to settle disputed issues.

Roosevelt's second term illustrates the transformation with remarkable clarity. His assumption that the landslide victory had given him a popular mandate no president before him had ever received turned out to be completely wrong. The constitutional crisis created by the Court's opposition was not going to be resolved by increasing his power over the Court. Nor was his definition of the need for greater managerial authority in the presidency going to be met. He was not going to be the last president to misinterpret a reelection landslide as a mandate to wipe out his enemies and strengthen his control. However, the legislative defeats he suffered in 1937 through 1938 are perceived as serious defeats only if what happened is held to a standard of victory that later observers ought to know is impossible in American politics. Like the Court fight and the battle over the reorganization of the executive branch, the immediate defeats did not mean that the changes being requested by the president were not, in some important sense, going to happen, but the fact that they did not happen the way Roosevelt had wanted them to happen is a point of some significance, particularly if one takes Roosevelt's celebrations of his seeming victories at face value. Chief among the defeats he suffered was Congress's scuttling of his effort to transform the way presidents managed the presidency.

Roosevelt's habits of administration, particularly during his first term of office, have been described by some historians with an enthusiasm Roosevelt himself did not feel, certainly by the end of that term. All of the supposedly successful techniques—the duplication of assignments and the overlapping responsibilities that had aides working at cross-purposes—he had come to regard as makeshift necessities, not virtues. In the spring of 1936, conscious of the need to restructure the executive branch of government, he appointed a committee—formally known as the President's Committee on Administrative Management but more generally known as the Brownlow Committee, after its chairman, Louis Brownlow—to recommend new forms of organization; but he deliberately separated the work of the committee from the public-works planning group in the Department of the Interior and the cabinet-level Planning Board. He wanted it to be solely dependent on him and governed by his wishes, not by those of his cabinet.

The Brownlow Committee's report, which Roosevelt received right after the election of 1936, called for a major centralization of executive authority. Its most important recommendation, perhaps, was abolition of the independent regulatory commissions that Congress had been setting up ever since 1887. The members of such commissions were appointed by the president, but they were never clearly under his control; nor were they under the control of Congress, though they were subject to congressional oversight. The Brownlow Committee proposed that all such regulatory bodies should be put under the jurisdiction of their appropriate cabinet departments. It seemed like a logical and simple step, particularly in light of the concern over separation of powers; for the commissions had become quasi-judicial bodies, and their regulations tended to operate as laws, yet they were executive bodies.

The report also recommended the creation of a permanent planning board in the White House. This board would have jurisdiction over the various regional planning boards and the many regional offices through which the executive branch exercised its authority in states and cities across the nation. All such changes seemed logical enough, particularly in light of the great expansion of federal services that had taken place during the first term. Roosevelt talked to reporters about consolidating the PWA and WPA, for example, but he insisted that consolidations of this kind were for the purpose of making government more efficient, not simply to save money. Given the fact that Roosevelt's personal influence on the recommendations was great, and given the fact that the most essential proposals were all excised by Congress from the reorganization bill he finally got, the victory celebrations, both by Roosevelt and by those students of public administration who continued to praise the work of the Brownlow Committee, obscure the fact that Roosevelt had tried to bring off a genuine revolution and had failed to do so. It was a remarkable plan, and it raises a number of major questions about the kind of presidency Roosevelt thought the country really needed.

It is necessary, too, to see the reorganization plan in isolation from the dramatic events of the period in 1937 in which it was presented to Congress, for these events have also obscured its significance. First, the recession, which began in August 1937, created a new atmosphere of mistrust, since it raised doubts about Roosevelt's economic policies, and these doubts, in turn, evoked defensive language from the administration. Second, the legislative session in which Roosevelt made his greatest push for the reorganization plan was a special session, called because of the economic recession. Roosevelt tried to create the emergency atmosphere of yet another Hundred Days, but he failed. The conflict generated by the Court fight had taken its toll. Third, the background rumbling emanating from authoritarian regimes in Europe and Asia was growing not only louder but more threatening, and some critics heard echoes of this in Roosevelt's reorganization proposals. They accused him of trying to become a dictator, of leading the country down the road to either socialism or fascism.

The Brownlow Committee's arguments for more effective national management, for stronger leadership, for control of the political forces that made congressional prerogatives a deterrent to effective government, were all classical progressive arguments, but in the context of the events of the period they were pictured as attacks on democracy itself.

The increasing soundness of the economy between 1935 and 1937 had been cause for celebration, despite the political turmoil of the period. But the market slump that occurred in late summer, 1937, cut the mood like a knife. Republicans chafing under the onus of the "Hoover Depression" were more than willing to announce the "Roosevelt Depression." At least one of the causes of the recession was the cutback in federal spending Roosevelt had ordered to counter the inflation some of his advisers were forecasting. His motives could be ascribed either to an inherent conservatism that led him to seek the traditional balanced budget or to the beginnings of a commitment to the new ideas of economic management being pressed upon him. Conspiracy theorists—of whom Roosevelt himself was one—added their belief that the recession was a deliberate maneuver on the part of the business community to discredit the administration and fulfill a desire for revenge, generated by the intensity of the 1936 campaign. Roosevelt himself seemed angry and confused; he ordered his spokesmen to stop sounding falsely optimistic, like Hoover, but he was unable to find alternative language in which to couch his own hopeful pronouncements.

The relation between New Deal economic policies and the theories of English economist John Maynard Keynes is not as easy to define as accounts of the New Deal would sometimes have it. Part of the problem comes from the nature of Keynesian theory itself. Keynes's major book appeared in 1936, and it provided a generation of young economists with the mathematical concepts with which they would launch a revolution. Keynes's theory fitted beautifully with issues that had already emerged as central to an understanding of the Depression. The belief that capitalism had reached a point where it could no longer sustain full employment as a natural or automatic consequence of investment and expansion was an integral part of a number of theories— fascist, socialist, and Marxist. What Keynesian theory offered was an answer to the problem of stagnation that accepted stagnation as a permanent condition of modern industrialization but provided a method of coping with it that required no revolutionary political change. By taking over the role of investor for a time, government could provide the balance of support that private investment would periodically be unable to provide. What it is important to see, however, is that Keynesianism involved an acceptance of the permanence both of stagnation and of the need for government intervention to counter it. Such intervention was neither emergency nor temporary.

The idea of government support of the economy was not in itself so revolutionary. As we have already seen, Hoover and other American industrial leaders had been advancing proposals for public-works investment. Bankers like Marriner Eccles had suggested similar functions for banks, to enable them to lend in hard times as a way of supporting sound businesses during cyclical declines. A wide range of countercyclical experiments had in fact been part of American economic theory since World War I. What was new in Keynesian theory, to put it simply, was the willingness to downplay the inflation that government investment would produce. That, in turn, required a willingness to accept the currency manipulation that inflation would require, and that, to put it in the language that so frightened Hoover, made the gold standard obsolete at worst and highly manipulable at best. Deficit spending, inflation, and currency devaluation would thus become devices for government to use in managing the economy rather than the ultimate enemies they had always appeared to be. The theory thus attacked the traditional logic of capital investment without attacking capitalism. In a sense, the theory turned the value structure of government's function in a capitalist state on its head. The traditional role of government as nothing more than the protector of the stability of the economic instruments on which commerce depended was to be transformed into a new role. Government economists would become the manipulators of those instruments, not as a bunch of mere theorizers but as a band of scientists armed with mathematical models and statistical indicators.

All of these matters made for highly charged intellectual and emotional commitments on the part of those who debated the theory and the policies that came out of it—as, indeed, they still do; but Keynesian theory added one central element that gave it meaning beyond the debates. The mathematical models that the theory provided and the techniques it offered for predicting economic behavior gave government action a precision, or an appearance of precision, that economists in the past had rarely been able to claim for it. The relation between government and business would then be more than a factor that economists would passively observe; it would become a dynamic relationship that economists would dominate as direct policymakers. Economics as a policymaking science came of age.

American economists, businessmen, and government policymakers were ripe for this transformation; they had been looking for a more fruitful kind of relationship for years, but the peculiar hostility between business and government that characterized the whole antitrust movement had made it difficult to find a meeting ground acceptable to both. However, the absence of the kind of centralized institutional structures that characterized Keynes's Great Britain kept academic economists and industrial managers in the United States apart to such a degree that there was small likelihood that a single theory would dominate national policymaking. What one could get was influence, and the New Deal was influenced by Keynesian theory. When Roosevelt appointed Marriner Eccles to be governor of the Federal Reserve Board in 1934, he was not transforming the board into a Keynesian instrument, but he was placing at the head of the board a man whose inherent sympathies for compensatory spending were already such that during the 1937 recession that policy could be adopted. In the debates preceding this policy move, Henry Morgenthau, Jr., as secretary of the Treasury, the administration's spokesman to the banking community, was preparing to go before a meeting of the nation's bankers to promise even more cutbacks in government spending. Marriner Eccles proposed exactly the opposite. Eccles won.

The economic crisis of 1937 transformed the New Deal. It was not a dramatic transformation, like that of 1933 and 1935, perhaps because transformation was by now a familiar event. But in the stalemate that ensued, what later critics of American government would label "the deadlock of democracy" took its modern form. It was less a deadlock than the persistent threat of deadlock; it was a stalemate broken by movements on the political gameboard that brought about useful changes without giving victory to either side.

What could be called a Third New Deal emerged, and it became the norm for American reform politics. A reform-minded president, assuming that his election victory had given him a national mandate to produce more systematic programs of change, faced a Congress each member of which was inclined to believe that his constituency wanted him to protect its interests, regardless of change. While partisan commentators might be inclined to see the relationship as a distinctly adversary one—that of an embattled president being deliberately thwarted by a hostile Congress—the image is inexact. The president's programs would be determined ultimately by his ability to find in Congress a majority whose political interests happened to coincide with various elements of his programs. A congressional program was and would remain an impossibility, for the conflicting regional and local interests represented there made consensus difficult if not impossible to achieve. The responsibility of the president as a *national* leader was to find in that anarchy of interests a significant number of allies to lead to victory, not enemies to defeat. As Roosevelt's efforts at congressional purge in the off-year elections of 1938 tended to prove, a president's hostility to a congressional candidate did not necessarily affect voter attitudes. The ability to anger a president—to stand up to him, they might have said—could be a virtue.

Virtuous or not, chronic opposition to the nation's chief executive manager was an odd way of governing a modern industrial state. It played havoc with the very idea of providing the nation with a consistent program that could be tested in the course of events and be proved successful or unsuccessful. Administrative theorists like Louis Brownlow could look for rational procedures that reflected their analyses of administrative management—just as their successors in the field would look to American versions of bureaucratic concepts Max Weber called "rational legal"—but to little or no avail. The only administrative reforms that were politically possible or popularly acceptable were those that met the ultimate tests of the political process, and they were neither administrative nor bureaucratic, at least as far as the public was concerned. Programmatic policymaking, like election campaigns based on systematic debate of complex issues, was not part of the outcome of the New Deal. Yet the very name New Deal implied a program, and the American people had become aware of the need for programs even if the idea of programming itself seemed threatening. This ambivalence would continue to be a problem in the years to come.

If the first Hundred Days produced emergency legislation masquerading as planning, the third Hundred Days proposed, in an important sense, the opposite. Some features of the program were intended as an immediate response to the economic crisis of 1937, but the program as a whole reflected ideas developed over the previous four years and legislative concepts that had far-reaching implications.

Throughout his first term Roosevelt had sought advice that would provide him with better, more systematic, machinery for responding to changing economic and social conditions. His Brain Trust was the first New Deal group to examine methods and programs used in social science, public administration, and the professions of law and social work. The planning board he placed in the Public Works Administration was another. Far more sensitive than Hoover to the political implications of social-science planning, he nonetheless faced some of the same problems. Moreover, Hoover had the luxury of supporting a vaguely defined conception of democratic planning that would be consistent, somehow, with American democracy, but Roosevelt was soon made aware that planning was increasingly associated in the public's mind with undemocratic ideas.

Planning also threatened congressional politicians, though they did not see it chiefly as an ideological threat, despite their tendency to use ideological arguments in opposition to planning. What they feared struck closer to the bone. The distribution of resources and federal funds was the lifeblood of a congressman's career. To turn that distribution over to the president, let alone to scientific planners, was a direct threat to congressional power.

An uneasy public was inclined to support the president and to take planning in a project-by-project fashion, avoiding generalizations unless someone or something called attention to its allegedly authoritarian features. The early critics of social security, for example, had told the American people that they would be carrying cards that identified them by number, like Germans or Russians. When Roosevelt set up an Unemployment Census in August 1937, he had to keep explaining that it was voluntary, that the postcards to be sent through the mail to each household, asking fourteen questions about employment, were not an attack on privacy. Even after the recession began, he was still forced to defend this census, though accurate employment statistics were essential to any measurement of economic conditions.

In the first phase of the New Deal, planning, including government intervention, seemed essential to meet the state of emergency, but it was considered temporary. As the sense of emergency diminished, the sense of a need for planning declined along with it. Americans from widely differing ideological perspectives had, in the twenties, looked at Soviet planning as a useful idea, capable of adaptation to American conditions. But the kind of planning that Soviet and other nondemocratic, foreign, ideologies represented ran counter to two traditional American beliefs. One was that the nation's resources were available to all and not subject to control by any bureaucratic elite. That idea could be traced back into the Jacksonian years of the nineteenth century, when small-town, middle-class people had perceived centralized planning as a threat to expanding opportunity.

The other idea was that planning threatened the traditions of regional and local politics. Washington was not close to home. That was not where the grass roots were. The fear of big government was real and capable of being used effectively by a congressman from his Washington office. Yet the movement of the federal government into the development of local programs and local administrations continued, justified initially as a response to the emergency. Staffs of administrators came too, and they, despite their inexperience, had a new perception of what "normal" American government should be.

In Washington itself a group known as "Frankfurter's Boys" because most of them had been recommended by the then dean of the Harvard Law School, Felix Frankfurter, were the best known of a generation of managers who set a special stamp on the late phase of the New Deal. They saw themselves as further left of center than their admired leader, FDR, but just as committed to a reformed capitalism as they fancied him to be. They were critical of business leadership, but they were willing to devise methods of bringing about social and political change through the normal processes of American democratic government.

They saw Roosevelt's presidency as the vehicle for liberal reform. They perceived the conservatism of Congress not as ideological but as representing self-interested localism versus nationalism. From their perspective, presidential leadership was the only instrument capable of effecting reform. Terms like "administrative management" replaced the older concepts of economy and efficiency as a way of describing the need for a leader who would do more than execute programs designed initially by Congress. The Brownlow Committee had recommended giving the president greater authority to control budgeting, to select personnel, and to plan future programs. Congress, perceiving the threat to its own authority, rejected the original plan, although by 1939, with war on the horizon, it agreed to adopt some of the Brownlow Committee's recommendations. Among these was the legislative veto, which gave Congress the power to disapprove of reorganization plans within sixty days of their submission to Congress by the president. The legislative veto was not viewed at the time as a revolutionary device, but it was destined to become the key element in future congressional efforts to control the administration of government.

The Temporary National Economic Committee (TNEC), created by a joint resolution of Congress, was charged with investigating the effects the New Deal had had on the American economy. Both the president's staff and congressional aides were represented on the investigating teams. Public hearings were held from December 1938 to April 1940; the end result was more than forty major studies of the American economy. One important finding was that the New Deal had done relatively little to slow the trend toward concentration of economic power in ever larger—and fewer—corporations.

The WPA planning board that Roosevelt had authorized in 1933 was finally transferred to the White House by the reorganizations of 1939. Now known as the National Resources Planning Board, its activities suggest the very limited role that technical and scientific planning could play, given the realities of national politics. Yet, both the NRPB and the TNEC opened issues for discussion and utilized the skills of the new technicians. The government, by providing economists and other academicians with information to organize and study, significantly expanded knowledge and method in the disciplines themselves, even if, ultimately, it chose not to apply the research it had sponsored. Congress continued to resent planning and to see it as a threat; but the final product of the movement, the creation of the Council of Economic Advisers in 1946, indicates the degree to which even Congress was forced, finally, to accept the realities of technological change.

Roosevelt's increasingly public use of the Planning Board suggests the degree to which planning had begun to govern his approach to his second term in office, and the fate of the legislation he proposed allows us to see the problematic relation between politics and planning. Even before the August 1937 slump produced the call for a special session, he had begun to submit legislation that was intended to give him the managerial authority he needed. The Court plan and the reorganization bill were, as it turned out, poor opening shots to fire; and the return of the sense of emergency late in the summer only made matters worse. It is useful, nonetheless, to view the plans as plans, outside the political context in which they were introduced.

In February 1937, two days before he unleashed his attack on the Supreme Court, the president asked Congress to consider a six-year program of public works. One feature of the program was that the president was empowered to set priorities. Priorities, particularly for projects that might stretch out for years, outliving congressional and presidential terms of office, offended congressional interests as well as the interests of agencies accustomed to giving congressmen programs tailored to their constituents' needs and wishes. Congress also preferred to consider itself the authority on priorities. Every congressman had constituents who stood to benefit from public works, either as investors in the local industries that ultimately did the work or as members of the labor force the projects would employ. "Pork barrel" was the term that critics applied to such projects, but it was a term that all too easily ignored some of the basic realities of projects funded by the federal government.

The theory behind the idea of public works was that the works themselves were what was ultimately useful. Dams would produce electric power for consumers and industry. Highways would carry citizens where they needed to go and help farmers bring their products to market. Schools would educate children; hospitals would heal the sick; government office buildings would usefully house the growing government services. Yet, as legislators competed with one another for projects for their districts, the project itself became all-important. The long-range utility urged by planners could not beat the needs of a representative trying to satisfy the demands of a powerful construction company, which may incidentally have contributed generously to his campaign, or the pressures of a job-hungry labor force. The old progressive battle against "the interests" had tried to weaken that power; but local politics still depended on it, particularly when the Depression made "recovery" a more important slogan than "reform."

By the beginning of his second term Roosevelt was willing to try, at least, to be bolder in his demands on industry and clearer in his resolve to make Congress meet genuine public needs first. He began to fight highway construction programs, which he considered relatively inefficient in terms of employment. The mechanization of highway-building meant that the dollars spent on roads employed fewer men in actual work hours than other building programs. There were, of course, side benefits to industries that supplied materials for highways, but there were better ways to serve public need, Roosevelt believed, than by building roads. It was a losing battle. Roads were a complex political symbol. Huey Long's experience in Louisiana certainly suggested that backwoods farmers could be convinced that new roads would ease their lot and increase their profits. The excitement of the automobile, even for those who could not afford to keep up the ones they had bought in the boom years, still sold roads to those who could only dream of traveling. Roosevelt's refusal to see highway expansion as the answer to the problem of employment, let alone as the best form of public works, was based on a realism that even later generations would find hard to acknowledge. By the end of his administration, Roosevelt had decided that toll roads ought to be the basis for a national highway system, with the heaviest burden to fall on the transportation industries that actually profited from the roads, not on the driving public that simply enjoyed them. But that, too, was for the most part a losing proposition.

The pressures that mediated against any form of systematic planning were thus complex. From the earliest days of our national history, the distribution of national resources had been governed by local and regional politics. Reformers could from time to time shout "corruption" and indict individual scoundrels, but the system in fact satisfied political needs. Fulfilling those needs elicited gratitude. Beneficiaries of the system glorified representatives who could bring railroad lines through ambitious small communities and give them the promise of growth. The same was true of highways. The political techniques required to bring about such useful ends could be considered shrewd rather than corrupt. Contributions to the electoral campaigns of such representatives amounted to support of the community's well-being. Planning that attempted to circumvent so satisfying a system spelled trouble.

In June 1937 Roosevelt submitted to Congress a proposal to establish seven regional authorities for planning the use of natural resources. The program was modeled in part on the TVA. It would utilize seven major river-valley basins as centers for a comprehensive system of planning. Arguing that "it is not wise to direct everything from Washington," the president went on to assert that "national planning should start at the bottom, or, in other words, the problems of townships, counties, and states, should be coordinated through large geographical regions and come to the Capital of the nation for final coordination."

This new program was based on a report the National Resources Committee had issued in 1935. It was tied into the Executive Reorganization legislation and the Planning Board it recommended. This board was to serve as the "coordinating" body established in the reorganized White House. Roosevelt's language sought to emphasize the localization of authority, but the meaning of "coordination" was clear, particularly to those who saw in it the threat of centralized executive power. Sinclair Lewis's novel *It Can't Happen Here* had appeared in 1935. A futurist fantasy, it depicted the takeover of American government by a fascist dictator whose first action was the abolition of the states and their replacement by eight "provinces." Roosevelt and his advisers found themselves trapped in a dilemma. They denied a "balkanization" of American politics through the creation of regional groupings, but they were forced into the untenable position of having to deny a reality: the centralization implicit in the concept of national planning.

The deliberate association of the plan with river valleys was meant to deflect attention from the comprehensiveness of the program by trying to focus on the apparent success of TVA and the public interest in flood control, aroused by the devastating Ohio River floods in the early spring of 1937. The Dust Bowl crisis, triggered by summer droughts, also lent a certain popular attractiveness to the basic theme: the control of nature by man. Yet the underlying purpose of the plan went considerably beyond the issues emphasized in the president's rhetoric. His Planning Board had started with an interest in water resources and the efficient use of land, but it then became involved in such complex social and economic issues as urban development, public housing, and consumer needs. Like Hoover's Committee on Social Trends, some of whose members were among Roosevelt's advisers, the National Resources Planning Board rationalized its place in the American political tradition by emphasizing classical conservation issues; in reality, however, natural resources were only a jumping-off point to a comprehensive system of social and economic planning. Both Hoover and Roosevelt knew that, and both accepted the useful tactic. The Tennessee Valley Authority had hidden a number of revolutionary social aims in a network of power lines that did nothing more extraordinary than produce and transmit electricity—the only acceptable "revolution." Roosevelt's plan for the regional authorities was unable to disguise its revolutionary aims, and so it failed.

The fate of the Seven TVA's bill (the program of regional planning authorities) is a remarkably good example of the complex fortunes faced by plans and planners in the American political system. Despite the fact that the basic idea came from the Planning Board's report, the Planning Board itself repudiated the form the bill actually took. To its members, the original TVA represented the defects of decentralized planning, not the national planning system they were calling for. Seven more agencies, all as decentralized as the TVA, would only compound the problem. Members of the technical committee of the board who had written the regionalism report opposed even the idea of using river valleys as the basis for defining "regions," partly because they thought it was too restrictive. They had in mind a much more rational basis for defining regional boundaries.

The degree of Roosevelt's support of the bill is still something of a mystery—he moved back and forth on it and finally appeared to drop it altogether—but one can speculate about what he was trying to do. Waterpower and flood control were highly visible and very popular projects. News and magazine—and now newsreel—reports of the yearly flood devastation along the nation's waterways and the more recent devastation in the Dust Bowl—which a more effective use of water resources might end—contributed to a public awareness that was politically useful. Whatever the board's technicians thought about the scientific utility of river valleys, their political utility was beyond question.

What disappeared from view entirely was Roosevelt's effort to connect the regional planning system to his reorganization of the presidency. The Brownlow Committee report underplayed the connection, but all of the members of the committee, as well as the president, were perfectly well aware of the complex interdependence of the two. The abortive Third New Deal was, in fact, the presidency that would have been created out of the Brownlow Committee's National Resources Planning Board, in the White House, and the Seven TVAs' regional planning system, decentralized or not. Roosevelt could easily sacrifice some centralization of the regional plans if he could get the centralized planning board. As it turned out, he got neither. The compromise planning board that Congress finally agreed to in the Executive Reorganization Act of 1939 was never given the authority to do what the original report called for because it was never given the national administrative system the board's regionalism report had recommended. Without that system, it was essentially powerless.

Congress was not solely responsible for killing the plan, for Congress reflects public attitudes in their crudest, most self-interested form. Americans could feel a sense of sympathetic concern for the Dust Bowl farmers, forced by a calamity of nature to give up their homes and migrate west; but Californians could band together to keep them out of California. Americans could sense the tragedy of the mountain poor in Erskine Caldwell's *Tobacco Road* even as they laughed at what then seemed the scandalous language of one of the period's most popular Broadway productions; but urbanites saw such poor folks as the unjustified recipients of government money. Dams on the Columbia River could indeed produce cheap electricity, but they also interfered with the spawning habits of salmon essential to the local fishing industry. States that had been progressive enough to use their own resources to control flooding were not pleased to see neighboring states, which had not been so foresighted, enjoying federal funding.

Any national system designed to create equality would threaten opportunities for those who had enjoyed previous advantages at the same time that it revealed the depths of inequality that remained to be overcome. One could ask for a definition of the national interest, but it was a question capable of exciting cries of anguish and screams of rage. Congress accurately reflected the conflicts that inhibited the presidential search for consensus and control.

The turmoil of the legislative sessions of 1937 did not prevent important programs from getting through, although most of the ones that did were efforts to remedy defects perceived in earlier New Deal programs. As part of the piecemeal restructuring of the principle of NRA, Congress passed the Miller-Tydings Enabling Act, which allowed manufacturers to make price-fixing agreements with retailers ("fair-trade agreements" these were often called, though the name misstates the purpose); the idea was to prevent price-cutting competition. The president signed it reluctantly, but freedom from the restrictions of the antitrust laws was a crucial concern of the business community.

The creation of the Farm Security Administration was part of the administration's effort to provide support for those pushed out of farming by the big farm interests; these were the sharecroppers, the migrant workers, and the small farmers who had lost their land. That such programs threatened the entire social base of southern farming by promising aid to cheap or seasonal labor not only generated congressional hostility but pointed to what became an increasingly clear feature of New Deal and post–New Deal politics: the fact that the economy of one region, the South, exercised an extraordinary shaping influence on the entirety of American politics. Migrant workers were essential for the operation of the large farms characteristic of the South and California, where seasonal crop-picking required armies of workers for brief periods. Senator Harry Flood Byrd of Virginia had built a prosperous business on the development of fruit orchards, where the use of seasonal labor was brutally obvious. His congressional power and his ideological opposition to the New Deal were important in the post-1937 period.

The National Housing Act of 1937 set up the United States Housing Administration. To the federal mortgage subsidies and protections of earlier public-housing programs, the new act added ideas more clearly associated with social intervention by the federal government. Slum clearance and, perhaps more important, rent subsidies to tenants suggested that the government, by its control of the purse strings, could help decide the shape of cities and the economic composition of housing residents. The act made it clear that the government was acting only because local communities could not provide adequate housing for poor citizens through mortgages alone, and compromises were struck with the building trades and with local customs—specifically, racial segregation. Over the next decade even conservatives like Robert Taft would support government construction of public housing as a practical necessity.

Such successes, along with the Revenue Act of 1937, which closed loopholes in previous legislation that had permitted tax evasion, seemed to portend a good, or at least an efficient, season for New Deal efforts. The calling of a five-week special session, to deal with the recession, could indeed have been an effort to use the new emergency as leverage for an even greater expansion of programs.

The session, which ran from the 15th of November to the 21st of December, was a disaster. Roosevelt's opening message called for agricultural legislation to replace the overturned AAA, plus a law to establish standards of wages and hours. He also reaffirmed his need for executive reorganization and the establishment of the regional units his Planning Board had recommended— the so-called "little TVAs." Congress rejected the entire list of requests. An alliance of southern Democrats and Republicans gave Roosevelt what was, perhaps, the most significant defeat of his presidency—more significant, though less well publicized, than his battle with the Court.

The era of even limited executive autonomy was over. If emergency and economic crisis were going to be the new way of life, then Congress was determined to find its own way of dealing with them. For the moment, that way seemed to consist largely of thwarting the president. It would ultimately emerge as a form of competitive revision, in which Congress would reshape the president's programs according to its own internal political compromises.

An increase in defense appropriations, early in 1938, while modest enough by later standards, was significant in terms of government spending to provide employment. Yet, as in 1937, the emphasis on domestic concerns remained. The revived Agricultural Adjustment Act, passed in February, contained elements of the old AAA, such as acreage allotments, but there were echoes of McNary-Haugenism as well. The act introduced crop insurance, "parity payments," and the "ever-normal granary" concept, according to which years of crop failure would be balanced by years of surplus, because the government would purchase and store the produce of "fat years" in order, supposedly, to sell it in "lean years." The obvious biblical reference to Joseph in Egypt had a certain appeal to the traditionally devout farm public.

Other legislation of 1938 met with considerable opposition. Roosevelt succeeded in obtaining a new emergency relief appropriation to expand WPA rolls and to provide funds for "pump-priming" to combat the business recession, but he did so only over loud objections from Democrats as well as Republicans. The Revenue Act of 1938 significantly reversed progressive tax policies Roosevelt had been trying to press. He allowed it to become law without his signature. The most important piece of legislation to bear the rapidly dimming mark of the New Deal was the Fair Labor Standards Act, which established a minimum wage of forty cents an hour, a maximum work week of forty hours, with time-and-a-half for overtime, and a minimum working age of sixteen. These items, which carried echoes of NRA, did not have the full backing even of labor or of Roosevelt's liberal advisers, some of whom feared that the wage floor might become a wage ceiling.

Congressional hostility to the administration's efforts to strengthen New Deal programs, particularly the WPA, was in part motivated by the increasingly popular suspicion that government agencies and labor organizations were filled with radicals. Caught up in and confused with a generalized popular fear of infiltration by foreign ideas, radicalism, both real and imagined, could serve as a reason for attacking projects that could be labeled radical or identified with supposedly radical causes. The House Committee to Investigate Un-American Activities, under the chairmanship of a Texas Democrat, Martin Dies, was created to investigate Nazi, fascist, or communist organizations or anything that could be called "un-American." The atmosphere was filled with strong fears of unnamed and unidentifiable invaders. On 30 October 1938, a Sunday evening, Orson Welles broadcast a dramatization of H. G. Wells's "The War of the Worlds" that set off what was virtually a national panic, despite the announcer's clear statement that it was fiction and despite the easy identifiability of what had become one of the medium's most popular voices. Residents of one block in Newark swarmed into the streets, faces covered with wet towels and handkerchiefs to protect themselves from the poison gases of the "Martian" invaders. The event evoked subconscious fears, as though the recollection of the first war remained, rankling in ways that called for a peaceful resolution that the world of 1938 could not provide.

The fear of internal subversion aroused during World War I had not ended with the war. The Russian Revolution and the Red Scare of 1919–20 had helped establish it as a continuing part of American life in the postwar era. The controversy surrounding the trial and execution of Nicola Sacco and Bartolomeo Vanzetti, two Italian anarchists, was based less on whether they had in fact been guilty of the Braintree, Massachusetts, robbery and murder of which they were accused than on whether their status as immigrants with radical beliefs had prevented them from receiving a fair trial. From the day in May 1920 when they were arrested until their execution in August 1927, the two served as symbolic reminders of the American nativism the war had triggered.

From 1920 to 1933 such actions were associated with a nativist Americanism many attributed to bigotry or naïveté; but by the mid-thirties a subtle change had begun to take place, and, by the end of the thirties, an intellectually supported Americanism had begun to emerge. The Americanism once promoted by American Legion attacks on history schoolbooks and by the at times tendentious energies of groups like the Daughters of the American Revolution was being transformed into a supportive patriotism with a much broader intellectual base. This had happened before. At least as far back as the progressive period it had been possible to graft radical reform on a very American root stock by appealing to Jefferson as the architect of the idea of useful revolution. Many of Roosevelt's followers saw him as a Jeffersonian revolutionary, and the tone he adopted in his 1936 campaign convinced them that they were right.

Between 1936 and 1940 there was a remarkable stirring of interest in the American past, a search for roots. Universities strengthened their course offerings in American history, literature, and art. American liberals, searching for an intellectually respectable kind of nationalism—one quite different, indeed, from the flag-waving nationalism of the American Legion and the D.A.R.—now read colonial history in a new way. In the twenties and before, it had been fashionable to dwell on the repressive Puritanism of the colonial mind; now the emphasis shifted to the eighteenth-century rationalism—and radicalism—of the Founding Fathers. Roosevelt's critics had called him a traitor to his class. Now he could be defended as one of a long line of religious liberals, the inheritor of one of the oldest traditions of American reform.

Popular interest in the past was stimulated by various celebrations of the one hundred fiftieth anniversary of the revolutionary and formative era of American history. Restoration projects, some of which were begun in the twenties, were now reaching completion. The reconstruction and preservation of George Washington's home at Mount Vernon had been under way for many years, and the opening of a new museum there in 1928, to house the growing collection of Washington materials, pointed to the increasing sophistication and professionalization of historic preservation. So did the remarkable reconstructions and restorations at Williamsburg, Virginia. The opening of the National Archives building in Washington climaxed the new approach, which emphasized scholarly accuracy.

The intellectual basis of New Deal liberalism is thus a complex mixture of historical conservatism, the search for an American radicalism, and the reform idealism that carried over from the old progressivism. The influence of revolutionary events abroad complicates what is already difficult enough to understand. The Spanish Civil War, which broke out in 1936, produced divisions in the American intellectual community between those who saw it as another stage in the European working-out of historical class conflicts—and therefore an event we ought to stay out of—and those who saw it as the beginning event in a war that would ultimately threaten liberal democracy throughout the world. The fact that both the Nazi government and the Soviet Union were involved in the conflict on opposite sides helped render judgment even more difficult. Yet the division itself is important. If American history was based on its own peculiar processes of development, then Americans were better off isolated from events that could only damage them. If the United States was now part of an interdependent world civilization, then it could not help being part of what happened elsewhere. The title Hemingway chose for his novel about the Spanish Civil War, *For Whom the Bell Tolls*, was taken from a poem of John Donne's that put the issue very clearly: "Never send to know for whom the bell tolls. It tolls for thee."

The voting for the 1939 New York Drama Critics' Circle award underscored the intellectual division. Robert Sherwood's *Abe Lincoln in Illinois* lost to Lillian Hellman's *The Little Foxes* by one vote. Hellman was defining her position as a critic of American materialism, and Sherwood had, in his earlier plays, explored similar critical ground. His Lincoln play, however, was a study in the tragedy of human leadership; we leave Lincoln on the eve of his journey to greatness and to death, portentous but unmistakably noble. Sherwood would go on to become one of Roosevelt's wartime speech-writers, while Hellman would move toward the group that envisaged a new international salvation.

In its late phase the New Deal sought to present to the public an understanding of social injustice that was neither explicitly nor implicitly revolutionary. By contrast with the Federal Theatre Project's bluntness, the photographic essays that Ben Shahn and Walker Evans prepared for the Farm Security Administration were moving depictions of poverty that touched emotions deeply without blaming or calling for solutions. Equally significant in artistic terms were the productions of the United States Film Service, which began as a branch of the Resettlement Administration in 1935, moved into the Farm Security Administration, and ended up as part of the Federal Security Administration after the reorganizations of 1939. Supported by the president as part of the New Deal's effort to educate the public, the Film Service under Pare Lorentz produced some of the best innovative art sponsored by the New Deal. Such films as *The Plow That Broke the Plains* in 1936, *The River* in 1937, *The Fight for Life* and *Power and the Land* in 1940, and *The Land* in 1941 utilized a wide range of talent. Virgil Thomson wrote the musical scores for *The Plow* and *The River*; Robert Flaherty was responsible for narration, script, and direction for *The Land*; and Pare Lorentz did direction, script, and editing for *The Plow, The River,* and *The Fight for Life.* These documentaries were funded by and for the government. Unlike the newsreel, which sought simply to reproduce newsworthy events, these films were intended to affect judgment, to stimulate attitudes and responses on public issues. It was education, to be sure, but for purposes designed and supported by the state. In short, it was propaganda.

Yet the idea of Americans as a whole, united people was belied by old nativist prejudices against Jews, Catholics, Orientals, and other groups and, far more, by the long and painful oppression of the Negro people. The inability of the American government to deal with the suppression of Negro rights, long written into local laws, came into the open as the conflict hardened between the president and the southerners within his own party. The options open to Roosevelt were complicated even further by the emergence of foreign policy as a critical issue, for in this area the southern Democrats were his most reliable allies.

The southern filibusters that continued to kill efforts to establish federal laws against lynching were inevitable, yet slow steps were being taken in the Federal courts to find ways of bridging the gap between state control of local justice and federal responsibility for civil rights. The *Scottsboro* case, in which nine Negroes were tried and convicted in Alabama in 1931 for raping two white girls, became a *cause célèbre* of the period. Defenders said that the charges were trumped up; the other side pointed to Communist lawyers on the defense team. The incident and its outcome, drawn out over succeeding decades, illustrates how deeply the divisions went and, what is perhaps more important, how helpless the political system then was for dealing with them. The Supreme Court twice overturned aspects of the trial in landmark decisions that would have more far-reaching effects on criminal justice than on the lives of the Scottsboro nine. The case was sent back for rehearing because the

Supreme Court questioned the provision of proper legal counsel and the methods used to select the jury; both issues had previously been reserved to state governments.

By 1937 four of the men had been released. Four more remained in jail for still another decade. The last was freed, finally, in 1950; but nine lives were damaged or effectively destroyed by what had clearly been a miscarriage of justice from the beginning. Yet the actual power of the federal government to intervene was limited. Formal action by the Supreme Court was still restricted to the power to force the State of Alabama to retry the case. Even a letter from Roosevelt to the governor of Alabama, asking him to free the remaining defendants late in the case, still had to be couched as a "friendly" letter, containing respectful advice only. On the race issue, as on so many other national issues, federalism still meant the supremacy of local governments with regard to powers—and prejudices—traditionally reserved to them. Not for another twenty years would presidents consider using federal officials, let alone federal troops, to resolve such issues, nor would the Supreme Court put them in the position of having to do so.

Southern opposition to Roosevelt's programs increased along with the increased national publicity being given to extreme forms of racial oppression in the South, chiefly, of course, lynching. The South needed federally funded programs, just as other regions did, but it needed to be able to restrict Negro access to them. Other regions of the country could be almost as restrictive in their own ways, but few commentators were calling attention to that. Periodic episodes of southern violence toward blacks dramatized the South's special problem, but many northern and western supporters of federal programs looked equally askance at New Deal liberalism if liberalism meant racial equality.

The American public was also being made more aware of repression in other parts of the world. Newspaper accounts were increasingly full, and these were supplemented by the weekly newsreels and the excellent photographic reports in *Life* magazine. Americans were seeing threatening behavior at home and abroad—a world in turmoil.

The 1936 Olympics raised the issue of Hitler's racism in the context of an American sports world that was still racially segregated. The Negro baseball league and the newly formed Harlem Globe Trotters basketball team were not taken entirely seriously, but runner Jesse Owens won medals for the United States in the Berlin games in 1936, and boxer Joe Louis finally beat Max Schmeling. Radio and newsreel coverage had begun—extremely cautiously—to create a national consciousness of the black athlete as an American hero.

When Roosevelt suggested that the money being earmarked by Congress for the Dies Committee might well be shared with La Follette's Civil Liberties Committee, he was told in no uncertain terms that there would be no

money for civil liberties. Roosevelt came to believe that the solution to the
South's racial problems lay in economics. By underwriting industrial—and,
when the time came, defense—spending in the region, he hoped to provide
an alternative route to reform. Jobs would lead to votes, and votes, in time,
would lead to rights. President Truman's later successful use of military
installations in the South as a wedge to secure desegregation suggests that
Roosevelt was headed in the right direction.

Eleanor Roosevelt's championship of minority rights now assumed special
importance. It is difficult to say whether her publicly voiced opinions were
deliberately intended to make up for the president's silence or represented
her independent views. Probably they were both. Nevertheless, from 1937
on, she was able to make assertions about minority rights that her husband
could only imply. Women of her social standing were traditionally concerned
with such causes, but she used methods to support them that no previous first
lady would have employed, including a newspaper column (entitled "My
Day") and a traveling and speaking schedule designed to bring her before
groups the president was not likely to reach. She attained a position in the
limelight that made her newsworthy on her own, and she attracted criticism
for her stands on many controversial issues. When the Daughters of the
American Revolution refused to rent their Constitution Hall in 1939 for a
concert by a black soprano, Marian Anderson, Eleanor Roosevelt resigned
her membership in the organization, and Harold Ickes, the Secretary of the
Interior, arranged for the concert to take place on the steps of the Lincoln
Memorial, to dramatize the situation. Mrs. Roosevelt described the affront to
the singer in her column, and though she chose not to mention the offending
organization by name or to identify the hall, the newspaper reporters had no
difficulty figuring out who was involved.

Four years later the D.A.R. opened Constitution Hall, not only to Marian
Anderson but to its first integrated audience; but it took this step simply to
acknowledge a previous wrong, not to signal a new social attitude toward
Negroes on the part of the D.A.R. Like many of the stages on the route to
reform, this event was less the result of a long-range intention than the
product of a mood generated by immediate circumstances—in this case the
wartime sense of fellowship, plus the fact that by 1943 even the D.A.R.
membership knew that Anderson's voice was one of the miracles of its time. It
is perhaps worth noting that by 1955, when the Metropolitan Opera finally
welcomed her to its stage, her miraculous voice was nearly gone.

Not only minority groups and labor dissidents, unprotected by union
power, but the poor and the oppressed in general came to look on Mrs.
Roosevelt not as an extension of presidential power but as embodying the
hope for what presidential power might someday accomplish. She prodded
and goaded and annoyed in ways that neither the public nor the president

they had elected to represent them found altogether comfortable. If the president from 1938 on tended at times to be ill at ease and uncertain about the domestic response to the growing crises, Mrs. Roosevelt's attitudes and activities reflected a classic Victorian female certitude. Yet, as her much more outspoken practices suggest, the benefit to be gained by speaking out in the face of political opposition and popular prejudice had to be measured against the costs to her husband's political maneuverability and public esteem.

In some crucial respects, it was Eleanor Roosevelt's positions on social and moral issues that post–New Deal young liberals—Hubert Humphrey, Eugene McCarthy, George McGovern, even Adlai Stevenson—remembered as the legacy of the New Deal. Franklin Roosevelt's willingness to champion liberal causes was limited to what was politically practical and publicly acceptable; this was the legacy effectively represented in the political careers and attitudes of Lyndon Johnson and John F. Kennedy.

Like most Americans of the thirties, the Roosevelts saw solutions for the problems of the chronically underprivileged as lying somewhere between benevolence and rights; probably they saw them as matters to be met by humanitarian responsibility rather than by law. Like most Americans they saw little relation between domestic attitudes and the events being played out abroad. Parallels tended to be obscured by the overriding fear of Hitler as a leader and Nazism as an increasingly militaristic opposition to world order and tranquillity.

International events themselves provided background for mass fears. In late August 1938 Prime Minister Neville Chamberlain met with Hitler, and the resulting Munich settlement promised "peace in our time" and brought relieved and congratulatory messages from Roosevelt and other world leaders. Then the Armistice Day riots occurred in Austria and Germany; roving bands of Nazis looted and burned Jewish synagogues, businesses, and homes—acts of mass vandalism one had to go back centuries to find duplicated in Western society. Roosevelt's formal message to Germany—the strongest such statement ever made by a president to a nation against which no hostilities were planned or even contemplated—had little effect. Roosevelt was later criticized for his failure to open the doors of America to the victims of the atrocities, but his efforts to find some acceptable "method" for doing so were stymied by traditional opponents of immigration, by the anti-Semitism that WASP America had always practiced politely, and by the fact that an economically depressed nation seemed to be in no position to increase its labor force by welcoming Jewish refugees. The suggestion made to Mussolini, that he allow Italian Jews to emigrate to Ethiopia, was angrily rejected. (This proposal illustrates the continuing popularity of the "homeland thesis," which saw geographical identity in some form as the answer to the problems of minority groups.) The growing horror of Hitler's Germany produced shock in societies accustomed to associating mass atrocities only with backward or primitive societies. Unable to digest such horrors, many preferred not to believe.

A marked increase in American anti-Semitism made it even more difficult for the government to show concern for the Jews. Restrictive quotas in the universities and professions and "restrictive covenants," which prevented Jews and others from buying houses in certain neighborhoods, had long been used. Now, in the late thirties, the want-ad columns of newspapers showed a remarkable upsurge of job opportunities "for white Christians only." Queried on its reason for refusing to employ Jewish women as telephone operators, a New York company explained that the decision was based entirely on physiology: their arms were too short to manage the switchboards. Advertisements for hotels and summer camps carried such coded statements as "restricted clientele" or "near Christian churches" to make their exclusivity clear.

Despite a universal desire to stay aloof from events abroad, these events affected—and often divided—American attitudes in numerous ways. *Time* named Hitler its man of the year in January 1939, but it did not use the traditional portrait as its cover illustraton. Instead there was a picture of an organ loft in a medieval cathedral. A tiny figure at the console, his back to the viewer but identifiable by uniform, played an instrument the pipes of which supported a huge wheel from which naked bodies hung. Figures in clerical garb stood in the background. *Time's* compromise—it had tried to base its yearly selection on importance rather than moral judgment—did not please all of its readers. Some objected to the implication that the German churches had accepted Hitler's deeds without protest. Others objected to the choice of Hitler in the first place, although it was certainly clear by January 1939 that Hitler, above all other men of the era, was controlling the course of world events.

The opening of the New York World's Fair in 1939 symbolized uncertainty about the future at the same time that it marked, in effect, the end of the Depression. Former stage designer Norman Bel Geddes created a memorable exhibit for General Motors that surveyed the future of the motor age from the perspective of the new city, an efficient urban environment linked to the countryside by highways that used scenic beauty as the stage setting for newly mobile Americans. The parkways built by the WPA along the lakefront in Chicago and the river in New York had already demonstrated the feasibility of such wonders. But there was a sense of strident urgency in the air, a sense that industrialism *had* to work. The same thing had been true at the Chicago fair, six years earlier, but then it was the Depression that inspired fear. Now there was a war on the horizon.

The summer visit of the king and queen of England, George VI and Elizabeth, generated a steady flow of headlines as they moved through Canada—where they visited the Dionne quintuplets, the five-year old sisters turned into a public-relations spectacle—and thence to Washington for a state visit to the president. Roosevelt took them to his Hyde Park estate for a good old American Fourth of July weenie roast on the immaculate lawn, overlooking the aristocratic landscape of the Hudson River. The royal visit to America, the first by a reigning British monarch, thus subtly joined the traditional Anglo-American aristocracies. It was intended to signify an alliance still beyond official consummation in an atmosphere at once sympathetic and intensely isolationist.

One of the most remarkable intellectual migrations of the century was also under way. Musicians, novelists, scientists—some of them "greats," like Arturo Toscanini and Thomas Mann, long accustomed to acceptance by American audiences, but many of them young professionals on the threshold of careers cut short by Hitler's repressions—fled their European homelands and took up residence in the United States. Large numbers of them resettled in American universities and became part of an intellectual transformation of America as significant, perhaps, as anything since the seventeenth century. Later commentators were inclined to emphasize the importance to atomic physics of Albert Einstein and Enrico Fermi; but their presence, critical as it was for the American development of the atomic bomb, was only the most dramatic instance of a phenomenal revolution.

Looked at from a distance of more than four decades, the impact of what was happening abroad is clear by 1939, before the outbreak of war in Europe and certainly before there was any discernible American consensus on world events; but the politics of the period, particularly as the election of 1940 approached, made it difficult then to see the direct impact that those events were in fact exerting.

By 1939 Congress was in open rebellion against the WPA, which had become the popular symbol of New Deal radicalism. Congress drastically cut administration requests for relief appropriations and forced a reduction in WPA rolls. It abolished the Federal Theatre Project and set an eighteen-month limit on the length of time one could be continuously employed by the WPA. The congressional reaction brought a reaction of its own, in the form of a nation-wide strike of WPA workers, which raised all of the essential issues of the meaning of public employment in New Deal terms. Were WPA workers employed as part of a permanent labor force funded by the government? Were they then entitled to rights that other workers enjoyed? Or were they public dependents in need of temporary aid—of charity or a dole, if one wanted to call it that—and hence in no position to claim such rights? Equally important, what was their status as citizens with political interests and rights? A society still dominated by an agrarian perspective and a middle-class work ethic was not inclined to view government employment as useful. Congress shared the public's hostility, and the WPA strike of 1939 seemed to underscore the basic unacceptability of the idea that those who were unfortunate enough to need public support had legitimate demands to make, let alone rights to defend. Accusations that they had engaged in political activities allied them, in the public's mind, with the traditional recipients of patronage dispensed by corrupt urban political "machines," and this led finally to the Hatch Act of 1939, which forbade political participation by federal employees below the top policymaking echelons.

The congressional rebellion against the WPA reflects an even more profound effect of New Deal politics. The fear of bureaucracy, of intellectuals managing government, and now of the very concept of government planning was no longer confined to a conservative minority. The factors that appeared to link bureaucracy and government expansion to intellectuals and radicalism were part of what Hoover had called "regimentation." Congress passed the Reorganization Act of 1939 and even gave Roosevelt his Planning Board, but congressional leaders proudly asserted that they and not the White House had written the act, despite the fact that Roosevelt had called in the Brownlow Committee, which had written the first act, to implement the new one. Always suspicious of the whole "Brain Trust" idea, Congress accurately reflected the popular belief that government should be kept uncomplicated and that the popular will should be the ultimate arbiter of public needs and the means of satisfying them. The series of Frank Capra movie comedies, from *Mr. Deeds Goes to Town* in 1936 to *Mr. Smith Goes to Washington* in 1939 and *Meet John Doe* in 1941, sounds variations on the same theme of innocence triumphing over manipulative politics in a victory of recurrent populist purity and small-town virtue. The newspaperwoman in *Meet John Doe*, who begins as the agent of evil and then, like some perverse Lilith, is seduced by the virtue of her intended victim, articulates the great American dream: the return to lost innocence.

The American people felt that their political system and its institutions were good but that politicians could be evil. Roosevelt countered by skillfully playing the role of the simple man who could refer to his wife as "the Missus" and speak of conversations with his gas-station attendant, implying that his life was no different from the lives of ordinary citizens. He could refer to himself as a farmer as though the crops produced on his Hyde Park land were like the crops of any Kansas wheat-grower. Yet between the "ordinary man" in the White House and the ordinary men on the Hill, a new group of intermediaries had begun to develop—specialists, experts, or, pejoratively, "bureaucrats." Earlier public consciousness of the government employee had been limited largely to the "civil servant," a term already glorified by two generations of civil-service reformers. The rest were political appointees, beneficiaries of patronage, looked on not as professionals but as products of a system no one admired. The patronage army that had for generations been accepted as one of the costs of urban government, to be subjected to periodic attack by reformers but still the basic economic support of significant groups in the population, suddenly seemed to include a federal work force that did nothing useful.

By 1939 "bureaucrats" could also be identified with labor radicals who engaged in politics and sought to establish a clear interest for themselves in the making of federal policy. Such politics, as exemplified by the WPA, were new on the American scene. Playwrights working for the Federal Theatre Project openly criticized American values and sought to use drama to define new ones. Social criticism like this, now identified with political radicalism, opened the administration to attack by those who found the New Deal programs threatening.

As the election of 1940 approached, Roosevelt wrapped himself in a silence no one knew how to interpret. He himself seemed puzzled and unsure in the weeks before the summer conventions, issuing conflicting statements regarding his own preferences for a successor to the presidency. He would not be a candidate, he insisted to friends and associates. Characteristically, he emphasized personal reasons for not continuing in the presidency, avoiding the third-term issue and the historic barrier it represented. His public statements tended to center on foreign affairs as he moved the country toward support of the increasingly embattled British and French; for the European war, stalemated and slow through the winter, was moving toward spring offensives and counteroffensives. Reporters quoted White House visitors to the effect that Roosevelt's choice was his secretary of state, Cordell Hull, but journalists and news analysts, seeking to describe the soft-spoken, dignified Tennesseean, were hard pressed to find words to make him seem a suitable heir-apparent.

Yet there was no dynamic Roosevelt to observe either, particularly after the Republican candidate, former Democrat Wendell Willkie, began a nationwide tour that revealed, quickly and persuasively, a warm and appealing intelligence and enthusiasm that were more than a match for the incumbent. Roosevelt's silence frustrated not only those looking for a battle but nervous advisers, who thought this presidential tactic was a mistake. Roosevelt chose not to battle for his third term, from the nomination, which he insisted take the form of a draft, until very close to the election itself, from which he deliberately distanced himself, busy being president and commander-in-chief. His aloofness seemed to fuel the panic and hostility of those who saw the shadow of tyranny in the breaking of the third-term tradition, and the campaign grew bitter and ugly as the election approached.

Willkie's line on foreign policy deftly skirted the center of the isolationist issue by arguing that the president had made secret agreements with foreign governments that would draw the United States into the war. Pressed finally to respond, Roosevelt informed a Boston audience that American boys would not be sent into any foreign wars—a statement he had made before. Those who wanted to see significance in his omission of the phrase "except in case of attack" were free to do so, though Roosevelt himself acknowledged that such an attack would mean that the war was no longer foreign.

In the Roosevelt of this period we see a conflict that reflects confused American attitudes. It is clear that he was increasingly sensitive to conservative criticism and even sympathized to some extent with the view that reform had gone far enough. Public-opinion polls supported that position, and some of Roosevelt's comments at this time indicate that he not only responded to this public attitude but shared it. At the same time, there is evidence that he was frustrated by political limitations, that he remained compassionately aware that there were fundamental problems still to be faced. The ill-clothed, ill-housed, and ill-fed remained, and government was still their only hope.

Roosevelt defeated Willkie in the election of 1940 but did so by the smallest plurality of his career—indeed, the smallest of any election since 1916. That was partly due, certainly, to concern over the third-term tradition, but it was also due to a problem that neither Roosevelt nor any of his successors could solve. The American fear of government had always to be measured against the American need for government. Expanding the national system, let alone trying to rationalize the expansions that had, from time to time, become necessary, posed a threat to something: to individualism, if one wanted to be philosophical about it; to the power of local politics, if one wanted to be more realistic.

The first two phases of the New Deal had sought for a balance between expansion and rationalization by basing new national programs on older, locally based reform programs. Increasingly, however, the experts who advised Roosevelt saw the limits of that method. Some of them continued to look for ways to bring new concepts in under the old umbrellas, but others were willing to have the need for changed conceptions announced openly and frankly; yet both groups saw the power of presidential leadership as the essential power. That the president himself saw his power as much more limited—a more realistic view—made him appear either as a secret conservative or a frustrated liberal. That on occasion he would angrily refer to his advisers as "longhairs" says something more profound about his actual point of view than one might at first be inclined to think. He was far less willing to see government as inherently benevolent than were many of the younger generation of New Dealers. The art of politics, as he had known it since his youthful days in the New York state legislature, had not changed. It had not been replaced by a profession of government—civil-service reform aside—nor did he intend that it should be. His attitude toward public opinion rested always on maintaining fundamental agreement with it, not on an elitist commitment to countering it with better knowledge.

Thermidor, the Third New Deal, had arrived. Roosevelt's first plan for his second term had failed and failed badly. The plan for a genuine regionalization of American government that would have made the presidency an effective

administrative agency for delivering federal services to state and local communities had fallen victim to two historical fears. One was the fear that
identified rationalization with dictatorship and fascism. The other was the fear
that rationalization would destroy state and local control of the federal government's power to distribute federal resources. Congress had always controlled
that power. Under the gradual pressures of technological change, it had
created various commissions and had managed its relation to the offices in the
executive branch in ways that enabled it to retain some form of control.
However corrupt and politicized that control might be, it was still preferable
to turning control over to the president. Dictatorship and fascism were the
terms that killed Roosevelt's plan, but they were little more than new buzz-
words in a very old political battle.

The third New Deal that did in fact emerge thus exhibits a much more
familiar pattern of American politics. It established a pattern of adversary
politics that made Congress responsible for negotiating the local and regional
adjustments to the national policies the president was advocating. If, in the
process of that adjustment, national policies became less rational than their
architects had planned and were perhaps even markedly changed, that, too,
was part of the pattern. As a reform movement, the New Deal had gone as far
as most Americans wanted it to go. Whether the president shared that feeling
remained a puzzle. Apparently, he was prepared to bide his time. Late in
World War II, when he made the decision to try to revive the New Deal for
postwar purposes, he failed. The machinery with which to do it—his defeated
reorganization plan—was not available to him. The fact that the inability of the
federal government to control the distribution of national resources would
remain the problem each of his successors would have to face suggests that
this is the ultimate issue.

It was at any rate at the heart of the questions that critics of American
government would always come back to. How strong a central government
did Americans need in order to fulfill the ideals they agreed were essential to
the nation's well-being? How strong a central government were they willing
to accept? Congress could continue to represent the varied interests of the
states assembled, but who would actually govern the administrative state that
Congress had created? Congress clearly could not govern, but the agencies to
which it had comfortably delegated its authority were its creation, not the
Constitution's. The Supreme Court's decision in the *Schechter* case had
attacked so peculiar an example of the problem of delegated authority that it
could, in time, be forgotten. The administrative state came into being, but the
question of who would administer it remained unresolved.

9

Ending the Twenty-Year Armistice

THE YEARS between the two world wars were frustrating years for American internationalists of all persuasions. They came through the twenties a badly divided community, still split over the utility of the League of Nations, the World Court, the rationality of war debts, ways of limiting arms buildups, and, ultimately, the appropriate role for the United States in world affairs. The Depression then widened the division by providing what some claimed was yet another lesson in the unfortunate consequences of international involvement.

Such debates ultimately helped establish various forms of isolation from European politics as the only common ground on which national policy could be built, although those who used the term were not in agreement on what it would mean in practice. "Isolationism" became a catchall term and a fairly comforting one as observers of the international scene watched the agreements of Versailles crumble. The tendency to blame congressional opponents of the League for America's failure to lead the world lessened as European governments and the League itself, paralyzed and confused by rapidly developing international events, provided even the old Wilsonian idealists with reasons to believe the effort had been in vain. By 1933 Wilsonian internationalism was looked on, even by most who once would have considered themselves sympathetic, as an old ideal tragically undone, but not by Wilson's American enemies alone. Americans may not have been ready for this idealism, but Europeans had proved themselves unworthy of it.

Mussolini's Italy, Stalin's Russia, Hitler's Germany, and Hirohito's Japan were all responding in similar ways to the postwar conditions of the 1920s, despite cultural differences and regardless of their positions as winners or losers in the war. Each viewed the world from an intensely nationalist perspective; each took not only its own economic interests but its racial and cultural values as the necessary basis for a regional or world order. Mussolini's concept of "monistic statism"—the view of the supremacy of the state over the individual, which European political theorists were calling "fascism"; Stalin's commitment to international communism; Hitler's belief in the superiority of an Aryan race; and Japan's expansionist policy, envisioning a structured hierarchy of Asian religious and cultural orders, with Japan at the top and the emperor occupying a special godlike position—all were revolutionary conceptions in which the world was to be governed and given order by a single dominant culture.

The Versailles Treaty had redrawn the national boundaries of Europe, in part to break up the power of the nineteenth-century empires of Germany and Austria-Hungary, but in part, too, to respond to the demand for self-determination by many of the subject peoples of those empires. The tension between the desire for national identity on the part of Poles, Czechs, Yugoslavs, and Hungarians and the need to free commerce from the national barriers that hindered trade was a legacy of the centuries-long partitioning of Europe; but in 1919 the demands for self-determination on the part of masses of people could not be denied.

What an American political scientist, William Yandell Elliott, was calling "the pragmatic revolt" was taking place. Mass publics were no longer prepared to accept class roles that denied them access to political power and the economic opportunity that went along with it. Old monarchical power and new parliamentary leaders were both being pressed by newer leaders, who promised that access now, not selectively or over time. Citizenship and participation had become identical; but the definition of citizenship was problematic to the extent that it could now be tied to some complex relation between nationality, with all of its ethnic overtones, and ideology, with its attachment now to party membership. "Party" became not simply an organization for pursuing certain defined political ends but a means of identifying true citizenship.

Americans had gone through stages in their own understanding of political parties from their almost accidental discovery of them at the end of the eighteenth century to an almost mystical sense of commitment to them in the nineteenth century. By the 1930s they had come to regard the two parties as loose confederations that offered suggestions rather than programs. Many Americans were learning to consider independence from party ties a virtue. When they looked at European politics, they saw either unstable multiparty systems or the religious fervor of single-party systems. The former produced constant stalemate; the "efficiency" of the latter depended on oppressive state control.

What most seemed to characterize both American and European views of the world after World War I was the sense that a choice had to be made between national self-development and a commitment to international order. National self-development meant improving the conditions of life for one's own citizens first. That required stabilizing the national economy, but at a cost that varied with the amount of internal discontent and popular perceptions of its causes. The Depression obviously exacerbated discontent, but tremors of discontent in the ranks of European labor groups had been felt long before the Depression began.

At the same time, however, the world outside could be seen as the only real source of solutions to the problems of national self-development. Again, that idea preceded the Depression and took a variety of forms, ranging from American efforts to stabilize the war-debts repayment, in order to aid European economic redevelopment, to the battle between the Trotskyites and the Stalinists in the Soviet Union. Both Japanese and German expansionists aims were argued, at least in part, on grounds that included the need to expand in order to provide living and working space for their own people—*Lebensraum*, as Hitler put it. The American version of that particular argument took the form of closing off immigration, an anti-internationalist act inspired by the presumed need to protect living and working space for Americans.

The American commitment to internationalism had in any case always been limited by the facts of American history. American policymakers had spent more than a century establishing hemispheric relationships that gave the United States a dominant position over its neighbors to the north and south. Ideas of conquest and invasion had surfaced from time to time, but the twenties and thirties were an era of stepping back, of trying to be what President Hoover was the first to call "a good neighbor." The United States had learned that it could control its relationships with its neighbors more effectively by economic management and industrial expansion than it could by invasion as long as it did not have to compete with the imperial ambitions of other nations. By using the Monroe Doctrine to close the door on those ambitions, the United States managed to establish a distinctive American empire in its own part of the world.

Even had American leaders wanted to emulate other nations in attempting some kind of world cultural conquest, their own history would always have stood in the way. The United States was, in its own terms, a liberating nation, not a conquering one. While its relations with its Asian protectorates like the Philippines and its colonies like Hawaii raised racial issues almost as complex as those raised by its relations with Puerto Rico and the Latin American protectorates like Cuba, the American sense of race and nationality made it impossible to conceive of the two as identical. The British, Germans, and French defined themselves as nationalities in a way that Americans could not without arousing conflicts that ranged from the meaning of "hyphenated

Americans" to the question of the supposed primary allegiance of Catholics to Rome. Questionnaires that asked Americans to list their "nationality" were usually asking for country of family origin, not citizenship. The anti-Germanism that had been so essential to the wartime fervor in 1917–18 demonstrated clearly enough that any effort to "purify" American culture or to come to grips with all of the meanings that underlay the term "stock" entailed injustices and potential repressions that could not be justified in a country devoted to democratic principles.

Rural communities, urban ghettos, suburban communities, even states, might claim homogeneous identities for themselves and pass laws supporting those identities or use social pressures where that sufficed. But the nation as a whole could not do so, and aggressive internationalism required a strong sense of national identity.

Throughout the twenties, Americans interested in fostering a benign internationalism had thought that American business could serve as a channel. In the prosperous twenties it was often asserted that "The business of America is business," and, to all but leftist critics of American policy, this business-based internationalism was equivalent to a benignly messianic materialism: Americans would improve the world by spreading prosperity, not by meddling in politics. Believers in American business internationalism, like Hoover, thought that improved standards of living in the rest of the world would, by producing the greatest good for the greatest number, render ideology irrelevant; capitalist materialism and Marxist materialism could be brought into a productive working relationship. The Depression only intensified a belief that was strong in the business community even before the Crash: that Soviet-American trade would be good for both nations. The intensification of that belief, together with the growing call among American industrialists for diplomatic recognition of the Soviet Union, was part of a general move toward internationalism in the pre-Depression years as nations throughout the world searched for ways of adapting the changed postwar world to the tradition of trading relationships. This was difficult, given the economic and geopolitical consequences of the Versailles settlement. New and inexperienced governments coming to grips with new constitutional forms and pressed by internal groups prepared to celebrate the liberation they had been fighting for for decades still had to deal with a world politics dominated not only by the remaining traditional empires but by the new and equally inexperienced giant, the United States. It was not the same world. The character and meaning of internationalism established by the Congress of Vienna had changed. The old balance-of-power diplomacy—romanticized even by liberal philosophers once the real effects of World War I and Versailles had become clear—had been replaced by untried forms of internationalism. Embodied in the hopes its proponents had pinned on the League of Nations, it still lacked definition, in part because the man many Europeans considered its most articulate proponent, Woodrow Wilson—and, along with him, the League— had seemingly been repudiated by his own countrymen.

Few Americans were inclined to recognize the fact that the United States had in fact changed the balance of power in Europe, but it was true. Nor did they see the consequences of their failure to supply a substitute for the system they had helped to destroy. They could argue that it was crumbling anyway, and that was certainly true enough.

The paradox that emerged once the Depression struck grew painfully clear. Only by establishing strict control over domestic commerce and employment could a government assure its citizens of stability, jobs, and a secure future, and some nations discovered that war, together with the military industry needed to keep it going, was the surest way to provide jobs for the unemployed masses. Moreover, if raw materials and markets were needed, the trade and monetary barriers other nations had erected to protect their domestic economies could be breached by troops. The relation between national self-preservation and aggression against others was troubling and confusing. National self-esteem became central to popular support of government policy. Japan and Germany in particular looked to expansion to relieve internal economic problems. Moreover, they needed to have access to basic raw materials, particularly oil, coal, and iron.

War production was an effective public-works system in itself, and so were the growing armies and navies. The Versailles Treaty and various other conferences and treaties throughout the twenties had sought to limit the growth of armed forces, but by 1935 it was clear that whatever system the twenties had created had fallen apart. Both Germany and Japan had repudiated the agreements they had signed, and both had withdrawn from the League of Nations; Italy was ignoring international criticisms and would eventually withdraw. All three had adopted expansion as their answer to the crisis, and the rest of the world looked on in despair.

Policies of aggression required a centralization of leadership that none of the other Western countries had achieved. Despite his commitment to international communism, Stalin's power was not yet sufficiently consolidated to enable him to ignore the pressures of domestic needs. Great Britain and France both faced internal political dissension that made centralized leadership difficult, even with respect to domestic affairs. Franklin Roosevelt was in a similar position. During the Manchurian crisis of 1933 he had considered acting against the Japanese but had rejected the idea almost at the same time as he rejected international currency stabilization. Within two years the strength of congressional opposition to military spending made it unlikely that he could take a strong international position, even if he could have reawakened the dynamic atmosphere of 1933.

As the thirties drew to a close, it was clear that the whole structure of international order, put together following World War I, was in ruins. War was in the air again, and some Americans were trying to assess what their role would be. The memory of their experience in 1917 colored all their considerations. America's entry in 1917 had determined the outcome of the war by assuring the total defeat of Germany and Austria-Hungary. The war had also transformed the role the United States had henceforth played in the international economy. Crudely put, it had become the world's banker—a creditor nation rather than a debtor. Yet Americans were not entirely sure what they had won from the war. They might not have been persuaded by a group of Germans who in the 1930s were publishing open letters to friends in the United States, saying that the Americans had made a mistake in 1917 by trying "to prevent history from following its proper course," but many of them felt that the nation's best interests lay in remaining outside any future conflict. American public opinion was not inclined to be sympathetic to international banking, to say the least, or to arguments in favor of gold as the basis for currency stabilization.

Sophisticated policymakers of the day had difficulty in persuading the American people to accept the consequences of the nation's new international involvement, and Congress accurately reflected the people's point of view. *Time's* tone of comic condescension when it described European dictators reflected the popular attitude, which did not take the new leaders seriously. Groucho Marx' portrayal of a dictator in *Duck Soup* was not so clearly directed a spoof as the later Chaplin movie, *The Great Dictator.* With Chaplin's caricature of Hitler and Jack Oakie's of Mussolini, audiences were treated to a complex fantasy that still allowed them the freedom of laughter. Children held black combs under their noses and stuck stiff arms in the air in imitation of the seemingly absurd Nazi salute. The goose step looked incredibly inane as a way of marching down a street. Radio comedians mimicked German accents. Yet beneath the comedy lurked fears, which grew more intense as the news from Europe grew more threatening.

When Roosevelt introduced the term "quarantine" in a speech in Chicago in October 1937, he seemed to be breaking the isolationist silence. He spoke of "aggressor nations" spreading disease and of the need for "peace-loving nations" to band together to protect themselves. He spoke of the "lawlessness" and "international gangsterism" that marked the behavior of the "aggressors"—a term he substituted for the more neutral term "belligerents." Japan's war in China was referred to as "the undeclared war," as though a proper declaration would have turned an act of presumed international immorality into a traditional dispute between sovereign states. Yet editorial writers puzzled at the meaning of the term "quarantine." Did it suggest some new kind of action? Roosevelt refused to say, indicating that he was not talking about "sanctions," and he dropped the idea entirely when it became clear that neither the American public nor British and French policymakers were eager to support any kind of action in late 1937.

That the first professional historians to examine American diplomatic policy from 1939 to 1941 with deliberate irony entitled their book *The Undeclared War* indicates the startling changes that took place after the outbreak of European hostilities in 1939. The increasing involvement of American naval forces in the battle of the North Atlantic, where they served both as patrols for the British and as convoys for ships carrying military supplies to Great Britain, meant that by the winter of 1940–41 Americans were effectively engaged in a war against Germany. The American entry into World War II necessitated a great deal of subterfuge as practical and realistic concerns increased the willingness of the president to take risks and the willingness of Congress and the public either to ignore or accept those risks.

To explain how that willingness came about is to open up another comparison between the two wars, perhaps the most complex of all. By 1917 Americans had been conditioned by propaganda to hate the "Hun," but that hatred had had to be created to counter a traditional and widespread respect for Germany. A large segment of the population was German in origin, and whole sections of cities were proudly German. By contrast, the rise of Nazism, combined with popular recollection of the old wartime hostility, represented in movies by the sinister roles played by Erich von Stroheim, kept anti-German sentiments alive in the years between the wars. It was not necessary for Roosevelt or anyone else to build moral justifications for an anti-German policy.

The creation of legal justifications for some kind of positive action was another matter. The decline of the League reflected a general decline of confidence in formal conceptions of international law as the basis for maintaining world peace. American theorists were still looking for legal devices to replace the complex system of neutral rights that World War I had in effect demolished. "Neutrality" was no longer a useful term for defining national behavior. Roosevelt's use of the term "quarantine" was an apparent effort to find some new kind of legal language, one that would suggest collective action intended to prevent aggressive behavior rather than individual action to protect oneself. It was an imaginative effort, but it produced no results. It came, in any event, after two years in which the American Congress had worked to create its own definition of neutrality.

The various pieces of neutrality legislation that Congress passed in the thirties were intended to prevent American involvement by restricting the sale of certain war materials, by preventing loans to belligerents, and by making it clear that the United States would not defend citizens who insisted on traveling abroad. When a congressional investigating committee, the Nye Committee, issued a report in 1935 suggesting that the armaments industry had been responsible for getting America into World War I, it fueled the suspicion that war preparations were dangerous in themselves. Such tactical needs as arming our Pacific bases were rejected outright or were supported reluctantly and minimally. Even the possession of such bases was looked on as a possible cause of involvement rather than as a protection of American interests. Yet the very existence of the bases makes it clear that the United States had interests, was involved, and would have to play some role in world affairs.

Many people who felt that the United States was destined to play a world role could conceive of it only in fantasy. The movie version of H. G. Wells's *The Shape of Things to Come* could have been understood by audiences as an allegory of what Americans should have done in 1917. The film depicts the coming of a new war that destroys most of the civilized order of the world. One society remains aloof, building its technological resources for the day when it can benevolently take over the world by putting the fighting barbarians to sleep and then reconstructing their civilization. The movie, the result of a collaboration between a British production company and an American director, stretches Wells's science-fiction fantasy beyond its author's original intentions, but it perfectly expressed a genuine American fantasy.

American historians, intentionally or not, had also begun to establish a view of American history that tended to emphasize the uselessness of war. This was true not only of those who, like Charles Beard and Harry Elmer Barnes, were providing intellectual support to those now questioning the purpose of World War I; it was also true of those who were examining America's involvement in even earlier wars. Samuel Flagg Bemis looked at the Spanish-American War, once called the "splendid little war," and found it to have been the product of American political mismanagement and misguided newspaper propaganda. James G. Randall was using similar terms to portray the Civil War as the product of blundering leadership and bad rhetoric. The basic charges—inflamed and inflaming language, plus poor leadership—became part of the cry against "warmongers" in the 1930s. Novels, too, from *All Quiet on the Western Front* at the beginning of the period to *Gone with the Wind* at the end, told different versions of the same theme—the theme that Hemingway repeated in all of its variations: that war is the individual's heroic confrontation with death, a ritual of self-understanding, not a nation's triumph. One could find a related idea in one of the most popular children's books of the period, *Ferdinand the Bull*. Appearing in 1940, it described a pacifistic bull, goaded into action not by others but, finally, by sitting on a bee. The story was a virtual parable of the American international dilemma. We wanted only to sit and smell the flowers.

The growing horror of events abroad also played a special role in the development of basic attitudes toward the war, attitudes that prepared Americans for conceptions of the war in terms much more dramatic than those implied by the traditional language of international law and neutral rights, let alone by the practical utility of war as an instrument in foreign affairs. The degree of violence associated not only with Nazism but with the activities of the Japanese in Manchuria and China added an element of racist primitivism that pervaded movies, comic strips, and popular literature. Atrocities committed against civilians or military troops had always been associated with war, but the whole Enlightenment tradition of "civilized" warfare had argued for their abolition. The Red Cross, the Geneva Convention, and the efforts to use international law to regulate methods of warfare had all marked the previous century as a century of progress, not necessarily toward the abolition of war but toward "humanizing" it. In the interwar years, and certainly by 1940, both Germany and Japan had succeeded in projecting the image of nations bent on abolishing the rules of war. Movies like *The Rape of Nanking* used newsreels to show scenes of dreadful brutality, and the bombing of Guernica during the Spanish Civil War and the Italians' bombardment of Ethiopian tribesmen were both examples of the new kind of atrocity made possible by the airplane.

While systematic torture had traditionally been used to extract information as well as to punish offenders of particularly heinous crimes, its removal from the canons of criminal law had been considered one of the triumphs of Western civilization in the nineteenth century. Various forms of flogging were still legal punishment in parts of the world, including the United States, but its use was regulated by limits on its severity, and there were strong movements to end it entirely. The reintroduction of torture in Hitler's Germany and in Stalin's Russia, not only to extract information and to punish but to compel ideological conformity and, simply, to kill, generated a new popular literature that detailed what could be viewed only as a nightmarish return to human bestiality. One of the Book-of-the-Month selections of 1941 was a Nazi prison memoir entitled *Out of the Night*, published under the pseudonym Jan Valtin. Excerpted by *Life* magazine and accompanied by drawings to supplement the lurid prose, it provided American audiences with the image of a world gone mad. Another club selection of the same year, Arthur Koestler's *Darkness at Noon*, presented a similar picture of the Soviet Union.

By contrast with August 1914, the outbreak of war in Europe in September 1939 surprised no one, even those who kept hoping that something could be done to avoid it. Hitler's drive to establish a new German empire in Europe had been made clear, and the series of compromises, culminating in the Munich agreements in September 1938, had all been Hitler victories. The signing of the pact between Germany and the Soviet Union in August 1939 was a virtual go-ahead signal, since it assured Germany against having to fight on two fronts simultaneously. Stalin, too, apparently needed the time he thought the pact would give him. The pact shook Western communist circles to their very roots, for fascism and communism had been regarded as the

Manichean opposites of modern history, but it was based on the pragmatic opportunism on which leadership in such uniquely troubled times had come to depend. Hitler's invasion of Poland in September 1939 triggered the defensive alliances and agreements among the great powers of Europe; these, unlike those of the years before 1914, had been arrived at in full public view. The outbreak of war in Europe thus proceeded almost like a slow-motion disaster scene in a movie, while the audience watched in frozen attitudes of horror but not surprise.

The events of 1940 gradually convinced many American leaders in both government and business that America would inevitably become involved, but how and when the involvement would begin no one ventured to predict. Roosevelt bluntly told Americans that he did not expect their thoughts to be neutral, but it was difficult for him to arouse a spirit of preparedness, particularly because memories of the previous war were still so clear. Those who continued to dream of the protection provided by the two oceans—and many did—were told by others that they were sticking their heads in the sand.

The United States still did not have a significant defense industry. The private industries that had produced munitions, weapons, and machinery for the Army and Navy during World War I had ceased producing them in the interwar period. Some were still smarting from the attacks of the Nye Committee, which had accused them of profiting from the horrors of war. Others recalled the difficulties they had had getting rid of the expanded war plants and the overproduced war goods at the end of World War I. All were aware of the reluctance of Congress to appropriate money for such production, let alone for the research that would be required. Nor had the notion of government-owned and operated war industries taken hold in the aftermath of wartime experiments. The idea of a continuing system of armaments production, backed by research and the stockpiling of strategic materials, was not accepted as a responsibility that government should undertake. Even a government-encouraged effort by private industry seemed unfeasible, for an effort to create a system of that kind had failed in 1934. Finally, America's productive energy had been so weakened by the years of depression that it was difficult to make the enormous switch from a consumer-oriented system to a military-industrial system. Leaders of industry were caught in a dilemma. They were not happy with the idea of allowing the government to go into the building and managing of war plants, but they were in no position to move enthusiastically into the transformations and retoolings that a private system would require.

Adding to the problem was the ingrained belief—which later generations would find it difficult to recall—that wars were temporary events, that peace was the normal condition of the world. Neither World War I nor the effort to revive Wilson's internationalist ideals, which many Americans still pursued in the years between the wars, had convinced most Americans that the United

States had the kind of continuing international interests that called for the maintenance of a ready, fully equipped, and up-to-the-minute war machine. Indeed, the belief that war machines and the professional class that used them were in themselves one of the chief causes of war was strongly represented in American thought even before World War I.

American labor was also unenthusiastic about the idea of government-operated plants. Government management during World War I had increased both wages and profits, but unevenly, unreliably, and at a cost to labor's unionizing campaigns that many looked back on bitterly when the patriotic glow dimmed. When financier and erstwhile presidential adviser Bernard Baruch suggested that the experience of the first war ought to be used to organize the industrial system for the second, he did not get an enthusiastic hearing from either the labor movement or the president.

For an industrial nation just beginning to sense release from the grip of economic uncertainty, the coming of a war was a disturbance, not an opportunity. Roosevelt's first idea, to build a separate war industry, which would then disappear at the war's end, seemed the best way to avoid disruption. The plan satisfied no one completely and disturbed everyone a little. Moreover, given the isolationist mood, it would have been politically impossible to get the necessary legislation through Congress. The plan was probably economically unrealistic as well.

With the outbreak of war in Europe, American suppliers of industrial materials and foodstuffs, recalling the increased sales abroad that had followed the beginning of hostilities in 1914, waited in vain for orders. None materialized. This was due in part, at least initially, to what the newspapers were calling the "phony war," the seeming unwillingness of either side to take significant action. But with the spring offensive of 1940 the picture changed, for the expected "customers"—France, the Netherlands, Belgium, and some of the Scandinavian countries—suddenly became conquered provinces of the German war machine. Great Britain stood virtually alone, isolated not only from the enemy-controlled Continent but from its own empire. Whether England could in fact pay for what it needed for defending itself was a question that played havoc with traditional approaches to international trade and underscored the inadequacy of the old conception of war debts incurred for war purchases.

Gradual awareness of a new reality—that an isolated England was all that stood in the way of German domination of Europe—made it clear that the defense of England was a defense of America's interest in the survival of the Atlantic community. The United States began to build a war machine whose overt purpose was to supply the British; but it was a machine that was limited by the government's ability to ship critical war materials abroad. As far as actual weapons were concerned, Roosevelt invented a method that enabled him to trade surplus, outdated, or "over-age" ships for the use of British bases.

This limited effort nevertheless produced a system of supply that paralleled a slow buildup of our own national defense industry. Congress supplemented the president's actions by step-by-step supports of its own; it passed a national-defense tax in June 1940 and increased the national debt limit from $45 billion to $49 billion. The Selective Training and Service Act in September authorized the first "peacetime" draft, but only for one year.

When Roosevelt told a news conference in December 1940 that we would have to "take the dollar sign" off our aid to Great Britain, he was using his customarily jovial tone to announce to the business community that it could no longer expect to use standard channels of international trade. Foreign trade was now to be governed by the president and his advisers, not by private enterprise.

Parrying and thrusting, government and industry cautiously sought methods of establishing ground rules for their new relationship. The government could build plants to make munitions or combat vessels of various kinds as long as private industry was not engaged in the same production or the government did not pay wages seriously out of line with those established locally in private industry. But disputes arose, and the newly appointed government administrators, staffing newly created agencies to manage national defense, were authorized to "coordinate," which in practice meant to persuade, to cajole, to manipulate, and to soothe—in short, to create no more political heat than necessary.

During this strange, uneasy year, the production of war materials gradually increased. Some of the war plants were directly owned and operated by the government, others were privately owned and managed but funded by the government, and still others were entirely private. Unemployment remained relatively high; it stood at 14.6 percent in December 1940, but it was unevenly distributed through the nation. Unable to acknowledge openly the coming of the war but committed to preparing for it, Roosevelt followed a characteristically opportunistic course, locating plants as much as possible in the needy and hospitable South and placating northern industry by not pressing for more disruption than he thought would be acceptable. For example, when automobile manufacturers accepted government orders for military vehicles, they were also permitted to build passenger cars, in anticipation not only of the material shortages the military expansion would produce but of the market for new cars that would be created when workers, reemployed by the war machine, would again have money to spend. That such decisions were not always made systematically, let alone confidently, has confused later analysts of war production.

The chief impediment to rational planning was the administration's inability openly to acknowledge the coming of the war. Support for the isolationist position still ran high. Political realities dictated caution on the part of the president lest he lose control of the Congress on which the gradual expansion of war production had to depend. In interpreting this period it is important to realize that Roosevelt lacked the power to command a war economy that later presidents would be given. The fact that 1940 was an election year, plus the years of criticisms Roosevelt had been subjected to for his supposed desire to be a dictator, severely limited his authority to move effectively in creating a war machine for a war that millions of Americans still believed would not involve the United States directly. By the end of the year steel production had gone well over 90 percent of capacity, up from 60 percent in April. Of aluminum, the key metal for the aircraft industry, there was a sufficient supply at the beginning of 1941 to keep production at capacity, but to meet the needs for aluminum forecast for 1942, plant capacity would have to be doubled. The memories of 1921 caused any experienced industrialist to look ahead and wonder what he would do with the excess capacity after the war. When Alcoa—the Aluminum Company of America—earmarked $150,000,000 of its own funds for expansion, it was looked on by some in the business community as a national patriot but by others as foolhardy.

Despite high sales, industry refused to be optimistic about the economy. Automobile dealers had trouble in keeping more than a month's stock of cars on the salesroom floor, but automobile manufacturers still were fearful of inventory overstock. Retail sales continued to rise, even at Sears and Montgomery Ward, whose customers were still primarily farmers; but ten years of Depression had taken their toll here as well. Every upward movement was viewed with suspicion. Every downward movement, no matter how small, was taken as the fulfillment of a prophecy. Looming in the background stood the specter of government intervention, of an impatient, frustrated New Deal, which could be unleashed now by the new authority that war management was bound to give to the president.

To fund the research needed for the creation of new military weapons, industry and government evolved what was to become a characteristic set of alternatives, ranging from private research investment and joint private-public ventures to research that depended exclusively on government initiatives. The reasons that led to one choice of funding rather than another were not always easy to define, but they always depended on the relation between profitability and utility as perceived in the changing circumstances produced by the coming of the war.

The Du Pont company had reduced its production of munitions chemicals to under 2 percent of its business, partly as the result of Nye Committee publicity. Its development of nylon, which it began to manufacture in 1940, was a spectacular technological achievement, one that was destined to have a critical impact on the making of parachutes for one of the war's most important tactical attack systems: parachute troops. Parachutes had been made most successfully from silk, and for that the United States was dependent on the Far East. Nylon was now being heralded as a substitute for silk in the stockings women coveted, freeing them from dependence on a product—Japanese silk—that they had been asked to boycott. But nylon stockings disappeared from the market within a year of their introduction as war needs took over.

The manufacture of synthetic rubber had been within the range of chemical knowledge for some time, but cheap supplies of natural rubber, primarily from Southeast Asia, made the costs of research and production uneconomical. Even the Japanese drive into Southeast Asia, which threatened American access to the rubber produced in the French colonies in Indo-China, had not stimulated research. One of the most trying restrictions of the war, gasoline rationing, was necessitated not by a shortage of gasoline but by a shortage of rubber tires. Government-supported research was central to the eventual production of synthetic rubber, and, as a by-product of that, to the postwar development of an entirely new industry: the world of plastic.

Finally, the war's most revolutionary contribution, the discovery and development of nuclear energy, was produced entirely at government expense and under government direction. In a remote section of the government-owned and managed power network, the Tennessee Valley Authority, the president established a branch of the Manhattan Project at Oak Ridge, Tennessee, to develop the atomic bomb on the basis of research directed by an Italian physicist, Enrico Fermi, in a secret laboratory under the stands of a football field at the University of Chicago.

The uneasy partnership between government and industry thus began before America's entry into the war. The initial relationships were ad hoc, based on suspicion, profitability, utility, and changing perceptions of national needs from different and at times hostile perspectives. The pattern that developed ultimately came to be known as the military-industrial complex; but it was by no means a planned pattern or one whose design reflected any long-range purpose.

The wartime association between government and the labor movement was quite different, for labor, unlike industry, had looked to the New Deal for support and had made advances that seemed promising. Yet the honeymoon was brief, and the promise was clouded by doubts based on labor's recollections of its experience during World War I and the twenties and, to some extent, during the New Deal itself.

The New Deal had strengthened labor, but unevenly and at times unwillingly, at least as far as Roosevelt himself was concerned. The Wagner Act of 1935, which created the National Labor Relations Board, had been a giant step, but it had been initiated by others, not by the president himself. The increasing number of defense contracts, particularly in the automobile industry, offered opportunities for further advances, but again the memories of labor's experiences in World War I, and the consequences of those experiences in the postwar years, produced caution. In the World War I years,

Samuel Gompers, the first president of the American Federation of Labor, had organized and headed the War Committee on Labor and had helped in other ways to hold labor loyal to the government's war programs. Later he was accused by some of selling out labor's interests to a war patriotism that cloaked a hostility to labor radicalism. He had extracted no-strike pledges in return for promises of greater power for unions in the future, and the hollowness of those promises, made evident during the 1919 strikes, and the subsequent decline of the labor movement in the twenties could be interpreted as proofs that if labor was indeed going to attain status in the national bargaining system, not only against the opposition of management but against the pressure of a public opinion that could be made to see unionism as synonymous with radicalism, it was going to have to take advantage of situations when the pressure was there, not afterwards.

In 1941 there was a series of serious disputes between management and labor. Philip Murray, president of the recently formed Congress of Industrial Organizations (CIO), called on management to cooperate with labor in the interests of national defense. Many of the industrial giants responded favorably—Bethlehem Steel for one, Henry Ford for another. Yet there were outbreaks of labor strife in various parts of the country, and demands were beginning to be made on the president to take action. In June, strikes began in the logging camps of the Northwest, in the San Francisco shipyards, and at the North American Aviation plant at Inglewood, California. All three were undertaken in defiance of presidential orders, and all were opposed by the CIO leadership. Roosevelt sent in armed troops against the strikers at Inglewood.

The United Mine Workers president, John L. Lewis, became a legendary figure of this era. Heavy-browed, with a gift for biblical invective, Lewis attacked Roosevelt and the New Deal as betrayers of American labor. He opposed Roosevelt's foreign policy and believed that the administration was overstating the threat Hitler posed. Most significant of all, Lewis's fervent dedication to the interests of the coal miners, whose hazardous occupation gave them a special set of needs that only government policy could deal with, made him the lion of the labor movement. A series of coal strikes in the fall of 1941 ended with an agreement in Lewis's favor; it was announced on the night of 7 December.

As preparations for war increased, the level of hostility rose among those who opposed America's involvement. Some isolationists had come to support military preparation, but they remained strongly opposed to participation in the war itself. The America First Committee had been formed in July 1940. Charles A. Lindbergh used its platform to speak against American involvement in the war; he blamed the pressure to become involved at least in part on American Jews. To counter the America-Firsters William Allen White, a midwestern journalist in the old progressive tradition, headed a Committee to Defend America by Aiding the Allies. By 1941 American ships were being sunk by German submarines in the North Atlantic. Roosevelt took the occasion of a German submarine's firing on the U.S.S. *Greer* to issue a shoot-on-sight order, despite the fact that the destroyer was actively aiding the British navy against submarine attacks. Earlier, in July, American naval forces had landed in Iceland, 2,800 miles from Berlin, 3,900 from New York. The United States was effectively at war.

When some Hollywood writers and film stars attempted to attack Nazism, they were criticized by congressional isolationists, who equated anti-fascism with pro-communism—an equation that stuck, because in some groups in Hollywood and New York that equation was quite clear. The Nazi-Soviet Pact had come as a tremendous shock to pro-Soviet Americans, especially coming as it did on the heels of the Moscow Trials; but the Nazi invasion of the Soviet Union had generated a new sense of sympathy if not support.

The successful movies of 1941 continued to provide entertainment from the worlds of fantasy and unreality, from the upper-class sophistication of *Philadelphia Story* to Walt Disney's fairytale, *Dumbo*. The first of the movies pairing crooner Bing Crosby and comedian Bob Hope, *The Road to Zanzibar*, began the series of spoofs of colonialism that were to become a familiar form of fantasy travel during the war years. A more serious attack on greed was the filming of Dashiell Hammett's *The Maltese Falcon*, with Humphrey Bogart in the role of Sam Spade, establishing for himself the beginnings of a career as a new type of hero, standing cynically at the edge of the law, passing judgment not only on the criminals he had been selected to bring to justice but on a system of justice that could be just as dishonest. Hammett's detectives had established a new position for themselves in detective literature. They were not only the classical logicians of the Sherlock Holmes tradition; they also administered the justice the system itself failed to mete out. Vulgarized in the postwar fiction of Mickey Spillane, Hammett's detectives were prepared to judge and to convict and to maintain justice in the face of official corruption. *The Maltese Falcon* was a study in the sinister, with Sidney Greenstreet, Peter Lorre, and Mary Astor playing parts that were to become models of an era. The later caricatures of these by Spillane were caricatures precisely because they failed to include Hammett's perception of the purity of justice. Spillane's detectives not only judged and convicted but executed their criminals, thus separating themselves from the system of justice Hammett's heroes were committed to forcing to work. Hammett's radicalism was clear enough in his criticisms of the corrupt system, but his hero's commitments were always closer to those of the New Deal, forcing the system to work rather than replacing it.

Bogart's performance opposite Ingrid Bergman in *Casablanca*, a movie destined to become a cult piece, epitomized the American dilemma on the eve of Pearl Harbor and its ideal resolution. As Rick, Bogart questions his responsibility to a world beset by demons willing enough to let him be—to run his saloon and simply watch them destroy others. He need not interfere. They will continue to do business with him after they have succeeded in reshaping the world to their own designs, and he can simply watch. It is his aroused moral sense, not a direct attack on his interests, that leads him to make the decision to leave the safety of his neutrality behind the bar. Pearl Harbor obviated the necessity of such a choice for most Americans. As Rick, Bogart represents the isolated American, persuaded that he has a duty to perform; he does not represent the United States, forced to make a decision about its international identity.

Among the film contributions from abroad, the most striking in the years of the undeclared war was the British production of George Bernard Shaw's *Major Barbara*, a play that poked embittered fun at munitions-makers and war. It was filmed, as American audiences learned, under extreme wartime conditions. Members of the cast had raced from the set to air-raid shelters and served as air-raid wardens at night. On one occasion the company, returning to finish a sequence begun in a row of houses in London's East End, discovered that the houses had been bombed into ruins.

The New York Drama Critics Circle split once again. This time the chief contenders were Lillian Hellman's *Watch on the Rhine* and William Saroyan's *The Beautiful People*, and again the closeness of the vote (the Hellman play won) suggests the essential division in American thought. *Watch on the Rhine* skillfully exploits the problem of the American response to Nazism without depicting a single clearly identifiable Nazi. The setting is a country house in the United States to which the daughter of a former American diplomat returns, together with the German she has married and their children, to visit her widowed antiwar mother. Even the chief villain is a Romanian, not a German; he discovers the husband's past as an anti-Nazi and tries to blackmail him. The husband kills the blackmailer and returns to Germany to fight underground, having finally converted his family to the necessity of his decision.

The Saroyan play could not have been more different, although it, too, contains a conversion. A father living with his two adolescent children in a rundown San Francisco mansion collects a monthly pension check addressed to a dead man. The relaxed, offbeat life of the household is reminiscent of that of the family in *You Can't Take It With You*, and the message is much the same: life is to be enjoyed day by day. This idyll is interrupted by the arrival of a bureaucrat, whose purpose is to bring this malefactor to justice. Convinced by the happiness and simplicity of the lives he sees—the daughter tends mice, the son composes one-word "books," the father relaxes with alcohol and poetry—he manages to protect the petty embezzler. The lives, suspended and directionless, are allowed to remain so.

Hellman's victory was slender, but it was significant. The play's setting—an elegant mansion and gardens outside Washington, where Hellman's ever-present servants patiently advise and lovingly tend their employers—keeps Hitler in the shadows; but the threat and the sense of evil are there as the play moves toward its resolution. Saroyan's fantasy expressed both the protection from the world outside and the romantic individualism that many Americans still believed in. If only they could be left to themselves. . . .

The news of the war, including nightly descriptions of the bombing of London, delivered in the familiar voices of Edward R. Murrow and Eric Sevareid, was producing tensions that had to be resolved. Roosevelt was in no position to produce such a resolution. Isolationist sentiment in Congress remained strong, the industrial community feared that he would use the threat of war to bring about New Deal economic reforms that Congress and the public had already begun to reject, and there was a general sense that another war would do no more than the previous one to correct the evils of the world. The election campaign of 1940 had already demonstrated the depth of the division, and when Wendell Willkie, Roosevelt's opponent in that campaign, turned internationalist after the election, the Republican party turned its back on him, despite his obvious popularity with the American voters. Internationalism was not a politically viable platform.

Even as the antiwar movement surged, however, an interventionist mood, backed by supporters of Roosevelt and the New Deal, who saw in Roosevelt the vindication of Woodrow Wilson, had begun to generate a liberal coalition behind a new Americanism. That Americanism was built now on a celebration of ethnic, even racial, amalgamation. Negro singer Paul Robeson recorded the "Ballad for Americans" in 1940. Written by John Latouche, with music by Earl Robinson, the record became a bestseller, and the cantata itself was picked up by amateur singing groups around the country in a spontaneous and urgent call for patriotic unity.

It was also increasingly clear that articulate spokesmen in the press and in the intellectual world were willing to do for the president what he could not do for himself. Henry Luce, in a *Life* editorial that appeared in February 1941, announced "The American Century." The United States, he argued, was going to have to take over the role Britain had played in the previous two centuries, sustaining the peace of the world through the power that they alone controlled. It was a position Roosevelt was, in effect, moving toward in his tentative meetings with Winston Churchill, whose ringing speeches were attracting a wide audience of American admirers. Secret meetings between American and British military planners had begun in January 1941, and the announcement of the Atlantic Charter in August was a public statement of common British and American aims, left sufficiently vague to avoid criticism from the increasingly strident isolationists.

In one portion of the intellectual community, where isolationism had created an alliance between left-wing critics of America's role as a greedy international power and writers who genuinely believed in the uselessness of war as an instrument of national policy, changes in attitude were under way. The Spanish Civil War and the Nazi-Soviet pact had already sparked some changes in the American communists' attitude toward American involvement in the war, and the growing view of Hitler, not simply as the agent of an antidemocratic ideology but as a demonic madman, bent on world conquest, overrode ideological commitments.

In 1941, Archibald MacLeish, the American poet Roosevelt had named Librarian of Congress, published an essay entitled "The Irresponsibles," an attack on the American intellectuals' withdrawal from political responsibility. Roosevelt brought playwright Robert Sherwood into the White House to help with the writing of speeches. Sherwood, whose antiwar play, *Idiot's Delight* (1936), had been made into one of the popular movies of the period, had, by 1940, indicated the shift in his own position by his play *There Shall Be No Night*, a moving portrayal of the tragedy the Nazi conquest was bringing upon Europe.

Drained of much of its intellectual strength, the isolationist movement grew more vitriolic in its attacks on Roosevelt's efforts to transform public opinion. Roosevelt was forced into a use of secrecy and manipulation that would make later efforts to understand the period particularly difficult. With public opinion in such flux, a leader with a strong political sense had few political guidelines to follow. Polls on the eve of Pearl Harbor still showed a majority against involvement, even though that same majority believed that Hitler should not be allowed to defeat Great Britain. The events that preceded the official declarations of war are intelligible only if they are reviewed against this background of political uncertainty. And that includes the attack on Pearl Harbor.

The surprise attack by the Japanese on Pearl Harbor on 7 December 1941 had in fact been preceded by a series of steps that left little doubt about the direction that events were taking. The Japanese bombing of the American gunboat *Panay* in the Yangtze in December 1937 killed two Americans and wounded thirty; but the effect of the incident on American public opinion was a mixture of anger and even further withdrawal. The United States demanded and received apologies and reparations, and the event spurred interest in the Ludlow Amendment, a proposed constitutional amendment requiring a national referendum for a declaration of war except in case of direct attack on the United States or its territories. A poll taken in 1937 showed that 73 percent of Americans questioned favored the amendment. Only a strenuous effort by the president prevented what seemed its sure passage by Congress.

The level of hostility between Japan and the United States had risen noticeably in the thirties in the wake of the well-publicized Japanese war against China. Americans had long portrayed the Japanese as an imitative and untrustworthy people, culturally inferior to the Chinese. The popularity of Pearl Buck's *The Good Earth* and the immense attractiveness of the American-educated Mme Chiang Kai-shek, the wife of China's General Chiang, helped generate support for the Chinese cause. Americans began to boycott Japanese merchandise. Strong racial overtones, even among top-level policy-makers, marked America's position in favor of China long before the United States had any direct cause for involvement.

Nonetheless, ambiguity and disagreement about America's proper role in the conflict was manifest in many areas right up to the attack on Pearl Harbor. As late as June 1941 Mississippi's Representative John Rankin told the House that the country was being pushed into the European war by "Wall Street and a little group of our international Jewish brethren." (New York's Representative Mike Edelstein replied angrily and then dropped dead of a heart attack.) The uncertainty about our position tended to increase internal hostilities and divisiveness. All of the major legislation, from the repeal of the arms embargo in November 1939 to passage of the Selective Service Act in September 1940 and the Lend-Lease Act in March 1941, was enacted by a Congress that was as much divided at the end as it had been at the beginning, and in August 1941, when Roosevelt requested extension of the Selective Service Act of 1940 beyond the one year initially allowed, the extension passed the House by a margin of just one vote, 203–202.

In its first year, the draft was popularly looked on as a temporary measure, even as a joke. The term "draft" was specifically avoided in favor of "Selective Service," and the draftees were called "selectees," to emphasize that this was not universal military service. One of the first Abbott and Costello movies, *Buck Privates*, set this comedy team in a boot camp, where everything was comic, temporary, and totally unrelated to anything that could remotely be called the horrors of war.

By 1941, Western pressures to stop Japanese expansion caused the United States to support the British, French, and Dutch governments, whose immediate colonial interests in Southeast Asia were being increasingly threatened. Japan's repudiation of the Open Door policy helped harden the American position, and by November 1941 the United States was prepared to demand Japanese capitulation to a list of restrictions that would have halted its expansionist drive. Americans stopped the sale of oil to Japan and joined with the other Western nations in freezing Japanese funds. That some form of Japanese action was bound to come was clear. The only question was where and when. Roosevelt and his advisers expected it to come in areas of Asia that produced materials the Japanese could no longer buy: in Borneo, Indo-China, perhaps Singapore. Oddly deflected from perceiving itself as the target, the United States thus anticipated hostilities between Japan and the colonies of the European Allies. Aware that Germany's invasion of the Soviet Union the previous June could release Japan to take aggressive action, American policy-makers waited. To avoid criticism that they had provoked an attack, they simply warned American commanders in the Pacific that hostilities were about to break out. They had already broken the Japanese diplomatic code, and they possessed the messages that were being sent to the Japanese Embassy in Washington, warning that hostilities would soon begin, though they did not say where. Thus, the attack on Pearl Harbor itself was a sur-prise—and a terribly damaging one—but it was the only surprise.

The success of the attack did nothing to change popular views of Japanese racial inferiority, although it did complicate them. The training of young Japanese air pilots to fly aircraft whose sole purpose was to crash and explode was taken as an example of Japanese racial character rather than military patriotism. Suicide was acceptable in Japan, perhaps, but not in the United States. Paradoxically, America's first war hero in the Pacific theater, Captain Colin Kelly, was described as having crashed his plane into a Japanese vessel because it was the only way to destroy it; but that was an act of patriotism, not suicide, because it was a choice he could have rejected, as the kamikaze pilots could not.

That the attack on Pearl Harbor was a sneak attack was also taken as demonstrating a character defect, and it was presumed to have been necessi-tated by another Japanese defect: that they were shoddy manufacturers whose equipment could not stand up in a proper battle. Still, it is important to note that when the American west-coast military command decided to remove Japanese-Americans from their homes and businesses and place them in relocation camps, the argument that was used was not the racial argument that most Americans were accustomed to accepting. The case made by California Attorney General Earl Warren was built on the belief that the allegiance of Japanese-Americans could not be trusted because Japanese-American chil-dren, taught in Japanese-American schools to respect their ethnic homeland, had been educated to a dual allegiance. This position held seeds of the argument that Chief Justice Warren would later use in his Supreme Court decision against segregated schools. Likewise, during the American military occupation of Japan, after the war, it was religion and emperor worship that were popularly considered the cause of Japanese aggression, not inherent racial characteristics. The racist justifications helped generate the hostility necessary to consider the enemy a beast and thus to justify any means of destruction, including the use of the atomic bomb; but the racism did not survive the war.

One more perception that governed America's entry into the second war and distinguished it from the first was the perception that the United States as a nation was becoming isolated in a totally hostile world. The Nazi invasion of Russia in June 1941 appeared to American policymakers to be an attack by an invincible power on a backward victim and bound therefore to succeed. It would be only a matter of time. The seemingly imminent fall of Great Britain, the prospective link-up of German and Japanese forces, once Russia was conquered, and the strength of Nazi movements in Latin American countries, whose governments seemed to need American economic support, made the approaching winter of 1941 particularly threatening. The destruction inflicted on the American fleet by the attack on Pearl Harbor added a final and devastating touch to a year marked increasingly by fear. Americans who knew the details of the situation had no reason to be certain that they would fight a war to victory, however strong their faith. Replying to one of Mrs. Roosevelt's early requests for postwar social planning, the president informed her brusquely that we first had to win the war to make certain that we would be the ones doing the planning. Americans marched into World War I to save the world for democracy, so the argument had gone. This time, though no one was inclined to admit it, they were pushed into war in order to save themselves.

The "surprise" attack on 7 December, a Sunday morning, was the kind of surprise that invited criticism of American policy. It was used at the time— and has been used in the years since—as proof of a White House conspiracy to get the United States into the war by inviting the only event that would unite American opinion: a direct attack. The charge is rendered particularly brutal by the degree of devastation sustained by the American naval and air installa-. tions in Hawaii and the Philippines. The sacrifice of American lives and the loss of extensive and irreplaceable equipment would be impossible to justify by claiming either incompetence on the part of policymakers and commanders in the field or a deliberate design on Roosevelt's part to achieve a political end.

One can remark that had Roosevelt had the audacity to announce an imminent Japanese attack, he would have had to announce it to his congressional opponents, who had repeatedly told him that their intelligence sources were better than his, that no aggressive action against the United States was pending. In addition, all of Roosevelt's tactics in preparing for war had for more than two years been based on subterfuge and delay. He had been fighting for time. Other nations, and particularly those now at war, had been building war machines openly and energetically for years, while the United States had debated both the morality and the utility of such action. The politics of American preparedness had been complex, and the president's role had been limited by that complexity. Only in the years after Pearl Harbor could analysts piece together the information available at the time and see in the assembled puzzle what could appear to be a clear picture of conspiracy. But it was hindsight alone that made the picture look clear.

The attack on Pearl Harbor dramatically transformed public opinion. It brought the United States into the war. But there were subtler transformations of attitude that also occurred in the immediate aftermath of the attack. The interwar period came to be seen as a twenty-year armistice. The once solid intellectual base of isolationism, the belief that Americans could form a utopia of their own in a world from which they could protect themselves, began to disappear. As a point of view, isolationism came to be identified as a hostile, naïve, and useless commitment to the past. That transformation took time; but it began with the simple sense of relief that the suspense of the years from 1939 to 1941 had come to an end. One could *win* a war. "We did it before, and we can do it again," was the way one popular song put it. The United States was returning to the world to "complete" its job. World War I blended into the reality of World War II, and the interwar years became an aberration. Yet the long-range view was unclear in 1941, despite efforts to promote the idea of an American Century. Isolationism was on the way out, but internationalism, as the postwar generation would come to understand it, had not yet come into being. The world's law-and-order police were back on the job, to pursue once more that short-range goal that required so simple and yet so complex a view of world history: the punishment of evil.

10

Managing War Again

M ANY AMERICANS feared that America's formal entry into the war had come too late. The English Channel alone protected the only sure base for a campaign, the British Isles themselves. Military observers expected a German invasion across the Channel; in the meantime, they puzzled over ways of getting American forces across the submarine-infested stretches of the Atlantic. Although the war would be remembered for its use of aircraft, essential aspects of war strategy were still heavily dependent on traditional naval support. Transatlantic air transportation did not yet exist, for the planes were small and their range was limited by the relatively low speed of their piston engines and their fuel capacity. The aircraft carrier, an innovation that combined traditional naval power with the airplane as a fighting weapon, still carried only small fighter planes. While the bombers that flew over the Channel on their nightly errands of destruction seemed gigantic by earlier standards, they too were limited in range, in part by the quantity of bombs they had to carry. Parachute troops were a highly specialized form of combat force that could be delivered in relatively small groups by aircraft; but for moving large numbers of regular troops over long distances, simultaneously protecting the troop carriers themselves from attack, and for supplying the needs of combat forces in distant places, naval vessels were still the only way.

The devastation at Pearl Harbor has to be seen in the light of this continuing dependence on the Navy. If mounting an invasion of continental Europe seemed difficult, the possibility of invading Japan rapidly came to be perceived as something that would have to wait for a fearfully distant future. The crippled Pacific fleet and the sudden vulnerability of the fortified island bases that Americans had wanted to believe were invincible made the islands of

Japan seem very far away indeed. Long conditioned to considering the threat to Europe the basic problem of the war and the "Japs" as a cowardly, technologically backward people, who could be "wiped up" with little effort, the American public faced an initial reorientation of major proportions, one they were going to have to deal with for seven agonizing months while American forces sought to reestablish a base of power in the Pacific strong enough to repel the currently successful Japanese advances.

The fall of Corregidor and the Philippines in the first half of 1942 and the flight of General Douglas MacArthur to Australia were only the dramatic preludes to depressing daily accounts of Japanese victories and the obvious move of Japanese power toward Australia, New Zealand, and Hawaii. The bad news from the Pacific could not have been covered up even had the government been inclined to try.

The decision to focus Allied energy on the battle in Europe did not improve the situation for American newspaper readers and newsreel audiences, who followed accounts of actions on the unfamiliar deserts of North Africa while the populations of urban Europe remained in German hands. Americans watched with alarm the establishment of puppet governments in invaded countries, headed by nationals under German control, while the omnipresent German military roamed the streets of Paris, Amsterdam, and Copenhagen with what appeared to be total impunity. Popular novels and movies portrayed the heroics of local citizens who found ways of frustrating their captors. John Steinbeck's *The Moon Is Down* was a successful play and motion picture that described the willingness of the citizenry of an occupied village to risk death to perform acts of sabotage against the invaders. The hiding of Allied soldiers caught behind enemy lines, the conflicts in local communities, as citizens fought fellow citizens who were willing to serve the enemy (such persons were called "Quislings" after the traitorous governor of Norway), were common themes. But apart from the Allied bombings of the Continent, which sought to match attacks on British cities, the war seemed to have reached a stalemate.

When in April 1942 an elaborately planned bombing of Tokyo took place, it was recognized less as a tactical step in military strategy than as an effort to assure Americans that some kind of retaliation might some day be possible. A popular movie, *The Purple Heart*, dramatized the incident by showing the heroics of the crew of the one plane shot down in the raid, in contrast to the brutality of their Japanese captors, who were trying them in a Japanese court. This trial scene was pure fiction, but it filled a popular need for reassurance.

The Allies disagreed on how to get the war headed in the right direction. The Russians were bearing the brunt of the invading German troops, but Stalin's pleas for a second front in the West led to a dispute between Churchill, who believed that control of the Mediterranean was the key to victory, and the American military advisers, who favored a more direct attack across the

Channel. Roosevelt's mediation of the dispute depended more on politics than on military strategy.

Roosevelt's management of the politics of the alliance was destined ultimately to subject him to criticism when later commentators sifted the agreements reached at the various wartime conferences and tried to separate policy-planning from the personal maneuvering among the three giant figures, each with his own national interest to preserve. Roosevelt's confidence in his own powers of persuasion and his respect for power in others led him to believe that he personally could influence Stalin's judgments about the future of Europe. His friendship with Churchill, a mutual respect that embodied the traditional Anglo-American relationship as a family relationship from which others could be excluded, convinced him that, one way or another, he could get the British to agree to America's basic war aims. On the other hand, Churchill was inclined to see the future of Europe as a matter that concerned Britain and Russia more than it did the United States, and he thought that a division of spheres of influence could be worked out between himself and Stalin, regardless of what Roosevelt thought. And Roosevelt was not inclined toward sympathy with colonialism, whether it was the traditional British variety or the kind expressed in the Soviet Union's desire to control eastern Europe. The relationship among the three was a political one in which real sympathies were balanced against real oppositions.

The compromises Roosevelt entered into in the wartime conferences among the three were based on his belief that the primary goals of the United States could be achieved by a postwar international organization with power to maintain peace and by a system of international economic agreements designed to stabilize world trade. He did not see ideological differences as a threat, an attitude that clearly paralleled his approach to ideological differences at home. His was committed to fulfilling the Wilsonian dream; in his view, America's misguided rejection of its international responsibilities in the aftermath of World War I had made the second war possible, and this view was shared by most international-minded Americans. The belief that they were still in the minority made a resurgence of isolationism at home seem a much greater threat than international communism. A Soviet Union already weakened by years of war and seemingly dependent on the United States for its recovery could be viewed as posing no immediate danger. Roosevelt had no reason to believe that Americans were any more committed to internationalism in 1945 than they had been in 1940; and there was still a war with Japan to be won, a campaign which, at that point, seemed clearly to require Soviet support. Roosevelt's options as a negotiator were still circumscribed by what he knew to be the mood of Congress and the American public.

From Pearl Harbor on, Roosevelt was therefore convinced of the necessity of generating political support for an international point of view; the country must not be allowed to drift back into isolationism or indifference. Two world wars in one generation had to be proof that what happened elsewhere in the world affected American interests. Yet the years of negotiating with a Congress that could not see any internationalist sentiment in the constituencies it represented was bound to have taught any president some important lessons. Even the most committed isolationist in Congress could find support from colleagues who might not have described themselves as isolationists but who nonetheless knew that the voters who had elected them either did not care what happened in the rest of the world or put it very low on their list of priorities. For years an interest in international affairs among congressional leaders had been the special concern of insiders, who saw it as a means of gaining influential positions on committees that had contact with members of the banking and financial communities who had a direct interest in the nation's foreign policy. The power that went with such positions was important in the government bureaus and legal offices of Washington, and it gave the holders of such positions important influence with a president concerned with foreign affairs. But their influence with the folks back home was nil, even in wartime, when "getting it over over there" and returning to normalcy were what the people desired. Throughout the war years Roosevelt was caught between the political necessity of projecting short-range goals to meet the emergency and his own consciousness of the need to plan for the future, to try to prevent international crises from recurring by giving the United States the power to influence international policy in a realistic way.

The battle cry of World War II was "Victory." The symbol of victory was the letter V, the Roman numeral for five, three dots and a dash in Morse code, the stentorian rhythm of the opening theme of Beethoven's Fifth Symphony. Winston Churchill provided the salute, the first two fingers raised to form a V. It was all there, symbol, song, salute, and battle cry; but concealed beneath this dramatic array was the real purpose of World War II as the Allies conceived of it: survival. The fall of France had been viewed by many Americans as proof of an innate European effeteness they had long suspected was there, a weakness underscored by the refusal to defend Paris lest the city's beauty be marred by battle scars. Churchill had promised defensive street fighting to the very end, and Soviet citizens were struggling to save besieged cities like Stalingrad in what were probably the bloodiest encounters of the war.

The attitude of American business on the eve of the World War II was quite different from its attitude in 1917. The industrial community of the Progressive Era had been caught up in at least part of the progressive movement. The years of "Preparedness," as the period just before America's entry into war in 1917 had been called, had been prosperous for American business. Whatever initial attractiveness the business community had initially seen in the New Deal had long disappeared by 1940, and a decade of economic depression had taken its toll of business confidence. While the actual experience of World

War I had taught American industry lessons it had not been inclined to forget, it had entered that war mobilization with an enthusiasm that could for a time blend with the spirit of progressive reform.

In 1940, by contrast, a far more cautious business community was determined not to be burned a second time. As individual patriots, they would come to their country's defense; but corporate experience could not be ignored, and it included the experience of being managed from Washington. Business managers and government officials entered World War I as partners and ended as adversaries. They entered World War II as adversaries and ended as partners; but the experience between the wars had established the difference in perspective. The New Deal had taught both sides important lessons. Their interdependence was clear; but so was the fact that their hostility to each other was based on a genuine incompatability.

Roosevelt built his management of the war in response to circumstances that gave him little opportunity to construct a logical system. In the years before the office of the National Security Adviser had been created, presidents were expected to rely on the appropriate cabinet officers—the secretaries of State, War, and Navy—for the formulation of war policy. It became clear in the years immediately preceding the war that this would be difficult for Roosevelt. Secretary of State Cordell Hull's close relationships with Congress and Roosevelt's desire to manage foreign affairs himself, coupled with his awareness of congressional opposition that had prompted his behind-the-scenes war planning all along, made use of Hull difficult. Harry Woodring, his secretary of war, was an isolationist, in addition to being ill part of the time. Roosevelt thus used his infinitely loyal friend, Secretary of the Treasury Henry Morgenthau, Jr., as his officer for secret arms negotiations with Britain and France. During the war itself, Harry Hopkins assumed the role of foreign-policy negotiator for the president.

Second, the powers given him by the Reorganization Act of 1939 enabled Roosevelt to create an Office of Emergency Management within the newly formed Executive Office of the President and to combine that with his authority as commander-in-chief to maintain an administrative control that allowed him to circumvent officials in the bureaucracy who either opposed his plans or were sympathetic with congressmen who might oppose them. Earlier in the New Deal Roosevelt had tried to place officials sympathetic to his aims in positions within the cabinet departments to serve as sources of information and instruments of management; but figures like Moley and Tugwell had not succeeded. The new managerial methods given to Roosevelt by the Reorganization Act now made such subterfuge unnecessary.

Third, Roosevelt appointed a committee on industrial mobilization, made up primarily of businessmen, not only to advise him but also to commit leaders in the industrial community to support the coming war effort. The committee produced an Industrial Mobilization Plan, which recommended the appointment of a single individual to control mobilization, a "czar" with extraordinary power, who would, presumably, be chosen from among industry's managerial leaders. It was an idea that Bernard Baruch, a financier and World War I adviser, was pressing on Roosevelt, but he rejected it and kept the plan secret for as long as he could. Roosevelt had no intention of turning such power over to industry or to one of its leaders. It was clear to him that he needed industrial support; but he wanted it to be organized by someone from within his administration, committed to his perception of the nation's needs. He compromised by selecting highly visible figures in industry and giving them an extremely limited managerial authority.

Fourth, Roosevelt quickly dropped his idea of building a war industry separate from the existing industrial system, and he embarked on a complex funding of private industry. As early as June 1940 the Reconstruction Finance Corporation was authorized to lend money for the stockpiling of strategic raw materials and for building or expanding plants producing war materials. By executive order in March 1942 the president authorized federal loan guarantees and even federal participation in loans made by private banks to finance war production. In June 1942 the government set up the Smaller War Plants Corporation to provide funding for small businesses that had received contracts for war production. Cost-plus contracts, which guaranteed payment at whatever the production cost plus a reasonable percentage of profit, were the government's acknowledgment of the fact that the necessities of war production overrode considerations of competitive bidding and productive efficiency. The government was also willing to forgive loans for new plants that remained in operation for a specified period of time. The wartime government moved into major support of the industrial system on a scale that dwarfed even the wildest ambitions of the NRA. At the same time, the Office of Price Administration, established in 1942, regulated prices and rationed such commodities as automobile tires, sugar, coffee, meat, and shoes. The result was a price stability that was remarkable by comparison with what happened during World War I. By August 1945 prices had risen only 31 percent compared to the 62 percent rise that had occurred by November 1918. (Such figures, of course, do not take into account the existence of an extensive Black Market, on which purchasers could buy scarce items at whatever price they were willing to pay.) The command economy created by the war was thus relatively effective, despite the clumsiness with which it was put together.

Finally, Roosevelt's method of staffing administrative agencies with personnel unwilling to use the strength of their agencies to the fullest meant that the war effort was hampered by the same problems Roosevelt had faced in the NRA under Hugh Johnson's leadership. Not only did Roosevelt refuse to appoint an industrial czar; he continued to place in positions of authority industrial leaders committed to some form of voluntarism. His practice of creating "watchdogs" with limited responsibilities successfully kept authority in his own hands but did so at the expense of a systematized coordination of efforts. It also blocked the tendency of his industrial administrators to central-ize production in a way that would turn the process of postwar conversion into a bonanza for the country's largest industries. Centralization meant efficien-cy, but it could also mean corruption and miscalculation. Senator Harry Truman's investigating committee watched over the mobilization process and put teeth into the system of regulations of industry that the president seemed unwilling to enforce. Truman, a life-long student of American history, knew that during the Civil War the Committee on the Conduct of the War had created havoc by its effort to take war management away from President Lincoln; that knowledge, plus his own populist attitude toward big business, helped establish his role as a feisty attacker of anyone who sought to slow down the war effort. He accused John L. Lewis of being "sassy" to his committee, and he defended Air Force inspectors whose superiors had tried to demote them for reporting leaky airplane engines.

The continuing view of the war as an unprecedented emergency helped contain criticism of Roosevelt's methods of war management; few asked him to defend his uses of power. Hitler, Nazism, and the Third Reich dream of world conquest provided a satanic threat that made the World War I images of Kaiser Bill and the Huns pale by comparison. Yet the wartime management was both establishing new patterns of relationship between business and government and solidifying changes that had already begun to take place in the New Deal. With a few exceptions—notably, the selection of former Republican Secretary of State Henry L. Stimson to be his secretary of war— Roosevelt did not go to the World War I industrial leadership for experienced staff or even for much advice. The selection of Stimson was in fact motivated fundamentally by Roosevelt's search for bipartisan support for the war effort. Roosevelt's new war leaders were men like Edward R. Stettinius, Jr., and Myron Taylor of U.S. Steel. Taylor and Stettinius had helped design Big Steel's compromise with the CIO, thereby breaking the united front against unionism that big business had been trying to sustain.

Another member of Roosevelt's team was James Forrestal, who reflected a point of view that was common among the younger members of the legal profession and Wall Street business firms. These men acknowledged the utility of closer relationships between business and government and recog-nized the justice of labor's claims and the growing responsibility of govern-ment for monitoring the welfare of the general public. The idea of a welfare state might have offended them, but they did not see concern for the general welfare as an ideological threat, nor did they see all forms of government intervention in the economy as a threat to free enterprise. In December 1944, when the Army took over the running of Montgomery Ward because of that company's refusal to obey a government order settling a strike, *Life* magazine displayed on its cover a photograph of Ward's director, Sewell Avery, being carried from his office in his chair, arms folded across his chest, mouth angrily shut. It was a kind of defiance that was going out of style.

Nevertheless, many of the younger war managers, recruited from business and industry, came out of the war with a feeling of having hung by their thumbs over an abyss. Their affection for Roosevelt did not conceal their belief that the chaotic, ad hoc war machine he had been forced to create was a precarious way of preserving the nation. If the managers of World War I had learned that wars were to be avoided because of the damage they did to the industrial system, the managers of World War II learned that military preparedness had to become a normal part of American industrial life, that never again should the United States allow its defense capacity to sink as low as it had in the 1930s. The lesson was not as universally clear in 1945 as it would become by 1950, but the first steps in learning it occurred during the war.

If Roosevelt's short-range domestic management had long-range implications he could not have foreseen, his long-range international planning was couched in the broadest of generalizations—in terms politically unassailable but also politically obscure. By contrast with the legal specificity of Wilson's Fourteen Points, Roosevelt's Four Freedoms—freedom of speech, freedom of religion, freedom from want, and freedom from fear—were beyond dispute as long as no one raised the question of ways for achieving them. Even by 1943, when Congressman William Fulbright of Arkansas introduced a joint resolution asking that "Congress hereby express itself as favoring the creation of appropriate international machinery with power adequate to establish and maintain a just and lasting peace among the nations of the world, and as favoring participation by the United States therein," the Senate Foreign Relations Subcommittee resolutely balked, despite overwhelming House approval. With aging Hiram Johnson speaking in opposition, the Senate finally agreed to support a statement asking that "the United States, acting through its constitutional processes, join with free and sovereign nations in the establishment and maintenance of an international authority with the power to prevent aggression and to preserve the peace of the world." It still took twenty-nine weeks to get Senate agreement.

Although the establishment of the United Nations was the ultimate result of the long debate, the issues involved in the struggle that began in 1943 seemed irresolvable initially, despite the fact that the prevention of future wars was, in general terms, a commitment most Americans tended to accept. But whether that responsibility was best exercised by collective agreement among nations or by maintaining the United States' military strength at a level that would assure its ability to act effectively was as open to debate as it had been throughout the war and even more debatable than it had been in 1920. The isolationism emerging in 1943 was different from the isolationism of 1920. Leaders like Senator Robert A. Taft were not supporting the old romantic ideals of separation from the evils of Europe but a position they considered much more realistic: they thought that the United States could best preserve the peace by retaining independent authority as a world power. Some of the League's opponents had taken a similar stance, but Taft and his associates envisioned a much more aggressive use of American power.

The question of how aggressive Americans would be willing to be in managing the postwar world was considerably less clear in the last years of the war than it would become over the next decade. Polls taken toward the end of the war indicated that most Americans were unwilling to provide aid to postwar Europe if it involved any sacrifice of the quality of life at home. Roosevelt in his negotiations with Stalin was almost too frank to confess his belief that it would be difficult to keep American military forces in Europe for very long after the end of hostilities, and the method chosen by Congress for demobilization even before the defeat of Japan proved him right. The point system Congress worked out released men on the basis of years of service, time in combat, and family status—factors that bore no relation to tactical service needs and were almost guaranteed to demoralize the remaining troops. Yet it accurately reflected the American view of the war: that it had been fought and won by an aroused citizenry, not by military professionals.

Roosevelt's position appears to have been based on a shrewd political compromise. He joined idealistic yet unexceptionable generalities to a harder realism that took account of the responsibilities of the more powerful nations to control the peace of the world through direct negotiations with each other and by overseeing the development of the smaller and newer countries. Political pressures at home inevitably dictated the language in which his arguments could be put. Vague war aims that spoke of human freedom and rights and an organization to support them still had to be seen in the context of the immediate war aim that Roosevelt had insisted upon and that he continued to enunciate: unconditional surrender. Peace, this time, was to come not through negotiation but through the total defeat of the enemy. Yet the long-range future was to be managed through negotiation and organization by a method left undefined, and deliberately so. Unconditional surrender met all the political needs Roosevelt saw immediately in front of him. It promised nothing but the end of the war and a defeat so devastating that the enemy could not rise again. In the circumstances, it was better to leave the future shrouded in idealistic mist.

The contrast and comparisons with Wilson's position in 1918 are important. Wilson had enunciated war aims and had promised negotiations that never took place, given the oppositions among the Allies. Germany was forced, in effect, into an unconditional surrender. Although Wilson would come to be known as an idealist in international affairs, it was the specificity of his aims and of his planned world organization that aroused opposition and disillusionment. Roosevelt was not going to entrap himself in the same way. Wilson's negotiations with the three other world leaders at Versailles had been an intense and tightly focused battle over specifics, and Wilson appeared immediately to have lost more than he had won. Roosevelt's negotiations with Churchill and Stalin, by contrast, took a variety of forms throughout the war. The agreements were left unclear; Roosevelt argued that the details should be spelled out when the new world organization had come into being. Whether or not that was good world politics, particularly where his compromises with Stalin were concerned, it was essential and effective domestic politics where Congress was concerned. Roosevelt gave his opposition moving targets, blurred and hard to hit. He was possibly aware, too, that the popular view of Stalin and the Russians as heroes was useful for war propaganda at home, at least for the short run. The congressional fear of radicalism and its identification with Soviet sympathizers in the United States had not been destroyed by the wartime alliance.

Domestic planning for postwar America ran into similar difficulties. Again Roosevelt struggled to balance the need for long-range planning—to deal with social and economic problems the New Deal had left unresolved—against the immediate desire of congressmen and the public to forget the past and tend to immediate needs: jobs, consumer goods, and business as usual. The identification of long-range planning with socialism and radicalism was still a part of congressional thinking, and the fact that many old-line progressives and New Deal liberals lost out to conservatives at the polls suggested that voters in many districts were not hospitable to the idea of a future planned by Washington bureaucrats.

Roosevelt's National Resources Planning Board had been preparing a report since before the war as part of its continuing concern for improving the social security program and instituting new programs for medical care, education, and hard-core poverty—areas that the 1935 legislation had ignored. Fearing that the report would arouse congressional hostility without necessarily generating support from the public, Roosevelt held it on his desk until 1943, when his hand was forced by Great Britain's announcement of the Beveridge Plan, a sweeping program of social reform designed by British reformers to forestall a recurrence of the radical discontent that had followed World War I.

The American public's response to the Planning Board's report is interesting. Most newspapers and magazines took it as a program for the 1944 presidential campaign and underplayed its seriousness. Critics labeled it a "cradle-to-the-grave plan," but even they were inclined to see it less as an immediate threat than as another ground on which to attack Roosevelt and the New Deal. Public-opinion polls showed that there was little general interest in the report but that it generated some suspicion among those who actually knew what it was about. Nonetheless, the contents of the report were central to Congress's attack on the National Resources Planning Board, which was branded as "socialist, fascist, and medieval." Roosevelt tried to defend the board, not on ideological grounds, but on the practical grounds that it could provide him with a "shelf" of public-works projects that would generate employment in the postwar recession that he and some other Americans were expecting.

This was a conservative and cautious support of an agency that had gone well beyond its public-works mandate in the course of its ten-year history and was now, in its postwar planning report, moving into broad areas of social and economic policy. Roosevelt's defense can be interpreted as an appropriate— and politically wise—response to congressional conservatism, but some of his own comments at the time—for example, his habit of referring to the group of young New Dealers who shared his wife's social-reform interests as the "Cherubs"—suggest that he may also have shared to some extent in the conservative reaction.

If British planners were anticipating a wave of radicalism at the war's end, American planners were learning to anticipate exactly the opposite. Some of those who had identified themselves as liberal in the New Deal years, even some who had been well to the left of the New Deal, were now taking positions that ranged from simply rejecting the radical positions they had once espoused to openly searching for an intellectually viable "new" conservatism. Americans like Reinhold Neibuhr, T. S. Eliot, and Peter Viereck were attempting to define a wide range of new alternatives, all of which disavowed Marxism. The more traditional conservatives found in Friedrich von Hayek's *The Road to Serfdom*, which appeared in 1944, one of the first academic justifications for their hostility to government intervention they had seen in almost a generation.

Among the general public there was a similar reaction against big government. Some of it echoed the complaints that were typical of the New Deal era, but the criticisms now were much influenced by the experience of wartime bureaucracy and its management of the national economy. Such bureaucracies had been remarkably successful in controlling wages and prices, in rationing scarce materials, and in financing the war. The introduction of payroll deduction of income taxes, the so-called "pay-as-you-go" plan, made the United States the last of the modern industrial societies to collect its taxes directly from wages, the "painless" way, before they were distributed. Rejected in 1942, the plan was "sweetened" in 1943, over the president's objections, by a provision that "forgave" 75 percent of the tax debt for 1942, supposedly to avoid having taxpayers pay the previous year's tax while they were also paying the current year's through payroll deductions. It was actually a sizable windfall for large taxpayers, but its public-relations effect on employed workers, many of whom were obligated to pay taxes for the first time in their lives, was undeniable.

Roosevelt's recollections of the excesses the Committee on Public Information had committed in drumming up war patriotism during World War I led him at first to reject the idea of domestic propaganda for the new war, but pressure from Mrs. Roosevelt made him decide in October 1941 to appoint Archibald MacLeish as head of the newly created Office of Facts and Figures (OFF). This agency utilized a more sophisticated kind of advertising and propaganda—Harold Lasswell, a University of Chicago political scientist, was one of its key advisers—to try to create an American view of the purpose of the war through radio programs that were frankly—and to some critics offensively—jingoistic and patriotic. Many of these critics were newspaper figures and political rivals who thought the agency overused the Roosevelt image and accused it of plotting a fourth-term campaign. The Office of War Information, the successor to OFF, was headed by a popular newspaperman, Elmer Davis, but it came under even greater fire. It was difficult *not* to sell the president, to use him as the symbol of a heroic America. It was difficult, also, not to promise a future democratic life for Americans that didn't reflect some New Deal ideas. For those who had never liked those ideas, almost any promise of future security had an unpleasant ring if the promise came from a federal agency.

A more sophisticated selling of government policy had been part of the New Deal program of 1939 and 1940, when agencies like the National Resources Planning Board, the National Youth Administration, and other reform-centered organizations used the radio to inform the public about their programs. Brief skits dramatized opportunities for job training and the like, assuring the listeners that "your government" would help prepare them for the future. Critics of the New Deal programs saw the threat that such assurances posed, the possibility that the architects of the programs were serving themselves by selling the public a dependence on government support.

At the same time, the wartime bureaucracy that administered prices and controlled wages was increasingly looked on as federal despite the effort to present it as a decentralized agency, administered by local boards having local jurisdiction. Draft boards, of course, were composed of "your neighbors and fellow citizens," but the "Greetings" came from the president of the United States. As in World War I, the federal government worked to sustain a commitment to localism, not only to lessen fears of a monolithic state, but to maintain public support for the war. Urged to collect scrap metal for the war effort, citizens went so far as to dismantle decorative old iron fences and pile them in city centers, along with discarded pots and pans, only to watch them rust and decay until confused and embarrassed officials carted them off, out of view. Yet the problem was there: the fear that geographical distance from the war would enable Americans to forget its importance to the nation's future.

Wartime regulations still tended to underscore the threat of centralized bureaucratic government that the supposed centralizations of the New Deal had already generated. The war enabled Congress to continue something it had already begun in 1937: recouping the powers that the Depression emergency had given to the president. Gradually it was Congress that cut down the authority of the president, limiting it effectively to the wartime emergency programs and removing from his control the New Deal domestic programs that still existed. The war sustained Roosevelt's personal popularity, but that aura, great as it was, could not sustain the New Deal. Roosevelt's advisers, among them many young Keynesians, who had moved into positions of leadership in university departments of economics and in government agencies, were predicting a postwar return to economic stagnation; but sentiment in Congress, caught up by the full employment stimulated by the war, worked against any concern for postwar problems. Even those who acknowledged that economic crisis might return thought that Congress, not the president, would have to lead.

Again, as in World War I, the assembling of American youth in the armed services made it possible to survey the quality of American education, and the results were not encouraging. The pockets of illiteracy among both whites and blacks, particularly among the southerners, revealed that providing equality of opportunity could come only through providing equality of education. Yet Congress, after the off-year election of 1942, was dominated by southern Democrats and small-town midwestern Republicans, whose faith in localism and individualism had survived the New Deal. What was added to that faith now was a militant antifederalism that associated programs formulated in Washington with radicalism, the term that, throughout the 1930s, had dogged New Deal reforms. Particularly offended were southerners, who saw federal programs being used to threaten them with racial equality. New Deal programs had in fact made it possible for southerners to avoid facing the issue. Despite the efforts of progressives like Harold Ickes to press for racial equality in federal programs, important agencies like TVA were allowed to discriminate in everything from housing to employment, and all New Deal public housing programs were segregated. Paradoxically, perhaps, the New Deal's acceptance of segregation, including the careful preservation of it in the armed services, did not relieve the fears of southerners, who, more accurate prophets than they could have known, now saw the move toward further federal programs as a move toward integration.

The Planning Board's report was bold enough to acknowledge openly that inequalities of treatment did exist; it also asserted, for the first time in an official government document, that there was such a thing as hard-core poverty—that there were individuals in America who were in no position to reach even the bottom rung of the economic ladder and that the government might have to assume life-long responsibility for them. To a society committed to the virtues of self-help and a faith in boundless opportunity, such ideas were appalling. They were perceived as radical not necessarily because they could be associated with Marxist ideology but because they called for national programs to eradicate local and regional differences. The equation of national programs with radicalism had long been the only basis for ideological attack on the New Deal. Wartime management only increased the sense of threat.

Aubrey Williams' efforts to keep the National Youth Administration afloat during the war illustrates what happened. Created in 1935, the NYA had concentrated on keeping students in school, on giving them the opportunity to obtain the kind of education that would make their entry into the job market as profitable as their intellects and skills would allow. It was directed at middle-class young people who under normal circumstances would have been in high school, college, or graduate school but whose opportunities were now being foreclosed by the Depression. Work-relief programs sponsored by the NYA enabled them to earn money while they continued in school. Once the war began, the NYA found itself emphasizing remedial programs for those not carried off by the armed services or war industry. These efforts were praised by industrial leaders, who appreciated government-funded programs capable of training manpower in the technical skills required for advanced war-technology. Even so, the program had drawn fire from the national education organizations, who saw it as a federal encroachment on the education profession's preserves. Such critics argued that the NYA was threatening the tradition of local control of education, and they raised the old specter of a federal system of educational management, which many equated with federal indoctrination of children's minds. In addition, as war employment absorbed the young who were in position to benefit most from NYA's support, those who were left had educational deficiencies so great that they required intensive remedial training. Many of these young people were poor and black. It took no planned collusion for southerners to join with education critics of the NYA to call for the end of the program. In a sense, the critics were correct. The war had changed the focus of the NYA. What had begun as the kind of middle-class support system that was so characteristic of the New Deal had taken on elements of social reform. The perception of that transformation as radical was rapidly becoming the standard response to the remaining vestiges of the New Deal.

Roosevelt had tried to muffle the rumblings of the civil-rights movement. He had bought off the threat of a march on Washington, headed by A. Philip Randolph, leader of the Brotherhood of Pullman Car Porters, with a promise to make equal-employment opportunity a condition of government contracts, but it was a promise honored more in the breach than in the observance. Southern congressmen, who refused to see the necessity of abandoning their well-preserved traditions, persisted in believing they could get wartime industrialization for the South without facing the consequences in racial policy. Their power in Congress, combined with the power of Republicans, for whom the racial issue was one of the ways of defining Roosevelt's supposed radicalism, was of decisive political importance to the president, for they could strip him of the authority he needed for the war. Equally important

from Roosevelt's point of view was his recollection of the ultimate consequences Wilson had seemed to bring on himself by making enemies in
Congress during the course of the first war. Political priorities had to begin
with the reality of a Democratic Congress dominated by southerners and with
a general public opinion that supported them and that equated radicalism
with racial equality and localism with the good old ways. These were ideas that
bred alliances between legislators who could otherwise have been political
opponents.

Other issues also won allies for the battle against the New Deal. The
language in which these issues were debated might dwell on the supposedly
radical nature of federal management, but what was really at stake was
something much older and simpler, namely, bureaucratic competition. The
New Deal had created new agencies to handle matters that were not necessarily new, even though the New Deal might have been trying to see them
from a new perspective. Army engineers had been building dams and managing the nation's waterways long before the National Resources Planning Board
came into existence to try to plan the process more systematically.

The Army Corps of Engineers had always had the authority to manage the
nation's rivers and harbors and to build dams and plan highways. They had
established good working relations with the committees of Congress that also
oversaw such activities. That supervision had been more political than systematic, and it had satisfied the interests of congressmen eager to win new
projects for the homefolks in their districts. In addition to its congressional
allies in its battle against the Planning Board, the Corps found a new ally in the
Bureau of the Budget. By 1940 the Bureau, particularly under the leadership
of Harold Smith, was committed to the position that it was better able to plan,
and to maintain control over planning, than were the academicians who ran
the Planning Board. Yet it was precisely to get around the pork-barrel
elements the Army Corps had always manipulated so skillfully and, moreover, to provide a planning center that was not dependent on the industrial
cost-accounting mentality of the Bureau that the Planning Board had been
created in the first place. One needed only to add the element of radicalism to
cement the potentially hostile bureaucratic and political alliances, and the
Planning Board did that for itself by championing the expansion and revision
of the social security program, along with the goal of full employment, issues
that again stirred racist sentiments in the South and conservative criticisms of
New Deal planning. Positions that appeared only mildly left of center in 1935
could now be painted red in the minds of those who saw planning itself as alien
to "the American way of life."

There were other aspects of wartime management that attached themselves
in recollection to the administration of the New Deal. The growing hostility to
the wartime agencies' invasion of private business enterprise at all levels gave
small business a clearer sense of the complaints that the large industries had

leveled at the NRA. The Office of Price Administration issued complex regulations governing not only the way in which prices were to be established but the way the manufacturing process was to be managed in the interest of the war effort. The elimination of vests and trouser-cuffs from men's suits did not bother those still in civilian clothing—though it helped the clothing industry somewhat by providing a significant style change—but the effect of regulations on the selling of meat by neighborhood butchers was another matter. The OPA not only set prices and controlled supply, but in its zeal to assure buyers of some semblance of a new equity it also required butchers to peruse page after page of orders, defining specific cuts of meat with a precision that required them to trim minutely specified amounts of fat. Directions on how meat was to be cut offended one of the country's more individualistic professional groups.

The establishment of regulations in all areas generated a new breed of regulators. They were generally young lawyers who were determined to administer the unadministerable and who, in the process, introduced Americans to a concept of bureaucratic rigidity they would come to associate with all federal management. Accustomed to viewing the inefficiencies of local administrators with a certain amount of patience, even pride, Americans looked on federal bureaucrats as presenting a new and serious threat. Young Richard Nixon began his government career as a lawyer for the OPA, and it was an experience he later used when he began his attacks on the federal bureaucracy. Other Americans who watched the process from their various civilian perspectives came to similar conclusions about the nature of bureaucracy. Wartime experiences of this kind inevitably tainted perceptions of the earlier New Deal programs and practices.

Roosevelt was puzzled by the hostility, particularly at reports that it was one of the important elements in what was, from his perspective, the disastrous off-year election of 1942; so he concentrated on selling the war. Sales of war bonds tested the ingenuity of the entertainment industry. Comedian Jack Benny's violin brought a million dollars in bond purchases from a cigar-maker who, when asked if he played the violin, replied that, if he were a violinist, he wouldn't have had the million to spend on bonds. An eighteen-hour radio marathon drive by singer Kate Smith sold $39 million in bonds and provided sociologist Robert Merton with a major case study in motivation. Buyers admitted that her argument had little to do with their decision to buy. Her personality, the qualities it symbolized, her identification as a patriotic figure—her recording of Irving Berlin's "God Bless America" was a best-seller—had been much more important.

Deliberately recalling World War I, Irving Berlin's *This Is the Army* used military personnel in a Broadway musical. Berlin had done the same with the first war's *Yip Yip Yaphank*, and he appeared in the new show in person, in a reprise of "Oh How I Hate to Get Up in the Morning," dressed in the old uniform with its pointed hat and the now-absurd leggings. War uniforms had been modernized, though the Navy insisted on retaining its bell-bottom trousers, complete with the thirteen-button drop front and the carefully folded cape-like collar, left over from the era of greased pigtails. Berlin's lyrics emphasized the basic theme, which was supposed to define the individual's relation to the war effort: this was a citizen's war, manned by "Mr. Jones" and "Mr. Brown," whose army it was. Proudly unprofessional, the citizen-soldiers were memorialized in journalistic accounts that emphasized their small-town origins. Ernie Pyle, who became a war casualty himself, wrote brilliantly unheroic prose, and Bill Mauldin's cartoons featured Willie and Joe, bemused and sometimes embittered fighters of the daily war, and Private Berger, the inveterate klutz. Not until after the war, with the appearance of James Jones's novel, *From Here to Eternity*, were Americans reminded of their professional soldiers, and then in not very flattering terms. Professional militarism was either un-American or corrupt. General Dwight Eisenhower, portrayed in cloth cap and a short battle jacket, exemplified the American contrast to the brightly uniformed and bemedaled Hermann Göring. Even the most heroic figure of them all, Douglas MacArthur, who enjoyed a sufficiency of gold braid, could appear in starched open collar, his pipe clenched in his teeth. The war's exception, General George Patton, who sported fancy helmets, boots, and pistols, was portrayed as a semivillain. His slapping of a soldier, hospitalized for an emotional breakdown, set off a national furor.

By 1943 Roosevelt himself seemed to be trying to play down even the term "New Deal." "Dr. Win the War" had replaced "Dr. New Deal," he told the press, and he used elaborate rhetorical stratagems to make the conservatives' destruction of the New Deal agencies appear to be triumphs. The WPA, he asserted, had won an "honorable discharge." A year later he confided to a reporter that he wished the press would simply stop talking about the New Deal. There was no need of a New Deal, he insisted.

Yet, in his State of the Union message in January 1945, at the beginning of his fourth term, he seemed to be suggesting important continuities. He called for a Second Bill of Rights, again in ringing generalizations, but he was suggesting that employment, the right to hold a job, was now to be given a new legal status. In the debates that would ensue over the next two years, critics of the idea of a new conception of "rights" would ask what the term was being stretched to mean. Constitutionalists asserted that the term used in that way had no historical status. The first Bill of Rights had established basic defenses against government incursions—protections *from* government. The new concept of rights appeared to be giving government a definite set of responsibilities. Would someone who could not get a job be entitled to sue in a court of law? Defenders hedged. It was simply a way of putting it, they insisted, partly rhetorical, to be sure, but really a way of giving the idea moral status.

The Servicemen's Readjustment Act of 1944 was nicknamed the "GI Bill of Rights," but its provisions were less comprehensive than those recommended by the Planning Board, whose plan Roosevelt had initially submitted. That plan would have tied benefits for the returning servicemen into the systematic social and economic readjustment envisaged in the NRPB's postwar plan, submitted to the president in 1943. The actual bill, pressed on Congress by the American Legion, was far simpler and involved only the immediate problem of getting the troops back into civilian life as painlessly as possible. It provided unemployment benefits for servicemen returning to the job market ($20 a week for fifty-two weeks), a promise of job preference, mortgage and business-loan support, and educational benefits to pay tuition for up to four years, with allowances for living costs and books. The plan proved to be a boon to the schools, which had suffered not only from the Depression but from the war, and it greatly benefited the textbook industry. But the loan-support features of the act were a not-so-tacit recognition of the relationship between returning veterans and the banking community, for they seemed to acknowledge that what lay ahead was, if not a depression, then something disturbingly close to one.

That same year, 1944, the president, for the first time in history, vetoed a tax bill, calling it a tax to benefit the "greedy," not the "needy." And Congress contributed to the historical anomaly by overriding his veto. What would in most other constitutional forms of government have been the ultimate statement of "no confidence"—the total inability of an executive and a legislature to agree on revenue policy—simply slid by as one of the inevitable mysteries of American politics. Yet it accurately measures the loss of Roosevelt's control over Congress. Later that year, when Americans once again went to the polls and elected Roosevelt president for an unprecedented fourth term, they also elected a Congress even more conservative than the one they had chosen in 1942.

By 1944 Roosevelt's leadership in domestic policy had become pure form; his authority was reduced to management of the war. There was little suggestion of direction for the future. The president was sixty-two, but an old sixty-two, in far weaker condition than anyone but his doctor suspected. Yet it was difficult to find an alternative candidate within the party he had dominated for such an unprecedented period of time. Vice-presidents were, in that era of American history, the discards of political leadership, not the presidents-in-waiting they would become. Vice President Henry Wallace was considered far too liberal by many in the party to remain on the ticket. Harry Truman, whom Roosevelt selected as Wallace's successor, was a completely traditional choice of a lesser-known party regular, acceptable to the party leaders but scarcely a stirring public figure. The fact that his experience in running the committee that oversaw war industry made him a remarkably good choice was the kind of information insiders respected and newspapermen understood; but it did little to suggest that he could succeed so giant a figure as Roosevelt.

The traditional split in the Republican party between its progressive and conservative factions had been widened by the increasingly liberal statements issued by the former candidate, Wendell Willkie. The selection of the young and vigorous Thomas E. Dewey over the more conservative Robert A. Taft was an effort to find a compromise. Even so, the future was less an issue in the 1944 campaign than the conclusion of the war, which the continuity of Roosevelt's leadership promised. It promised little else.

The news of Roosevelt's death in April 1945 set off tremors of disbelief. Caesar was dead; and whether one feared him as a tyrant or worshiped him as a god, one knew that a mighty leader had fallen. Most Americans simply wept, openly and unashamedly. He had given them as much leadership as they were willing to accept when they most needed it. Even so, they hoped they would never need it again. In the coming years, as if to enshrine that hope in the secular scripture his programs had seemed to threaten if not violate, they would initiate and approve a constitutional amendment limiting presidential terms to two. There would be no more New Deals.

Epilogue

T HE PHRASE "no more New Deals" is bound to have a peculiar resonance for twentieth-century Americans. Roosevelt promised his followers a return to the New Deal, and the drama of his last State of the Union message, in which he used the Planning Board's idea of a new bill of rights that would make employment a basic right, suggests that he meant it. Yet Truman's efforts to implement that plan ended in resounding failure. The Employment Act of 1946 (Congress was unwilling to accept the bill's original title, "Full Employment Act") gave the nation a Council of Economic Advisers but gave the president less power than the Employment Stabilization Act of 1931 had given Hoover. The passage of the Twenty-first Amendment, limiting presidents to two terms, helped to sustain the belief that Americans in general did not want to return to the kind of extended and strengthened presidency the New Deal seemed to require. Truman's struggle for a Fair Deal brought some significant changes in existing programs but did little to encourage those who looked at that last Roosevelt message and wondered where the blueprint for the future had gone. Support for health care, one of the logical next steps for reform, was one of Truman's major losses; America was not ready to follow other societies in the Western world, which had long accepted it in some form. One has only to recall the trip Lyndon Johnson made to Independence, Missouri, in 1965 to sign the Medicare bill in the presence of the aged Truman to realize the length of time it would take for American logic to work its way toward the future.

There were, nonetheless, recurring reform moods, and the reformers always evoked the New Deal. Kennedy's New Frontier and Johnson's Great Society both appeared to reflect New Deal aims. Expansion of government

programs in all areas—in the arts for the first time since the New Deal—
moved with surprising ease from the Johnson administration into the Nixon
administration. The equation—familiar since the New Deal days—of expanded federal programs and a strong presidency with liberalism, the opposite with conservatism, no longer applied, for Nixon as much as Johnson
wanted to centralize control of the bureaucracy in the White House.

In these years the term "planning" fell more or less into disuse in areas
other than foreign policy, but concern with management of government
programs and with the relation between that management and the political
structure that all presidents had to use in order to govern at all grew ever more
intense. Both Johnson and Nixon took their overwhelming electoral victories
as occasions for expanding their control, and both lost, not because the
appropriateness of that control was challenged but because other issues—Viet
Nam and Watergate—made the question of presidential power seem particularly threatening. The recurrence of the great issue raised by the New
Deal—the threat of presidential power—has never been given the attention it
deserves. We prefer to periodize our history, mythologize its various segments, and avoid the problem of continuity, particularly where it might
damage our image of the past.

No period since the Civil War has had such a continuing effect on American
political debate as the New Deal. Its leader and its programs have turned into
images and sounds that reverberate through time. "Happy Days Are Here
Again" continues to ring out as the Democratic party's theme song, and
Roosevelt's elegant phrases have a bipartisan quotability that even Ronald
Reagan has found useful. Critics and defenders of the New Deal alike point to
it as the origin of America's version of the welfare state, and the former attack
it for what it presumably did as well as as for what it failed to do. Searchers for
the origins of the nation's problems with social security, welfare, unemployment, and industrial planning treat it like a grab bag of evidence that will
prove both the evils and the virtues of state intervention in economic and
social affairs. Still, if Roosevelt had indeed done all of the things he has been
condemned or praised for doing, the society we live in today would look quite
different from the way it looks to us now.

There is no question that the New Deal transformed many aspects of
American life, most notably, perhaps, American popular attitudes toward the
role of the federal government in the management of public policy. Americans
prior to the New Deal did not look to Washington for management of the
problems of everyday life. They accepted unemployment and poverty, just as
they accepted successful businessmen and wealthy individuals, as products of
a whole system of social and economic life, only part of which could be affected
by the federal government. National policies seemed to be set by congressional legislation, not by presidential decision. The New Deal began a process

of change that put the president in the center of the picture of government but not as a manager with prime responsibility for administering programs. Roosevelt and his successors became spokesmen for their programs and, as such, became adversaries of Congress in a contest that Congress still controlled. The reputation of presidents from Roosevelt on seems to depend not on whether they get their programs through but on whether they present convincing cases for them.

Hoover, for example, knew what he wanted but was unable to articulate it effectively to the public, even though Congress refused him little of what he actually requested. So his reputation is poor. Yet, if one looks at the outpouring of legislation in the first term of the New Deal, one is hard pressed to find enduring and workable programs beyond such obvious examples as Social Security and the TVA. Throughout the New Deal, Congress continued to shape programs, often in directions Roosevelt found it difficult to accept; but accept them he did, and with that shrewd skill that required him to celebrate a limited victory as though it were better than what he had wanted in the first place. The point, simply, is this: Roosevelt was no more the master of the programs he found himself championing than is any president. The fact that frustration led him to seek greater control does not distinguish him from any other president.

Americans do not want an effectively managed government if it limits their individual control over access to the opportunities for personal advancement that government can offer. Congressmen seeking votes and a sensitive bureaucracy seeking appropriations can assure that access better than any president with a program. Wars and economic crises may generate moments of distress that lead to calls for strong presidential leadership, but they will be only moments. In the aftermath of the crisis, the popular will will reassert itself.

The New Deal became, in fact, the chief deterrent to the reforms that reformers have continued to call for in American government. If one looks at the crisis that brought Roosevelt into office, a crisis that was immeasurably heightened by the long interregnum the Twentieth Amendment now makes impossible, one sees that an occasion for presidential drama of the Rooseveltian kind no longer exists. The crisis atmosphere that in March 1933 fueled public enthusiasm for reform is not likely to recur, given the range of supportive programs that now protect everything from bank deposits to mortgages and supply unemployment benefits and welfare aid; one sees a system of safety nets and a public expectation that they will, in some form, remain in place. It could be argued that the confidence the public placed in Roosevelt depended much more on the sense of crisis and on his charismatic management of it than on the actual programs initially put in place by the New Deal. At the very least, we ought to examine more carefully than we tend to do the relation between leadership and programs. That requires neither attacking the New Deal for what it did or didn't do nor celebrating it as a liberal, even a revolutionary, reform movement.

It was possible in the aftermath of the New Deal to see it as a triumph of liberal reform, but those who did so were chiefly the younger postwar liberals, who were eager to sustain reform enthusiasm in the Truman and Eisenhower years. New Dealers themselves, particularly the more radical of Roosevelt's supporters, saw a different picture. A Wisconsin congressman, Thomas Ainslie, viewed the failure of the New Deal as an indication that the true character of the American middle classes was deeply conservative. Robert Sherwood, writing the movie script for *The Best Years of Our Lives*, predicted that the postwar years would bring another depression but that it would not be perceived as a crisis. Those who had gone through the late years of the New Deal, particularly the period from 1937 to 1939, felt that the American voters' tolerance for stagnation had grown greater with time. That sense of decline and stultification continued through the Truman years as President Truman and his followers unsuccessfully sought to revive the New Deal that Roosevelt had planned in the last years of his life. His efforts, moreover, won Truman no honor among former New Dealers or younger liberals, who saw him as a tool of conservative interests and an inept one at that. When David Riesman's *The Lonely Crowd* appeared in 1950, it discovered a sense of apathy and decline in a nation that had lost its sense of both the past and the future.

The fact that these phenomena were not solely American and the fact that their own focus on the New Deal might be obscuring larger issues did not seem to occur to most observers, although the questions were being asked in a larger world literature, even by some Americans. James Burnham's *The Managerial Revolution* (1941) attacked the New Deal as an effort to create an American benevolent fascism, but it was either ignored or castigated as an intemperate and inaccurate statement. Karl Polanyi's *The Great Transformation* (1944) took a larger frame in which to place the history of the era since World War I; the nineteenth century was ended now, he argued, and with it the essential stabilizing factors that had given that era its effectiveness and order. Karl Mannheim's posthumous collection of essays, *Freedom, Power, and Democratic Planning* (1950) tolled the knell of the expansive energies of the preceding one hundred years. "As we contemplate the chaotic state of unregulated capitalist society," he wrote, "one thing becomes quite clear: the present state of society cannot last long." And he called for democratic planning that would be neither communist nor fascist, although what it would be is buried in a program for spiritual revival that is not easy to understand.

A new conservatism, heralded by writers as different as Friedrich von Hayek, T. S. Eliot, and a group of scholars reviving the writings of Edmund Burke, called for various versions of a new social order. The one thing these writers had in common was their sense of the doom that a misguided liberalism was leading us to. They agreed, at least in part, with the neo-Calvinists in castigating those who promised utopias that human beings by their very nature could not achieve. Reinhold Niebuhr's *The Children of Light and the Children of Darkness* (1944) was a somewhat more hopeful version of the same critique, while Joseph Schumpeter's *Capitalism, Socialism, and Democracy* (1942) projected a long-range view of the inevitable collapse of the known managerial world, not in a dramatic cataclysm, but by the weight of its own ineptitude.

By 1944, when many of these books appeared, thirty years had elapsed since the outbreak of World War I, the event that seemed somehow to have triggered a strange slow-motion Armaggedon to mark the end of the utopian dream of nineteenth-century progress. Two major wars and a devastating international economic collapse certainly underscored a sense of ending without the promise of a future—unless, of course, one took the communist revolutions as the sign of the future. But they, too, seemed to develop an embattled grimness. Futures of that kind had little appeal for those imbued with what they liked to call "the American dream," a dream of success based on individual competitiveness, a leveling-upward that promised unlimited wealth for all.

Americans had had special reasons to puzzle over limits ever since the end of the nineteenth century, when free land and everything it symbolized had gone the way of the buffalo. The closing of the frontier and the gateways to opportunity that it represented continued to be remarked by writers well into the 1930s. John Steinbeck's *The Red Pony* (1937) played on the theme of "westering" in a much more depressed tone than he used in *The Grapes of Wrath* (1939). Tom Joad and his family looked to California as the land of hope, but Jody's old grandfather stared forlornly at the Pacific, realizing that the energy of the westward-moving "great beast" was gone, drained away by success.

That mood disappeared by the end of the 1950s, when an international economic boom, totally unanticipated by the New Deal generation, took off. Economist Alvin Hansen's gloomy predictions of economic stagnation were forgotten in a literature that turned now to discussions of stages of economic growth and "take-off" societies. Viewed in that context, the New Deal could be remembered as a triumph of pragmatic politics, with Roosevelt cast as a kind of jovial inventor whose genius lay in his own mystical sense of experiment. But that required taking the New Deal out of the context of the two world wars and putting it into the context of the affluent fifties and sixties. It looked much better against that background.

This is not to argue the incorrectness of the later view of the New Deal or the inappropriateness of the shift in context that produced it. The boom did occur, despite predictions to the contrary. The New Deal years were probably responsible, in part, for the conditions that made it possible. But we have recently been living in a period marked by a depression mood reminiscent of the one that launched the New Deal—a mood in which it is easy to question the whole idea of progress. The questions being asked now are as significant as the ones that were asked fifty years ago, and it may be important to look at these current questions of ours in the context of the New Deal.

Put in its place in the order of events of the first half of the twentieth century, the New Deal raises all of the most fundamental questions about the character of American government and its relation to governments elsewhere in the world. Searchers for the appropriate forms of democratic government for industrialized and industrializing societies all struggle with the same basic issues: the role of leadership and planning, the role of the popular will and the political institutions for expressing it, and the relation between leadership and the people that is most likely to assure a just distribution of available resources.

If one sees industrialism and technological change simply as enhancements of human abilities, producing machines that do more efficiently what human beings have always done, it is easy to adapt any governmental form to the process and let individuals make whatever judgment they want to about their appropriate relation to the economic and governmental system. That is the approach most Americans have preferred to take. Arguing the flexibility of the Constitution of 1787, they have allowed a wide range of governmental and administrative change to adjust the basic structure to the conditions of industrial society. The relation between the federal government and the state governments has always been productive of disputes, and the ad hoc arrangements each generation has created to resolve these have made it possible for government to continue, though it rests on a collection of political structures that have nothing to do with the Constitution, chief among them the agencies of the administrative state legitimized by the New Deal. The president, as chief executive, now manages a great number of administrative offices created by Congress, but the regulatory bodies Congress has been creating since 1887 have never been under the control of either the executive or the Congress. Yet these agencies issue regulations enforceable in the courts, and they govern the way individuals under their authority conduct their lives. The New Deal did nothing to increase the president's control over these agencies, nor did it resolve the age-old dispute between the president and Congress on the question of who would control the executive branch. The problem of administration remained on the battlefield of partisan politics, where the president was constantly negotiating truces with Congress. Despite its ruling in the *Schechter* case, the Supreme Court has come to accept various forms of extraconstitutional delegation of authority as the norm. Only in recent years has Congress come to object to its own executive creatures, the regulatory agencies and the order-issuing bodies in the executive branch. Its use of legislative vetoes to overrule such orders has now raised constitutional problems that, given the elapsed time, will make *Schechter* look simple.

If one sees industrialism and technological change not as providing extensions of powers humans have always had but as genuine revolutions against traditional practices and therefore requiring new forms of government, one is also within a major tradition of the Western world, dating back at least to Karl Marx. The belief that control over the new industrial structures can be gained only through a major change in the political structures has fueled both communist and fascist theories of government. Indeed, the belief that liberal democracy is essentially inept at industrial management, that by its very nature it is subject to takeover by antidemocratic conspirators, has been a central element in revolutionary theory.

Americans have traditionally believed that their democracy is so strong and flexible that it is immune to that threat. Yet, as I have tried to argue in this book, they have been forced to ask so many questions about the effectiveness of their control over the changes that industrialism and technological change have produced that their sense of strength may be deceptive if not dangerous. Ever since the Progressive Era, they have debated the efficacy of political parties; they have even regarded them as conspiracies against democracy, just as Michels and Mosca did in an earlier time. They have argued not only about the propriety but about the effectiveness of centralized government controls, and they have argued about the role of charismatic presidents, the equality of citizens, and the appropriate distribution of the nation's wealth. From the Progressive Era through World War II, Americans disputed, with one another and with their government, the same issues that Europeans were concerned about.

The New Deal can serve as the last major battleground for that dispute only if one sees it in the center of the period—1915 to 1945—in which the dispute received its most open and sustained hearing. Our acceptance of the consequences of industrialism and technology no longer allows us to regard the agrarian past as an alternative, and perhaps this heightens the agonies and the uncertainties. Americans still resist the controls that modern technology seems to require. We still rest our faith on some kind of populism, an inner sense of the rightness of individual choice over scientific knowledge and community self-control over even a benevolent management by the state. Politics, by which we mean our right to run our government, not simply to comment on it, is still our only protection against tyranny.

A century before the New Deal, Tocqueville called attention to what seemed to him the peculiar American preoccupation with politics. Later European observers like James Bryce puzzled over the American suspicion of administrative solutions to political problems even though, true to his own British heritage, he accepted the American hostility to bureaucracy that his compatriot, Thomas Carlyle shared (Carlyle called it "the continental nuisance"). Yet the worldwide crisis of the thirties raised the issue of politics versus management in its most striking form when the seeming breakdown of parliamentary democracies led thoughtful people in many parts of the world, including the United States, to call for a leadership free of the constraints imposed by political debate. As if in anticipation, Germany's Weimar Constitution had provided for just such an authoritative leadership in time of crisis, and Hitler used it to set up what became his dictatorship.

Roosevelt was the last American president to have what would have been, in effect, that same option, and it has been foreclosed to us, in part because he refused to take it. Hoover had not called a special session of Congress in the aftermath of the off-year elections of 1930 because he thought administrative government would be more effective if congressional interference was muted. Roosevelt could have used the emergency of March 1933 as an occasion to set the process of reform in motion by himself, as Lincoln, indeed, had done in 1861; but he did not.

Calling Congress into special session immediately, rather than governing by executive order, was perhaps the most crucial decision of Roosevelt's presidency and the most characteristic. Roosevelt was essentially a professional politician. He knew that administrative management did not operate in a vacuum; it took all his skills in manipulating the very traditional political machinery available to him to make it work. His thinking was untouched by that side of progressivism that insisted on sharp distinctions between politics and administration. Even when politics failed to work to his advantage, there were, for him, no alternatives, as there were for Hoover. Unlike Hoover, Roosevelt saw political battles as wars against adversaries he regarded as equals, and he accepted the structures of politics as the only structures available to him.

In that sense, even his own view of his plan to reform the Supreme Court provides evidence of the depth of his political commitment. It was a tuck in the familiar political fabric, not a redesign of the pattern. His abortive attempt to restructure the presidency was similarly based on a political view of administrative structure; it was not an effort to supplant politics with administration. As the nation's political leader, he believed that a modern American political system required political control at the top, strong enough to manage the growing bureaucracy. That ran counter to Congress's own desire to retain political power over the administration of government; it also ran counter to the progressives' belief that keeping politics and administration separate was the only way to protect the management of government from patronage and partisan control.

All of the legislation that brought the New Deal programs into being continued the tradition of local political control, even with the infusion of federal money. Federal policymakers had to encourage and cajole, holding out large carrots and brandishing very little in the way of enforcement. They had to hope that experience with the programs would educate the public and provide a sense of security that would make further expansion possible. Neither the political system nor the courts would allow anything else, as Roosevelt's most professorial appointee to the Supreme Court, Felix Frankfurter, kept insisting. It was the ballot box, not the Court, that would have to point the way to reform, and Roosevelt accepted that approach, not as a limit, but as an opportunity for the kind of political education he enjoyed providing.

He believed that an educated and informed public could exercise its will on the entire political system. The new instruments available to him, radio and film, and his immensely theatrical instinct in the use of them, were threats his opposition learned to fear. Kenneth Wherry, the conservative Nebraskan who in 1942 replaced George W. Norris, an old-line Progressive, in the Senate, put it well when he said, "No man who has that persuasive power, such personal charm, should serve more than two terms. We've got to safeguard the American people."

Such fears underscore our need to see the period as a whole, nationally and internationally, and the New Deal as part of it. For what is central to fulfilling the democratic prophecy, "the American Dream," is not only provision of material well-being for all Americans—for that hope the American Dream shares with all utopian promises—but maintenance of the hope of progressive improvement, of unfolding opportunity, for generation after generation. But it was also a part of the American dream that this opportunity was to be there without significant interference by the state; it was to be created by individual efforts at self-improvement. This was the key to the American meaning of individualism. Individual achievers would thus be beholden only to themselves, not to the government, and they would, out of their own sense of benevolence, form communities devoted to preserving the environments that had made their achievements possible. Huey Long may have summed it up better than anyone else in his time when he titled his book *Every Man a King*.

The belief that democracy begins at home has been one of the basic canons of democratic theory as far back as Plato. The writers of the *Federalist Papers* had to defend themselves against the classical belief that democracies must be limited geographically because participatory government necessarily demanded a reasonably small number of participants. Nineteenth-century racial theorists made similar claims for the natural limits of democratic government. To geographical space and size of population they added a demand for homogeneity of language, culture, and religion—in effect, homogeneity of "race." The problems the introduction of such limits posed for American democratic theory were intractable, given the hugeness of the country and the cultural diversity of its inhabitants—a diversity constantly renewed by each new wave of immigrants.

By the turn of the century, the words "local autonomy" had become a code signal, not of democracy for all, but of democracy for some. Local majorities exercised their power to limit democracy on grounds of race, national origin, and sex. The call for federal action to extend democracy could be viewed as an attack on local culture and the traditional bases of local democracy. The Progressive movement seemed to threaten local traditions of selective democracy in the interests of a national promise of greater democracy. It became possible to view Progressives as revolutionaries; but whether one saw them as radical revolutionaries or as conservative revolutionaries depended on where one stood on the local-national continuum. Whose traditional beliefs were going to be tampered with for what ultimate purpose became a question that could be asked as openly by southerners defending the separation of races as by generations of European immigrants being forced to change their drinking habits and give up the languages their parents had spoken to them and that they in turn wished to speak to their own children.

The two world wars raised the issue of national loyalty and, with it, the need to define a national culture to which loyalty could be given and by which it could be measured. Simply raising the issue seemed to underline the differences that did exist. The first war was fought to make the world safe for democracy, the second to preserve democracy in nations still attempting to practice it. Both experiences revealed the ultimate fragility of democracy, even in nations willing to sacrifice lives in its defense. And the United States, whose sense of itself as one nation was the product of more than a century of compromise and of a Civil War that had left some of its fundamental issues unresolved, was faced with bearing the burdens of world leadership.

To understand the way the world was when Americans felt themselves called on to save it in 1941 is crucial to an understanding of the peculiarities of the American role. Participatory democracy had either disappeared or was under attack in the very cultures historians had pointed to as the seedbeds of democracy. No matter what American policymakers had thought about the possibility of encouraging—or enforcing—their form of democracy in the Far East, Latin America, or Russia, the collapse of democratic governments in Italy, Germany, and Spain and the critical threat to it in the remaining nations of western Europe represented the first sustained ideological and practical assault on democratic government since its establishment in the eighteenth century, save for the Napoleonic challenge, which had been defeated. Moreover, the scientific, technological, and economic changes that made the new attack viable in new and challenging ways were also part of the American experience with industrialization. The fact that similar questions about democracy were being raised here, and that some of the solutions Americans were suggesting bore more than a passing resemblance to those being raised abroad, might allow us to see the American experience in broader, even richer, terms. We were in fact looking to leaders and leadership in ways that we hadn't in our earlier history, when establishment figures like Woodrow Wilson were asking fundamental questions about the effectiveness of our forms of government. The Progressive party of 1912 was as much an attack on the whole concept of political parties as it was an effort to create a single party whose doctrinal clarity and moral purity would represent the true interest of the nation as a whole. We continued to see American democracy as a governmental concept the whole world could benefit from adopting. We were attempting to create a single nation out of our diverse internal interests.

The crisis of the 1930s pushed some European governments to extremes that we were forced to perceive as threatening, but primarily because those governments adopted world conquest as their ultimate aim, not because their questions about the effectiveness of traditional liberal democracy in governing industrial societies were so strange to us. Many Americans admired Mussolini, and some admired Hitler at first, or at least respected the problems with which he was trying to cope. Nor, as I have already suggested, did the war end responsible speculation on the meaning of the whole experience of the first half of the twentieth century. The threat to capitalism and capitalist democracy seemed real enough, no matter where you stood on the ideological spectrum.

Yet by the end of the 1950s the threat was gone for Americans or was at least transformed into the shape given it by the Cold War. The democracies of western Europe were restored, in large part by the Marshall Plan, and Japan was transformed by the American occupation under MacArthur. A new era—which future historians will have to define—had been brought into being. The utopianism of the first half of the century disappeared as those who had sought permanent international peace through the creation of global political organizations were replaced by a new generation of realists, who looked to basic realignments of world power and balances built into terms like "containment" and "brinkmanship." They sought to create a warless world that was, somehow, a peaceless world as well.

The United States adjusted itself to this new view of internationalism by making social reform—even in areas such as race relations and civil rights—a requirement for maintaining America's position in the eyes of the world, particularly in what was now being called the Third World. It was no longer simply a matter of morality or social justice. Americans had to rebuild their society to serve as a model for democratic hopes throughout the world. The history of the New Deal became part of that model.

The tendency of historians, even those who personally experienced the New Deal, to see it for what it might have been rather than for what it was has led to criticisms, justifications, and judgments that perpetuate the myth that the New Deal was a liberal reform crusade that was finally defeated by a conservative minority and that it stands somewhere in the wings, waiting to reenter the stage on which American history is played. This myth sees Roosevelt as more of a frustrated liberal reformer than he was. More important, it perpetuates the notion that an efficient centralization of political and economic power in the United States is compatible with our commitment to democracy. Our historical experience suggests both the dangers of such a centralization and the practical difficulties that stand in its way. But what it is essential to understand is that local government and community control remain at the heart of our most intuitive conceptions of American democracy, even though they may also represent bastions of political corruption and locally condoned injustice. Federalism, the term we use to describe our historic localism, contains within it the basic paradoxes of American history. Dynamic presidents who symbolize the vitality of the democratic ideal can use the power of the federal government to do a great many things, but when they touch the nerve centers that register a threat to individual autonomy, they inevitably arouse the protests that lead, in turn, to reaction. The issue may be taxation—certainly the oldest cause of American rebellion against authority—or a war that violates our individual sense of justice.

These are the circumstances in which Americans encounter the conditions and demands created by modern management in a technological age. Limited, clumsy, based ultimately on a fundamental self-interest, American political management relies on perceptions of what is politically possible in the short run and on an abiding faith in the unpredictability of the future. Together, politics and the unknowable future will enable us to find solutions and to outwit the wisdom of experts claiming dire knowledge of what is to come. That's what Franklin Roosevelt was all about. This method not only demands tremendous political skills; it also entails the kind of risks and insecurity that intellectuals of each generation find troubling and that Roosevelt himself might have found disturbing had he lived to see the consequences of certain events. He had in fact begun to perceive some of them at the time of his death.

In 1937 Stephen Vincent Benét published a short story entitled "The Devil and Daniel Webster." It was a political parable, and it struck a note of triumph, the victory of an articulate and poetic voice over evil, of true conscience and the voice of God, speaking through the American statesman, over the terms of contracts exacted by the harsh realities of economic life. It is a folktale kind of narrative, set in mid-nineteenth-century New Hampshire, and it tells the story of an encounter between Webster, the great orator of American politics, whom some considered satanically inspired, and Old Scratch. They engage in battle for the soul of a fellow New Hampshireman, Jabez Stone. Seven years earlier Stone had sold his soul to the Devil for release from the agonizing hardships of New England farm life, and now the time is up. Webster insists on the right of trial by jury, the American way, but he leaves the choice of jurors and judge up to his opponent. Scratch proceeds to empanel twelve American villains—traitors, murderers, and thieves—and, to sit on the bench, a Salem witch-trial judge.

Webster wins, but it is his eloquence that wins, not the legality of the contract. His words have brought the ghostly jurors briefly back to life, and they see a fellow sinner, a human like themselves. Having conquered the Devil, and therefore free of any reason to fear his power, Webster grabs him by the scruff of the neck and demands information about the future. He learns that he will not be president, that the Civil War will indeed take place, but that the Union will be preserved. Assured of the safety of his beloved Union, Webster claims his victory and triumphantly kicks the Devil in the seat of the pants, propelling him out of New Hampshire forever.

The story was turned into one of the successful movies of 1941, *All That Money Can Buy*. As the title suggests, the movie plays more on Stone's greed than the story did, partly to provide a seduction scene, but partly, too, to suggest that the responsibility for Stone's difficulties was not simply the harshness of his fortunes but his hunger for something more than he deserved. Nonetheless, the salvation the story had promised was still intact, and the triumphant patriotism was still loud and clear.

Thirty years later, Archibald MacLeish used the story as the basis for a Broadway play, *Scratch*; but audiences and critics in 1971 failed to see the point, even in MacLeish's subtle and elegant reinterpretation. In the context of those years the vibrant patriotism seemed anachronistic, and this perhaps obscured the fact that the questions MacLeish was raising were the questions they and their contemporaries were asking: What are the real costs of beating the Devil? Does one really win such battles? Do human beings really understand the cataclysmic nature of justice in the confrontation between good and evil?

MacLeish's Webster still wins, but, unlike Benét's, he knows the price of his victory: a war that will resolve nothing. He takes no pride in the power of his oratory and claims no control over his defeated opponent, who vanishes by his own magic, not by being kicked in the pants. This Webster looks at the complex bargains of American history, the irrational compromises that hold, for a time, but will have to be remade, patched up again. He knows, too, that what won him the victory in the eyes of the jury was not that he had made them see a fellow man through the eyes of pity and compassion rather than justice but the fact that his jurors know that what they are weighing are their own contracts, their own bargains. It is impossible for them to repudiate these, but they can enjoy letting Stone off the hook, creating an exception in his case. And it is an exception. They all know it, even the Devil.

MacLeish's Webster is wiser than Benét's. He knows that not even New Hampshire will be protected from evil in the future. There are no bargains with evil, only periodic escapes from it. He is not arrogant in victory, partly because he knows that he has yet to find out exactly what, in fact, he has won. His patriotism is the rock on which he rests his hopes; it is not a weapon to be waved in triumph.

But MacLeish's audience had been through the 1960s, not the 1930s, and they did not seem to see his point. Benét's Webster could well have been the

Roosevelt of the thirties, triumphant and confident, assured of the justice of his cause and willing to pay the price of victory. MacLeish's Webster was the Roosevelt who might have survived into the sixties, less sure of the meaning of victory but just as determined to pursue it. As Americans were learning in the seventies, it was getting harder to measure success, and victory had become an angry term in the debates over Viet Nam. Lyndon Johnson's efforts to emulate Roosevelt in his championing of programs that dwarfed the New Deal in their ambitions had ended in a war that could not be won, and the symbols of patriotism had become weapons in a new civil war.

If the play about Webster is a parable on the tragedy of historical inevitability, it is also a glorification of the virtues of truth and compassion, to be practiced even in the face of what seem impossible odds, buoyed by the optimistic hope that chance will intervene. Webster saves his neighbor's soul, but he does so at the price of a war he had wanted to avoid.

Americans have always preferred to avoid the consequences of their commitment to individual choice by assuming that, somehow, the sum total of such choices will be compatible with larger historic goals. They have preferred to pay the price of mismanagement rather than suffer the restrictions that effective management places on the individual's right to choose. Our fundamental populism, our faith in our own intuitions and in the forms of government in which we believe them to be embodied, is essential to our sense of security in ourselves as citizens.

For over a century now we have been trying to transfer that security from the state and local governments where it originated to the federal government. Not even the authors of the *Federalist Papers* really foresaw how persistent the problem would be, although they would certainly have understood it. The transfer has involved a weakening of the independent authority of governments close to home in order to produce national uniformities some of us wished to impose on all of us. The civil-rights movement presented us with this issue full face, and we still are working to resolve it. Those now engaged in dismantling the national regulatory state, created to replace the chaotic system of state-by-state regulation, are moved by a faith that freedom from regulation will produce equity.

We want governments to protect our self-interest. Fearful from the beginning of our national history that a national government would not meet that fundamental need, we nonetheless found it necessary to look to it for redress when the industrialization of the nation and its emergence as an international power required us to think with a single national mind and speak with a single national voice. To the extent that those requirements have severed our contacts with the more familiar state and local governments, they have threatened our sense of ourselves as citizens. Like the closing of the frontier, that transformation, it can be argued, was inevitable. Modern industry is national industry, and the American role in the world is a product of national development. But the transformation has left us accepting an uneasy State as our primary method of self-government, a State we have always suspected and will continue to suspect. It may be ironic that at a moment in history when the technology of communication is improving by quantum leaps our suspicions of the truth of what we are told and what we know are greater than they have ever been. These suspicions have their source in our oldest and most profound need: our need to govern ourselves.

It is time, perhaps, to transfer our loyalties to the State, not as an act of militant patriotism of the kind we have traditionally performed in order to fight our wars but as part of the tradition of politics with which we have governed the communities in which we live. The transference will not be easy, but it may open the only path we have to a viable future. It will require rebuilding local governments as part of a national system; local governments will then serve not as an escape from the authority of the State but as a means of controlling it. This new federalism, if it is to come, cannot be founded on the desire to replace the role the federal government has come to play in our lives since the transformations wrought by the New Deal. A new federalism must share with the old federalism the realization that both national and local responsibilities for governing are essential to our conception of democracy. There is no choice to be made between them. There are balances to be struck, tensions to be resolved, and continuing battles to be waged to preserve our special commitment to participation as the soul of democracy. The New Deal preserved that. Remembering it for that victory and remembering it correctly may help us recapture our understanding of what we are as a democratic people.

Index